THE LEGAL TREATMENT OF MUSLIM MINORITIES IN ITALY

AF714336

'Andrea Pin's book offers an encompassing account of the legal treatment of religious minorities in Italy. Interestingly enough, it shows that the Italian constitutional culture and its state–religion model look well equipped to address one of the biggest challenges of our times: the place of Islam in the West.'

Marta Cartabia, Italian Constitutional Court

'Islam challenges both the secular and the Catholic tradition of Italy. This book designs a triangle, where the Italian Catholic background and secular legal system react to the Islamic presence through judicial accommodations and political negotiations fostering the contamination of models and identities. A key contribution to understand one of the most interesting patterns of integration in Europe.'

Silvio Ferrari, University of Milan, Italy

'The countries of Europe have adapted in different ways to the collapse of their monolithic Christian inheritance and the rise of Muslim traditions, laws and practices. Professor Pin explores the extent to which Islam has become integrated into civil society and church–state relations in Italy. His study reveals the self-made difficulties which have arisen in consequence of insufficient attention being given to adapting existing structures, modelled on Vatican concordats, to the requirements of an unfamiliar faith which is neither fully accepted nor properly understood. This book is a thoughtful and profound analysis of the current dysfunctionality of Italy's governmental engagement with Islam, and a convincing plea for it to be revisited through a more honest, focussed and pragmatic dialogue.'

Mark Hill QC, Cardiff University, UK

'Professor Pin has done yeoman service in bringing this revealing and promising story of Muslim religious culture and religious freedom in Italy to the attention of the English speaking world. His writing is deeply researched, refreshingly comparative, boldly proffered, and often wise beyond his youthful years. It is a privilege and pleasure to commend this important study.'

John Witte, Jr., Emory University, USA

The Legal Treatment of Muslim Minorities in Italy

Islam and the Neutral State

ANDREA PIN
University of Padua, Italy

Routledge
Taylor & Francis Group
LONDON AND NEW YORK

First published 2016 by Ashgate Publishing

2 Park Square, Milton Park, Abingdon, Oxfordshire OX14 4RN
52 Vanderbilt Avenue, New York, NY 10017

Routledge is an imprint of the Taylor & Francis Group, an informa business

First issued in paperback 2020

Copyright © 2016 Andrea Pin

Andrea Pin has asserted his right under the Copyright, Designs and Patents Act, 1988, to be identified as the author of this work.

All rights reserved. No part of this book may be reprinted or reproduced or utilised in any form or by any electronic, mechanical, or other means, now known or hereafter invented, including photocopying and recording, or in any information storage or retrieval system, without permission in writing from the publishers.

Notice:
Product or corporate names may be trademarks or registered trademarks, and are used only for identification and explanation without intent to infringe.

British Library Cataloguing in Publication Data
A catalogue record for this book is available from the British Library.

The Library of Congress has cataloged the printed edition as follows:
Pin, Andrea, author.
The legal treatment of Muslim minorities in Italy : Islam and the neutral state / by Andrea Pin.
pages cm
Includes bibliographical references and index.
ISBN 978-1-4724-5023-4 (hardback)
1. Muslim minorities–Legal status, laws, etc.–Italy.
2. Islamic law–Italy. 3. Islam and state–Italy. I. Title.

KKH2467.M56P56 2015
342.4508'5297–dc23

2015021232

ISBN 978-1-4724-5023-4 (hbk)
ISBN 978-0-367-59744-3 (pbk)

Contents

Foreword

Since 9/11, the place of Islam in Western society has become an ever more urgent question. Other tragic events in the West since 9/11 have kept the question in the headlines. Think of Fort Hood, 7/7, the Spanish train station bombings, the carnage at the Boston Marathon, the Canadian Parliament and *Charlie Hebdo*, among others, let alone the ongoing wars in Afghanistan, Iraq and Syria, and the repeated acts of violence in North Africa, the Middle East, Russia, Eurasia and the Indian subcontinent. To be sure, it is now commonplace to distinguish between radical Islamicism and authentic Islam, and to view terrorism and jihadism as a betrayal of the Prophet's abiding message of peace, love and justice that the vast majority of Muslims around the world have embraced. But for many Westerners, it has been hard to look beyond the gratuitous bloodshed and carnage that Islamicist terrorism has inflicted and the massive costs to life, liberty and property that have been imposed by the necessary military, security and police responses to terrorism. Anti-Muslim sentiment has developed quickly in many Western nations over the past 15 years. Major battles over the place of Islam in the West have broken out on the streets and in the courts, in schools and in churches, in scholarly tracts and in legislative initiatives targeting Islam.

Italy has been largely spared from Islamicist terrorism to date, though it sits perilously close to several hotbeds of Islamicist radicalism around the Mediterranean. And the diverse Muslim communities of Italy, more than a million strong in number, have found ways of living peaceably in this ancient Catholic land that was long at the heart of Western Christendom. In this first book-length study of Islam and Italy to be published in English, Professor Andrea Pin of the University of Padua explores how and why Islam and Italy have so far reached a rapproachment and what the prospects are for this peaceful coexistence to continue.

One reason for this rapproachment, Professor Pin shows, lies in the immense diversity of Italian Muslims, who represent numerous cultural, linguistic, regional, ethnic, tribal and religious sectors of global Islam, each with their own views on Islamic public and private life. This pluralism has provided an effective internal check and balance against any one group or ideology dominating or radicalizing Italian Muslims. And it has empowered a number of émigré Muslims to assimilate more easily in Italy than their compatriots abroad might have countenanced.

A second reason lies in the commitment to religious freedom of Italian Catholicism. Since the Second Vatican Council in the mid-1960s, the Catholic Church has been a champion of religious freedom for all peaceable souls around the world, not least Muslims. Particularly during the long reign of Pope John Paul II and now again under Pope Francis, the Catholic Church has reached out generously to its Muslim neighbors at home and around the Mediterranean, finding common cause in issues like marriage and family life, and building mutual understanding among the sundry children of Abraham. This has made the dominant Catholic culture of Italy, with its nerve center in Rome, more welcoming to Muslims than many other cultures in Europe.

A third reason lies in Italy's distinct approach to religious freedom. The Italian constitutional principle of "laicità" counsels a basic separation of church and state and a basic commitment to religious neutrality by the state—principles that are confirmed by the case law of the European Court of Human Rights. But Italy also seeks to balance traditional Catholic values of Italy with the needs of new immigrants and modern cultures. Unlike its French namesake "laicité," which often promotes aggressive secularism against both traditional and new religions, Italian "laicità" remains more open to retaining old traditions that were once rooted in religious teachings, but are now woven into Italian culture. Alongside this principle, however, Italy has worked out individual concordats or peace treaties between the state and religious groups that allow for carefully tailored legal accommodations of the special needs and concerns of its minority faiths. Despite their diversity, most Muslims in Italy (and elsewhere) need accommodations for Friday worship and other holidays, access to mosques and Muslim cemeteries, *halal* slaughtering methods and proper food, religious education in sex-segregated Muslim schools, protections for head coverings and other distinct forms of dress and ornamentation in public. So far, Italy (unlike Spain) has been unable to build a general concordat with its diverse Muslim citizens. But Italian courts and legislatures have tried to build piecemeal accommodations as steps along the way to reaching a broader consensus that might one day yield a concordat.

Professor Pin has done yeoman service in bringing this revealing and promising story of Muslim religious culture and religious freedom in Italy to the attention of the English-speaking world. He is ideally suited for this task. He is a distinguished scholar of comparative religious freedom, constitutional law and human rights viewed in comparative legal and religious perspectives. For years, he and his colleagues at the University of Padua and at the Oasis Foundation in Venice have worked at fostering deep dialogue and conversation about these topics among various Jewish, Muslim and Christian constituents all around the Mediterranean basin. He and his colleagues have translated into Italian a number of books and articles from different parts of the world in an effort to build greater mutual understanding about the fundamentals of faith and freedom, historically and today. And he has generously shared his experiences and expertise in public lectures, courses and publications in the UK and the US, not least in our Center for the Study of Law and Religion at Emory University, where he serves as a senior fellow. His writing is deeply researched, refreshingly comparative, boldly proffered and often wise beyond his youthful years. It is a privilege and pleasure to commend this important study to you.

John Witte, Jr.
Director, Center for the Study of Law and Religion
Emory University

Acknowledgments

Few accomplishments can be attained without the help and support of friends and colleagues, but some are literally inconceivable without them. This book never would have seen the light of day without the generous support and encouragement of John Witte, Jr., who urged me to prepare this English edition of *Laicità e islam nell'ordinamento italiano. Una questione di metodo*, which first appeared in Italian in 2010 with Cedam, and watched over the whole process. John was so attentive and paternal to me that I wonder where he found time to work on his own books in the meantime.

I am deeply thankful to the Center for the Study of Law and Religion at Emory University at large for supporting the preparation of this work. In particular, I would like to thank Amy Wheeler and Anita Mann for their excellent administrative support and two fine law students associated with the Center, Wes Pickard and Anna Beaton, for their extensive and expert editorial help with the English edition. The Center has been an invaluable hub of ideas and people, food for the mind and relief for the soul, and I am proud of having befriended a lot of great folks with whom my friendship goes on.

I remember with gratitude conversations I had and corrections I received from Abdullahi Ahmed An-Na'im, Luca Antonini, Marta Cartabia, Stefano Ceccanti, Silvio Ferrari, Massimo Papa and Javier Prades, all of whom contributed to the ideas that the reader may find thought-provoking here, but not to my mistakes.

I am also thankful to the Department of Public, International and Community Law, at which I work, and to the University of Padua at large, which gave initial financial support to this book as part of a broader research project on *Law and Development*.

My memory spontaneously goes to him who has always been with me. In a storm I could wake him up and he was able to turn the tide. I always wished that I were spared from storms, but all I have always needed is him beside me. As I do right now.

Time hasn't left me as I was, for many reasons. Here it will suffice to say that when I began thinking about this book, I thought that seeing it in print in the future would be a true success. Now my greatest achievement happens every day and consists in shutting down the laptop and playing with my son Carlo. Right in the middle of a storm.

Introduction

The Way to Religious Freedom for Muslims in Italy

> There may be religious denominations for which some adjustment is necessary, even in the absence of any requests from the religions themselves; this might happen if Islam were to request formal recognition by the Italian government. Adaptation will be required, at least with regards to institutions like polygamy that conflict with the Italian legal system.[1]

Over the last 50 years, the situation hypothesized by this quote from President Ruini at the 1947 Italian Constituent Assembly has become a reality. The framers of the Italian Constitution used President Ruini's views to mold Art. 8 para. 3, which foresaw and implemented state–religion agreements as the method by which church and state would interact. The conviction that religions such as Islam present elements of deep conflict with the basic tenets of Italian law has informed the debate over the relationship between church and state and judicial interpretation about the provisions of Art. 8.

Despite President Ruini's initial skepticism, Italy has consistently believed it conveys a welcoming attitude towards religious minorities, including Islam. Recently, at the European Court of Human Rights (ECtHR), the Italian government has depicted Italy's approach as "benevolent" towards religious minorities, especially in public schools, which are undoubtedly an extremely sensitive environment.[2] The famous 2011 ECtHR *Lautsi v. Italy* decision itself highlighted Italy's treatment of Islam in particular by admitting that "it was not forbidden for pupils to wear Islamic headscarves or other symbols or apparel having a religious connotation; alternative arrangements were possible to help schooling fit in with non-majority religious practices; the beginning and end of Ramadan were 'often celebrated' in schools."[3]

In fact, Italy's attitude towards Islam is rather accommodating compared with much of the rest of Europe. The ECtHR and, more generally, international human rights agencies have demonstrated a skeptical approach to embracing the religion. Narratives centered on prejudices towards Muslims have mushroomed:

---

1 Constituent Assembly meeting of April 12, 1947—Proceedings, p. 2783, available at: http://archivio.camera.it/patrimonio/archivi_della_transizione_costituzionale_1944_1948/atc04/struttura.

2 *Lautsi v. Italy* (App. no. 30814/06) Grand Chamber decision, March 18, 2011.

3 Par. 74.

the ECtHR, for example, has dismissed a considerable number of cases seeking to vindicate the right to wear a headscarf at French public schools. The fact that Italy has demonstrated an inclusive attitude towards Islam is encouraging.

Nonetheless, Italy's benevolence towards Islam is provisional and piecemeal. There is no systematic or comprehensive understanding of the political and religious needs of Muslims and how to address them. Further, there is no solution proposed to addressing these needs in the foreseeable future, nor will there be until the government promulgates a state–religion agreement with Muslim community leaders, although Art. 8 of the Italian Constitution places this kind of agreement at the intersection of religious freedom for groups of believers and the need of the state to balance such right with other relevant interests. In other words, Italy's positive attitude towards Islam remains confined mainly to the non-legal and non-constitutional domain, and is therefore highly exposed to increasing scepticism against Islam, if not proper Islamophobia.[4]

That is not to say there have not been efforts at achieving the total incorporation of Islam into the Italian political and legal community. The first concrete initiatives to enact a state–religion agreement date back to the 1990s. The Italian Islamic community had been showing a marked increase both in population and in internal tensions (owing to the differences among the various Islamic groups in the country). Some initiatives to address these problems were undoubtedly overly ambitious; others demonstrated a real involvement and engagement with the Islamic community. Italy's political officials and legal scholars met (without success) to consider the possibility of crafting a state–religion agreement. Although nothing came from this (and other) attempts to formally recognize Islam, the need for an agreement has increased in the two decades since the initial attempts were made: 2012 statistics report that 33 percent of the five million or so immigrants are Muslim.[5] This is a sizeable percentage in a country of 61 million inhabitants.[6]

These efforts have been part of a broader movement of which the evolution of Italian law plays a part. The Muslim footprint in Europe has increased both in terms of population and social visibility—the growing Islamic presence is an integral part of a larger religious resurgence in Europe that was predicted

4 See the recent Pew Research on *Faith in European Project Reviving*, available at: http://www.pewglobal.org/2015/06/02/faith-in-european-project-reviving/, which emphasizes that the rampant anti-minority sentiments among Italians outnumber those of other countries.

5 http://www.dossierimmigrazione.it/docnews/file/2012_Dossier_Scheda.pdf. But see http://www.zenit.org/it/articles/le-religioni-in-italia-censite-oltre-600-fedi-e-vie-spirituali, which gives an account of different statistics, calculating around 850,000 practicing Muslims in Italy.

6 http://www.istat.it/it/popolazione.

by sociologists back in the 1980s. European communities are seeing the amplification of more traditional ways of living one's religion and the elevation of new forms of the relationship between the worshipper and the divine in response to contemporary individualistic trends.

Contemporary Tendencies and Growing Tensions in the Field of Religious Freedom

The revival of the issue of individual and collective religious identity has found its way into the Italian legal realm thanks to international legal trends and new modes of thought in Italian constitutionalism. Advocates for legal and political acceptance of Islam in Italy have utilized legal theories such as multiculturalism (which first inspired Canadian policies and from there gained global attention) to support this movement. But long before multiculturalism took hold, Italians promulgated their 1948 Constitution, which perpetuated a new and broader understanding of religious freedom. From the old mentality that the only religion to be protected by the Constitution was Catholicism, through building upon its Constitution, Italian legal culture has moved to a new understanding that sees virtually all religions protected.

Scholars regard such protection as one of the core features of personalism, a fundamental principle that is enshrined in Art. 2 of the Constitution itself. It is now commonly held that the Italian Constitution protects the development of the human personality, insofar as it signifies human connection through the medium of cultural and religious groups. The rights of the religious and cultural groups to which individuals belong find their first protection under the constitutional umbrella in this way, through Art 2. This reading has created an expectation among religious groups: when they have needs requiring a political solution, they expect public authorities to implement new policies to address them, protecting their diversity and helping them to flourish.

The multiplication of cultural identities, as a trademark consequence of contemporary pluralistic societies, has encountered difficulties in being accepted in Italy as elsewhere in Europe and beyond. The recent religious revival has not provoked unanimously friendly state policies. Western constitutional systems are seasoned veterans at handling social pluralism, which aspires to equality between different genders and social classes through institutional devices like universal suffrage and social rights. The same cannot be said for these systems handling cultural and religious pluralism, which aspires to equality between religious and cultural groups. This type of pluralism, as has been shown by political scientists,[7]

7 See, for example, Panebianco A., *Il potere, lo Stato, la libertà. La gracile costituzione della società libera*, Il Mulino, Bologna, 2004. Significantly, certain doctrines warn that social

is harder to manage.[8] The scattered skepticism about the possibility of handling cultural and religious pluralism can be easily traced in the results of a study that were released by an authoritative French political division called the *High Council for Integration* in 2007. This suggested that frameworks of cultural policies in Europe that would most reinforce and expand cultural differences would be the ones most subject to social tensions and displays of radicalism.[9]

These tensions emanate from the structure of state and religious legal systems. These systems place concurrent and parallel obligations on the individuals so that they are in constant competition with each other. This conflict places the average religious person in the uncomfortable position of choosing loyalty to religion or loyalty to the political society and state structure in which they live. The state can and does provide a solution to this dilemma through political accommodations for religious needs; these are supposed to strike a balance between the importance of the religious practice and the political right being infringed.

Overall, these political accommodations are piecemeal, transient or otherwise unsatisfactory. For example, the American legal regime is familiar with the problems created by this accommodation-based way of dealing with conflicts of loyalties. The US Supreme Court has found it difficult to pinpoint a consistently reliable criterion to distinguish between appropriate and inappropriate religious exemptions. In *Sherbert v. Verner* (1963),[10] the Court created the "compelling governmental interest" test,[11] which allowed the federal government to infringe upon a religious right if it had a specific and weighty interest in the matter. Two decades later, the Court largely abandoned the test in *Employment Division v. Smith* (1990),[12] recognizing that to restrict religious practice merely on the basis of a particular area of conflict with the law was to oversimplify the complexity of

---

pluralism is much more conducive to the maintenance of the democratic system than cultural pluralism, arguing that while the former is both sought after and closely guarded, as necessary for democracy's very survival, the second is merely defended: Llamazares Fernandez D., *Derecho a la libertad de Conciencia I*, Civitas, Madrid, 1997, 106–07.

8 "If the lack of social homogeneity requires positive actions aimed at eliminating the causes of inequality, then the lack of ethnic and cultural homogeneity demands—conversely—interventions designed to recognize diversity": Rolla G., Caratteri di una società libera e democratica secondo la giurisprudenza della Corte suprema del Canada, in Rolla G. (ed.), *Eguali, ma diversi. Identità ed autonomia secondo la giurisprudenza della Corte Suprema del Canada*, Giuffrè, Milan, 2006, 24.

9 *Charte de la laïcité dans les services publics et autres avis*, issued on March 31, 2007 by the Haut Conseil à l'intégration, available at: http://www.ladocumentationfrancaise.fr/rapports-publics/074000341.

10 374 U.S. 398.

11 374 U.S. 398, 406.

12 494 U.S. 872.

the issues involved.[13] Given the continued increase in immigrant groups and affiliations, an approach like the "compelling governmental interest" test would have probably resulted in undermining the country's legal system. Each generally applicable law would be riddled with legislatively or judicially created exemptions for the needs of the hundreds of distinct religions in the US.[14] This decision was greeted with widespread criticism from scholars and citizens alike,[15] and has created an ongoing debate[16] between Congress and the judiciary as to the method by which difficult cases regarding religious rights should be resolved.[17]

Even the success of Canada's unique approach to treating religious and cultural diversity is problematic. Canadian policies likely would not work in different cultures because political officials promulgated them in response to a very specific and peculiar relationship of the citizens native to Canada: the Anglophile majority and the Francophile minority.[18] Specifically, the policies might not be easily adapted to the situation of recent immigrants and their descendants, which is the standard situation throughout Europe. Most importantly, even the term "multiculturalism" is a term of art in Canada, suggesting that there is much doubt as to its meaning and the implications thereof. This doubt can be seen in the *Adler* case, which divided the Supreme Court of Canada on the extension of public funding to denominational schools. In a series of opinions, the judges were split in the way they used the word "multiculturalism":[19] they also advocated different interpretations of it in the service of differing viewpoints.

---

13 See Helfand M.A., When Religious Practices Become Legal Obligations: Extending the Foreign Compulsion Defense, in *Journal of Law and Religion*, 2008, XXIII, 102.

14 *Employment Division v. Smith*, 494 U.S. 889 (1990), Judge Scalia: "If the 'compelling interest' test is to be applied at all, then, it must be applied across the board, to all actions thought to be religiously commanded. Moreover, if 'compelling interest' really means what it says (and watering it down here would subvert its rigor in the other fields where it is applied), many laws will not meet the test. Any society adopting such a system would be courting anarchy, but that danger increases in direct proportion to the society's diversity of religious beliefs, and its determination to coerce or suppress none of them."

15 See, among many others, Nussbaum M., *Liberty of Conscience. In Defense of America's Tradition of Religious Liberty*, Basic Books, New York, 2008.

16 The intervention of the Court resulted in the *Religious Freedom Restoration Act* (1993), which allowed for the expansion of religious freedom. However, the same new regulation was revised by the Supreme Court, which maintained that the law infringed upon the powers of the states.

17 Witte J. Jr. and Nichols J.A., *Religion and the American Constitutional Experiment*, 3rd edn, Westview Press, Boulder, 2011, 137–39.

18 Ceccherini E., *Multiculturalismo (dir.comp.) Digesto—Discipline pubblicistiche*, UTET, Turin, 2008.

19 I am referring to *Adler v. Ontario* (1996), which concerned the legitimacy of the extension of public funding to religious schools. An opinion that *dissented in part* claimed,

In Europe, the religious conflicts have been handled through political pragmatism, which has provided the necessary guidance in identifying room to maneuver for religious groups that request political sanction. The treatment of new religions in a country throws this pragmatism into relief. The new religious group first establishes roots in a country through immigration; then, it begins making demands for religious exemptions. These demands create a debate between the new religious group and the state, new religious institutions and generally applicable laws, and the majority and the minority, assuming different guises in different countries. In Germany and France, the debate is between foreigners and citizens; in Sweden and the Netherlands, it is between niche cultures and mass society; and in the UK, it is between different ethnicities.[20] This debate, which should in theory address the religious needs of the denomination as compared to the fundamental tenets of the legal system, gives way to a permissive negotiation conducted on the basis of the demographic and political weight of each party involved. A balancing of pros and cons ensues, putting the new religious group and its requests for special treatment against

in fact, that not to finance religious schools would encourage different segments of the population to resort to public schools, leading to their actual cohabitation. In this way, the state could have incentivized multiculturalism: "These students, instead of being educated in public multi-cultural multi-religious schools, would be educated with homogeneous groups of people of similar beliefs. In short, secular schools might become less diverse and the number of students receiving parochial educations would increase. The overall effect would be to diminish the exposure of children in multicultural schools. This lack of exposure, in turn, would diminish the mutual tolerance and understanding of different cultures and religions of Ontarians for one another" (Justice McLachlin). Another *dissenting opinion*, on the other hand, supported financing private schools, because in this way it would help conserve each cultural group's heritage, which would have had their own schools/educational institutions of reference: "Denial of any funding to the appellants constitutes not only a financial prejudice, but also a complete non-recognition of their children's educational needs and the children's and parents' fundamental interest in the continuation of their faith … The interests at stake for the appellants, being the recognition and continuation of these communities, are clearly recognized as relevant to the fundamental purposes of the Charter. This conclusion can be drawn from the incorporation of the principle of accommodation in the interpretation of s. 2(a) and s. 15. Moreover, it is consonant with the interpretive guidance of s. 27, which reads as follows: 'This Charter shall be interpreted in a manner consistent with the preservation and enhancement of the multicultural heritage of Canadians'" (Justice L'Heureux-Dubé).

20 See the Gallup poll on the worldwide Islamic community, the data of which was partially reported in the British journal *Islamic Emel*, July 2008, p. 24: "the majority of the general public (62%) asserted that minorities must be more flexible to blend in with the majority, whereas in London majority of Muslims (54%) believe the majority should do more to accommodate minorities' religious customs."

the historical majority and its desire that everyone conform to traditional rules and values.[21]

The pragmatic approach is not entirely satisfactory. It blurs the distinction between immigration and race with religious rights and needs, and it fails to fully respect the religious rights requested in accordance with their constitutional value. Religious freedom for immigrants often becomes a second-class right, placed behind other rights in terms of its priority. Many governments view the immigrants' religion as a factor that conflicts with a desirable integration into the host society rather than the more healthy perspective of the religion as an intrinsic part of their identity. Unfortunately, this view has been amplified and widely embraced given the nascent threat of terrorism in the last decade.[22] The threat of terrorism and the government perspective of new immigrant groups have become inseparable.[23]

Even the most progressive and advanced endeavors of governments to manage their cultural and religious pluralism are not entirely satisfactory to all sides. Majority policies and political criteria do not sufficiently recognize the depth of religious and cultural differences; at the same time, the solution cannot lie in the indiscriminate approval of any minority demand predicated on core fundamental rights recognized by law. Contemporary Italian and Western constitutionalism lacks effective criteria to resolve those issues central to religious pluralism even in their original context. Thus, a reflection upon what kind of principle might play a similar role within the Italian legal system is needed, especially when dealing with the needs of the Muslim community.

The Purpose and Structure of the Book

This book will be both descriptive and prescriptive. First, I plan to analyze the emerging Islamic presence in Italy by placing it in the broadest perspective of the Italian religious environment, and to analyze the challenges it presents in the context of ecclesiastical law over the last 25 years. By comparing Islamic

---

21 Nussbaum, *Liberty of Conscience*, 4: "Jews, Mormons, Jehovah's Witnesses, Seventh-Day Adventists, atheists, members of non-theistic religions such as Buddhism or Taoism, Native Americans, Santeria worshipers—all these religious have suffered disabilities at the hands of the majority."

22 Nussbaum M.C., *La nuova intolleranza. Superare la paura dell'islam e vivere in una società più libera*, Laterza, Rome-Bari, 2012, 21.

23 The vast bibliography on this matter demonstrates the pragmatism of Posner E.A. and Vermeule A., *Terror in the Balance: Security, Liberty and the Courts*, Oxford University Press, New York, 2007. In vivid terms: "As more and more Muslims enter the U.S., the rhetoric of war makes people wonder whether they are trustworthy citizens": Nussbaum, *Liberty of Conscience*, 9.

doctrine and regulation of religion in traditionally Muslim countries, I will provide a clear picture of the obstacles for a comprehensive regulation of Islam–state relations in Italy and other European states.

Next, I will use the principle of "laicità," or of state neutrality, in the field of religious freedom, as developed in Italian constitutional case law, to construct a method that will establish a healthier and more enduring relationship between Italian institutions and the Islamic community.

The issue of state neutrality, its relationship with religious freedom and secularism, and its constitutional scope will be played out at this point because the purpose of this book is not to treat state neutrality by itself. Throughout the book I maintain that state neutrality is a constitutional device that aims to protect religious freedom and secure religious pluralism, and must therefore be analyzed only after considering the challenges that pluralism and religious freedom are facing in Italy now.

The focus on the Italian conception of neutrality will provide the ground for further elaboration in the field of religious freedom for Muslims: I will utilize it to address some of the most problematic issues that arise from Islamic presence in Italy and explore the possibilities of their realization.

Italian Constitutional Court decisions demonstrate that the Italian reading of the relationship between church and state provides a more benevolent and nuanced approach with valuable insights that will help settle problems created by integration of the Islamic faith and its cultural and religious needs. I will draw comparative examples and lessons from the Spanish model of religious liberty (which is similar, but more advanced, than the Italian model), ECtHR case law, and the contributions of Italian and foreign doctrines to justify the value of this approach.

However, this exercise on the understanding and the scope of state neutrality will benefit religious pluralism in a much broader sense. Whatever proposals that address the needs of Muslim communities could equally apply to other religions and affiliations in Italy. The issues of religious freedom that Islam is facing and how state neutrality addresses them are a good template for the challenges to come. More specifically, the exercise will be an asset to other states that have a similar constitutional structure and that decide to adopt a model of state–religion relationships based on state–religion agreements as broadly understood. This model includes systems that grant churches full or ample autonomy, but adopt collaborative methods through state–religion negotiations and agreements: this is the case in Austria, Belgium, Germany, Italy, Poland, Portugal and Spain, among others.[24]

---

24 Minnerath R., Church Autonomy in Europe, in Robbers G. (ed.), *Church Autonomy: A Comparative Survey*, Peter Lang, Frankfurt am Main, 2001.

To summarize, the challenges of religious freedom for Muslims suggest that the idea of state neutrality needs to be sharpened in Italy and, more broadly, in Europe. This book assumes that the Italian experiment on religious freedom and state neutrality provides a legal framework to address Islamic needs in the country, but also legal scholarship in Europe with fresh elements for reflection in an era in which an elaboration of such concepts is particularly needed.

It is necessary to underline the fact that the scope of the book is limited in two senses. First, it does not deal with problems that have yet to reach the legal field in Italy.[25] The normativity of Islamic law traditionally covers both the religious and the legal spheres, as they have been distinguished by Western legal thinking.[26] But Islamic rules pertaining to family law, penal law or succession law, for instance, have received widely different receptions in European legal systems; some countries have given them some official recognition, while others have offered more resistance and have forced such practices to remain outside state law, confining them to societal practices.[27] Italy is one of the states that have taken the latter approach; dealing with such topics would therefore request a sociological profile that lies outside the scope of this work. If we follow framer Ruini's intuition about polygamy quoted at the beginning of this book, we would need to leave the legal field and dive into the sociological sphere. The only notable exception is the celebration of marriage, since it is closely tied to the legal status of religious figures and therefore will be considered here.

Second, the book will devote the largest part of its attention to the state level. The local level is almost absent here. Local accommodations of Islamic needs are not absent, but they are nonetheless piecemeal, undertheorized and rather undeveloped—and, more importantly, they lie outside the spectrum of the state–religion agreement, which is the only tool that the Constitution explicitly provides to address the specific necessities of religious groups. Moreover, the scattered accommodation practices that local bodies have put into place have been channeled mainly through welfare policies and practical measures that have largely ignored the needs of Muslims *qua* Muslims. Therefore, although they may be socially significant, they do not really help in framing the debate on religious freedom for Muslims in Italy. In addition, here an exception applies: the construction of mosques falls within the competences of regions, and a word will be said on that issue.

25 Obviously, sometimes it happens that domestic controversies involve Islamic laws pertaining to family or penal law, because the parties belong to countries that enforce it. Such events, however, are normally resolved through the recourse to the categories of conflict of laws.

26 Rohe M., Sharia and the Muslim Diaspora, in Peters R. and Bearman P. (eds), *The Ashgate Research Companion to Islamic Law*, Ashgate, Farnham, 2014, 261 and 269.

27 Ibid., 263.

In Chapter 1, I briefly analyze the Muslim presence in Italy, placing it within a broader European context, and sketch the different issues it has created. In Chapter 2, I consider how Italian law has addressed the needs of religious liberty requested by religious groups, highlighting both the merits and shortcomings of the Italian policies in the field and contrasting them with the Spanish system briefly. Chapter 3 portrays the relationship between church and state in some Muslim states, and compares it to European states with large Muslim populations: the focus on the state–religion relationships in such states will show that the difficulty in accommodating Islamic needs largely derives from structural differences between the Western and Islamic models of this relationship. Chapter 4 focuses on the possibility of finding a reliable interlocutor within the Italian Muslim community, given its structure and the past experience of creating state–religion agreements. Chapter 5 maintains that the method through which agreements are negotiated and promulgated should be reconsidered: the focus should be the actual needs of the Islamic community rather than the needs of those negotiating the agreement. Chapter 6 describes traditional Italian understanding of the relationship between church and state, demonstrating that it can be understood either as an obstacle or as a vehicle for fulfilling the religious needs of Italy's Muslims; following the Italian constitutional text and the Constitutional Court's wording, I will not use the concept of "secularism," which is largely ambiguous,[28] and will prefer the utilization of concepts such as "laicità" and "neutrality," which are still hard to handle, but nonetheless have been largely utilized by the Constitutional Court. Finally, Chapter 7 demonstrates through case studies how separation of church and state, if understood in a positive sense, can be conducive to religious freedom.

28 See, most recently, Zucca L., A Secular Manifesto for Europe, available at: http://ssrn.com/abstract=2574165.

Chapter 1
Islam in Italy

Islam in Italy and the Emergence of New Issues for Religious Freedom

Italy has an immigrant Muslim population of multivarious ethnic diversity, which stems from two factors: first, Italy has not retained a relationship with its former colonies, which encourages immigration; and, second, because it is squeezed between the Arab-African South and the Balkans in the East. This "ethnic mosaic"[1] has distinguished Italy from other nations where there was (at least until recent times) a single dominant ethnic immigrant origin,[2] whether it is the Maghreb in France, Indo-Pakistani in Great Britain or Turkish in Germany.[3]

The largest Muslim communities in Italy are Albanian, Moroccan, Tunisian, Egyptian and Bangladeshi. Other significant Muslim communities come from Senegal, Pakistan, Nigeria and Algeria.[4] The diversity of origins among these groups demonstrates the variety of ways Islam is practiced and defined in Italy.[5] For example, even though 70 percent of the Albanians in Italy are formally Muslim, their community is highly secularized,[6] meaning that the religious identity of Albanians in Italy is less pronounced and somewhat absent from the ongoing debate between the country's various Muslim communities.[7]

---

1 Fouad Allam K., L'islam contemporaneo in Europa e in Italia tra affermazione identitaria e nuova religione minoritaria in Zincone G. (ed.), *Secondo rapporto sull'integrazione degli immigrati in Italia*, il Mulino, Bologna, 2001, 602.

2 Pew Research Center, *Faith on the Move. The Religious Affiliation of International Migrants*, Report, March 8, 2012, 32.

3 Fouad Allam, L'islam contemporaneo in Europa e in Italia tra affermazione identitaria e nuova religione minoritaria, 602.

4 See La popolazione straniera residente in Italia, available at: www.istat.it.

5 Pacini A., I musulmani in Italia. Dinamiche organizzative e processi di interazione con la società e le istituzioni italiane, in Ferrari S. (ed.), *Musulmani in Italia. La condizione giuridica delle comunità islamiche*, il Mulino, Bologna, 2000, 33.

6 Pew Research Center, *The World's Muslims: Unity and Diversity*, Report, August 9, 2012, 41.

7 The Albanian Islamic community's current lack of impact on the religious landscape may change over time, due especially to the evolution of the social context in the areas of their origin. As well as the institutional changes, Albania, Kosovo and Bosnia-Herzegovina are witnessing the arrival of key religious figures arriving from the Arab Islamic world whose objectives, amongst others, include the Islamization of the local population. See Conte M.L., Kosovo, the Unknown Face of Euro-Islam, available at: www.oasiscenter.eu.

Each minority's strategy for social inclusion depends upon its specific origins and many other factors. Muslims with Moroccan, Tunisian or Albanian ethnicity seem to be those most interested in absorbing Italian culture and grounding themselves in Italian society.[8] The Senegalese Muslims, by contrast, have generally focused on returning to their homeland.[9] The Senegalese are different from other Muslim communities: they belong to brotherhoods within their ethnicity whose rules differ from mainstream Islamic doctrine in that they put a greater emphasis on the nurturing of their relationship with God.[10] As a result, members of these brotherhoods build close personal bonds of support with each other, developing their relationship with the divine on the basis of affection rather than codices.[11] This phenomenon effectively eschews the organizational dynamics of Islam in Italy, because the Senegalese convene in separate gatherings motivated by different goals.[12]

Religion plays differing roles within Muslim communities. This is not to suggest that religion is the sole factor, but merely that it plays a role in cultural adaptation. The more secularized the immigrant Muslim group, the less difficulty it has in assimilating with the Italian culture and way of life. This works in reverse as well, as very religious Muslim groups with a wealth of tradition and established customs have difficulty fitting in. Another variable is the collective intent of the Muslim group, whether to settle in Italy or return to their homeland like the Senegalese. The diversity of attitudes among Muslim groups in Italy transcends their different places of birth and derives from the era and cultural cluster immigrants experienced before leaving their country. Ancient immigration patterns involved traditionally religious newcomers; milder religious practices characterize more recent expatriations.[13]

It is worth noting that Muslims' customs and traditions, which are promoted by the political and social institutions of their homeland (including regular calls to prayer throughout towns and cities),[14] stand out in Italy as unusual, if not eccentric. In Muslim countries, religious identity is substantially supported by institutional and social structure, perhaps more so than other religions. Civil

8 Pacini, I musulmani in Italia, 32.

9 Ibid., 32.

10 See Pew Research Center, *The World's Muslims: Unity and Diversity*, 31.

11 Pacini, I musulmani in Italia, 40.

12 Notes on the situation of Senegalese brotherhoods can be found in Piga A., Ordini soufi a confronto nel Senegal contemporaneo: un excursus storico, paper presented at the International Conference *Il ruolo del Sufismo e delle confraternite musulmane nell'islam contemporaneo. Un'alternativa all'islam politico?* Turin, November 20–22, 2002, available at: www.centroedoardoagnelli.it.

13 Pew Research Center, *The World's Muslims: Unity and Diversity*, 46.

14 Fouad Allam, L'islam contemporaneo in Europa e in Italia tra affermazione identitaria e nuova religione minoritaria, 595.

authority, social structure and the religious forum are intractably interweaved together, as can be seen in the considerable influence of Islamic religious law over state law.[15]

All these dynamics come into play in the fashioning of the identity of the average Italian Muslim. It is inevitable that European Muslims will experience a rupture between territorial identity and religious identity.[16] In an environment largely shaped by Christian culture, but which has for centuries experienced a process of gradual separation between the religious and civil world, they find it doubly hard to identify with the Italy's basic social and institutional framework.[17] In past centuries, religious Muslims (as opposed to more secular Muslims) would have felt alienated by the majoritarian Catholic faith. Now, most Muslims (whether religious or not) feel alienated by the fact that religion eschews the bond between the individual, community and institutions.

The dynamic between the Muslim immigrants' own cultural and religious heritage and their new social and cultural context in Italy has led to various adapted forms of Islam in Europe. The first such form of Islam is neo-fundamental communalism, according to which a Muslim does not define his identity in terms of his origins, but in terms of a system of standards and codes of conduct, which are based primarily on the conflict between right and wrong. The unifying factor here is not so much common Islamic tradition, but religious practice, which binds individual members of the Muslim community. The second such form is neo-ethnic communalism, which underscores the immigrant's affiliation and connection with Islam (elevating shared traditions) rather than the inherent orthopraxis connected to being a Muslim. The third such form represents a secularized approach to Islam based on the immigrant's separation of private from public life and the internalization of his religious experience. This is a private and individual religious experience, focusing on spiritual, mystical and ethical aspects of the Islamic faith. It derives from constant contact with Islam in an incremental process of religious absorption and is seen mainly in European countries with strong Christian faith (which may have influenced this form by its own individualized approach to religion).[18]

A growing number of Muslim immigrants and new converts to Islam do not intend to give up or radically change their religiosity as they move to Italy; rather, they negotiate with the government to obtain legal exemptions to meet their religious needs. On the one hand, this phenomenon is inherent in the integration process of several other new religions now appearing on

15 Ibid., 579–81.

16 Ibid., 596.

17 Ibid., 596.

18 Ibid., 591–94.

Italy's landscape: their requests are usually initiated with the aim of creating a limited special status suited to their own particular characteristics. From this perspective, the attitude adopted by Italian Muslims is similar to those adopted by other religious minorities who have put forward similar demands (whether or not they were granted). On the other hand, the Muslim presence in Italy is generating tensions, which might be of a very different magnitude from those religions that the law has already tacitly supported through state–religion agreements. Islam raises new and different issues that the Italian legal system is not accustomed to handling. Accepting some of the more incisive demands of the Muslim community could precipitate a major impact on the state of religious freedom in Italy. The pressure on the legal system to meet Islamic demands from a qualitative perspective is decidedly novel and significantly greater.

See, for example, the practice of polygamy[19] and the role of the mosque in political and religious aggregation. Polygamy impinges significantly on legally protected values like established models of institutions such as marriage.[20] Mosques often take on a strong role in political leadership, raising sensitive issues in an international context, through which Islamic terrorism has made a big impact. Moreover, Muslim immigrants in Italy are unlikely to let such demands lapse because of the passage of time or their potential impact on the law; they are also not likely to limit themselves to private religious practice.[21] While a substantial number of Muslims appear inclined to embrace a more

19 For the history and events surrounding polygamy in the countries of emigration, see Aluffi Beck-Peccoz R., *Le leggi del diritto di famiglia negli stati arabi del Nord-Africa*, UTET, Turin, 1997; Tedeschi M. (ed.), *Quaderni della scuola di specializzazione in diritto ecclesiastico e canonico*, 4, *La presenza islamica nell'ordinamento giuridico italiano*, Jovene, Naples, 1996. Regarding the problems of polygamy in context of the European continent, see Campiglio C., Famiglia e diritto islamico. Profili internazional-privatistici, in Ferrari (ed.), *Musulmani in Italia. La condizione giuridica delle comunità islamiche*; Cardia C., Matrimonio, famiglia, vita privata. Spunti di analisi ricostruttiva, in *Quaderni di diritto e politica ecclesiastica*, 2002, 31–61; Colaianni N., Poligamia e principi del "diritto europeo," in *Quaderni di diritto e politica ecclesiastica*, 2002, 227–61; Mancini L., *Immigrazione musulmana e cultura giuridica. Osservazioni empiriche su due comunità di egiziani*, Giuffré, Milan, 1998.

20 Rohe M., The Current Debate on Islam, in Ferrari S. and Cristofori R. (eds), *Law and Religion in the 21st Century. Relations between States and Religious Communities*, Ashgate, Farnham, 2010, 336.

21 See Aluffi Beck-Peccoz R., The Legal Treatment of the Muslim Minority in Italy, in Aluffi Beck-Peccoz R. and Zincone G. (eds), *The Legal Treatment of Islamic Minorities in Europe*, Peeters, Leuven, 2004, 156: "integration does not seem to be a major objective for all Muslims. Some experts underline that certain groups focus on a neo-communal project, involving the claim for collective rights, rather than individual ones and for economic and social integration, doubled with cultural separateness."

spiritualized, less public and socially relevant practice, indications from the whole of the European continent would suggest the contrary.

The Charter of Muslims in Europe, for example, signed on January 10, 2008 by more than 400 Muslim organizations that all gathered at the *Federation des Organisations Islamiques en Europe* in Brussels[22] positions the European Muslim community directly at the forefront of Islam's long-standing religious tradition. It affirms the prescriptive nature of the immutable rules of the Qur'an and the Sunnah of the Prophet Muhammad,[23] advocates the rapprochement between the many different component forms of European Islam in accordance with customary Islamic sensibilities that conceive of Muslims as a single fraternity, and expresses the need for Muslim immigrants to be granted the status of a religious community throughout Europe. As such, the concord highlights the will of the Muslim community to gain ground on the European continent through a communitarian approach. Although benign and positive on its face, this approach is not without issues. Several themes presented in the paper are vague, such as the assertion that men and women "complement" each other. This idea appears to elide the problem of legal equality between genders (which is symptomatic of Islamic law generally).[24]

At first glance, the Muslim community seems to be characterized by peculiar aspects, both in the way it conceives its presence in Europe and in its demands for religious freedom. This is also true with regard to Italy. Although Italian law has not had to address highly critical issues such as polygamous marriages, which have never been openly advocated, it has nevertheless experienced other sensitive issues for Muslims, such as ritual slaughter and the use of the Muslim headscarf. It is good to briefly consider these two issues as meaningful examples: in fact, Islamic ritual slaughter has received a reasonable, albeit partial, accommodation on the same basis as Jewish slaughter. On the contrary, the use of the headscarf has been welcomed by the judiciary but sometimes impeded by state officials, and is still debated.

---

22 The document can be found at: www.olir.it.

23 The body of words and deeds attributed to Muhammad. Other elements found in the document that demonstrate an endeavor to position itself in the wake of orthodoxy are the mention of the Shari'a and the various classic law schools which are accepted as being equally valid.

24 See, for example, Schacht J., *An Introductioni to Islamic Law*, Oxford University Press, Oxford, 1982. Another problematic issue mentioned in the Charter concerns the analogy between the ancient custom of making political decisions through the consultation of the religious community versus the practice of modern democracy: an ever-recurring theme, at least since the early twentieth century in literature regarding the compatibility of Islam with modern and contemporary constitutionalism.

Ritual Slaughter

Islam prohibits the consumption of all pork and other meat from animals that have died in particular circumstances.[25] It also prescribes detailed conditions to the slaughtering of permitted meats in order to make them *halal*. These conditions are similar (in form and in origin) to the Jewish *kosher* customs found in the Torah.[26] The traditional conflict in this context arises between differences in terms of what the state will permit and what the religion requires. For example, Italian law has for some time regulated animal slaughter, increasing the protection of the animal to prevent its unnecessary suffering (i.e. by stunning the animal prior to the slaughter itself).[27] At the time of slaughter, the animal must be completely healthy and fully alert. Islamic slaughter must be carried out by severing the jugular vein with the aid of a sharp blade and without making any preliminary incisions in order to sever the trachea and esophagus with a single cut (this ensures that the animal is fully bled). While they appear incompatible, neither Jewish nor Muslim ritual slaughter is intended to constitute a voluntary act of abuse;[28] rather, it is apparent that the intention behind ritual slaughtering (as understood by the knowledge and techniques available at the time that it was created) was finding a relatively quick and painless way to procure the death of animals for human consumption.[29]

---

25 It is, first and foremost, the Qu'ran itself which provides that: "Forbidden to you is that which dies of itself, and blood, and flesh of swine, and that on which any other name than that of Allah has been invoked, and the strangled (animal) and that beaten to death, and that killed by a fall and that killed by being smitten with the horn, and that which wild beasts have eaten, except what you slaughter, and what is sacrificed on stones set up (for idols) and that you divide by the arrows; that is a transgression. This day have those who disbelieve despaired of your religion, so fear them not, and fear Me." Sura 5, verse 3.

26 Roccella A., Macellazione e alimentazione, in Ferrari (ed.), *Musulmani in Italia La condizione giuridica delle comunità islamiche*, 201.

27 Ibid., 204.

28 See the Opinion issued by the National Bioethics Committee released on September 19, 2003, *Macellazioni rituali e sofferenza animale*, 13: "Considering that the special constitutional protection of religious freedom as recognized in our system suggests legally permissible ritual slaughter, the [Council] considers it to be bio-ethically permissible when accompanied by all those practices which do not conflict with the actual rituals of the slaughter and which minimize the animals' suffering." The Opinion can be found at: www.governo.it/bioetica/pareri.html.

29 Roccella A., I musulmani in Italia: macellazione e alimentazione, available at: www.olir.it, 3.

For almost a century, European states have sought to strike a balance between the values at stake: a practice promoted by religious precepts and the protection of animal health and well-being.[30] In recent decades, however, the impetus for the evolution of state laws has come from the growth of laws guiding the European Union, the directives to which Italy has duly adhered. These directives provide for the safeguarding of the animal's welfare as well as exemptions that allow for ritual slaughter on the condition that specific protocols to minimize animal suffering are respected.

This religion–state balance culminated in the Ministerial Decree of June 11, 1980, which was issued by the Ministry of Health in conjunction with the Ministry of the Interior and was entitled *Authorization for the Slaughter of Animals According to Jewish and Islamic Religious Rites*. The decree implemented Law no. 439 (1978), an Italian law that was issued in compliance with a European Community directive on the procedures for ritual slaughter.[31] Further, the decree referred specifically to requests from the Union of Italian Jewish communities and the Islamic Cultural Center of Italy to authorize them to slaughter animals according to Jewish and Islamic rituals.[32] As was hoped, the needs of these communities appear to have been met by the decree. A state–religion agreement between Italy and the Jewish community referenced it and further consecrated and stabilized the right to practice ritual slaughter. Formally, until either party decides to amend the agreement, Italian governing bodies will be allowed to approve ritual slaughtering rites as they see fit.

The aftershocks of this decree can be seen in the state–religion agreements of various religions that were put forth according to Art. 8 of the Italian Constitution. In 1998, when a new European Directive was issued[33] and a subsequent Legislative Decree implemented it,[34] the new law safeguarded ritual slaughter under the same conditions as the previous decree had done.[35] Note,

30 Roccella, Macellazione e alimentazione, 205. Royal Decree no. 3298 issued in 1928, aims to protect animals from suffering inflicted during slaughter, but ensures "observance of religious precepts," in case they conflict with the duty to avoid animals' suffering (Art. 9).

31 Namely, Directive 74/577/EEC, 18/11/74.

32 Roccella, I musulmani in Italia: macellazione e alimentazione, 5.

33 93/119/EC, released December 22, 1993.

34 In reality, EU legislation has also been put in place, and thus implemented by the Italian legislature (Legislative Decree no. 286 of 1994 and no. 193 of 2007), aimed at regulating the release of fresh meat onto the market.

35 Directive 93/119/EC was repealed and supplanted by the Council Regulation (EC) no. 1099/2009, September 24, 2009. It has not directly abrogated the Italian legislation, but has confirmed that "Derogation from stunning in case of religious slaughter taking place in slaughterhouses was granted by Directive 93/119/EC. Since Community provisions applicable to religious slaughter have been transposed

however, that the new decree was issued without consulting the Jewish or Muslim communities.[36] The Jewish state–religion agreement had made specific reference to the earlier decree; as such, the new law was technically a violation of the state–religion agreement.[37] Although there does not appear to have been any complaints from the Jewish community regarding this violation, the experience suggests that state–religion agreements should not make specific reference to internal guidelines, which may be affected by the evolution of European Union law.

That said, this success of religious slaughter is not without its drawbacks: spread over the whole of Islamic and Jewish culture, the situation is still fragmented and disjointed. For example, while the Islamic community at large has the right to practice ritual slaughter, it is not clear whether these regulations apply to detention facilities,[38] hospitals and school cafeterias. The Italian state could have (but currently has not) ensured that all Muslims who make use of public services could eat with accordance with the requirements. This is also the case for the Jewish community: the availability of the *kashruth* diet for public services is complicated (owing to different needs of different Jewish communities) and has received a scattered application throught the country. This is in sharp contrast to the situation of these communities in Spain, where the state–religion agreements address these issues.[39]

---

differently depending on national contexts and considering that national rules take into account dimensions that go beyond the purpose of this Regulation, it is important that derogation from stunning animals prior to slaughter should be maintained, leaving, however, a certain level of subsidiarity to each Member State. As a consequence, this Regulation respects the freedom of religion and the right to manifest religion or belief in worship, teaching, practice and observance, as enshrined in Article 10 of the Charter of Fundamental Rights of the European Union" (no. 18).

36 Roccella, I musulmani in Italia: macellazione e alimentazione, 9.

37 Roccella, Macellazione e alimentazione, 9–10.

38 Moreover, another potential conflict may occur for the Islamic holiday of *Aid al Kabir*, during which the head of the family should personally carry out an animal sacrifice—usually a sheep. For further clarification, see Barberis E., Problemi di regolazione della macellazione islamica in Italia: note da una ricerca empirica, in *Sociologia del diritto*, 2004, 3, 77–98.

39 Cooperation agreement with the Islamic Commission of Spain (Law 26 of 10.11.92): "La alimentación en centros de los internados o establecimientos públicos dependencias militares, y la de los centros de los alumnos musulmanes docentes públicos y privados concertados que lo soliciten, se procurará adecuar a los preceptos religious islámicos, así como el horario de comidas durante elmes de ayuno (Ramadàn)" (Art. 14, fourth paragraph).

The Muslim Veil

The wearing of a headscarf by Muslim women is a hotly debated issue. The law has not explicitly accommodated the custom; as such, I will highlight the different strategies that have been used and which ones have prevailed.

The use of a veil by Muslim women has attracted the attention of some European states as well as the European Court of Human Rights (ECtHR). France has infamously introduced two pieces of legislation, one that outlawed the use of visible religious signs in public schools[40] and the other that outlawed the use of garments that hide a person's identity in public.[41] While these laws purported to provide a neutral framework that covers all religions in France,[42] they were provoked by an intense debate over the presence of Islam in the public sphere and came after long-standing legal disputes between Islam and the state.[43] Interestingly, given that the laws purported to be neutral, but stemmed from issues with Islam, their effect created problems for the other religions in France (for example, Jewish students were not allowed to wear their *kippah* in public schools).

The enforcement of similar provisions to those in France is common in Europe. For example, Germany's *Länder* have provisions that ban the Muslim veil in public schools or prohibit teachers from wearing religious symbols.[44] Likewise, Belgium also passed a ban on the wearing of garments in public places that hide one's identity.[45] The European Court of Human Rights has repeatedly justified bans on the use of Muslim veil and their jurisprudence has approved of any limitations on the use of headscarves on Muslim schoolteachers[46] or students,[47] or the use of the complete veil (the *niqab* or the *burqa*) in public places.[48] One rationale for the French law conceives of the use of such veils as hidden forms of gender discrimination and menaces to the secular character of

40 Law no. 228, 2004.

41 Law no. 1192, 2010.

42 *Charte de la laïcité dans les services publics et autres avis*, delivered March 31, 2007 by the Haut Conseil à l'intégration, available at: http://www.hci.gouv.fr/rubrique.php3?id_rubrique=16.

43 Cavana P., *Interpretazioni della laicità. Esperienza francese ed esperienza italiana a confronto*, A.V.E., Rome, 1998.

44 Mancini S. and Rosenfeld M., Unveiling the Limits of Tolerance: Comparing the Treatment of Majority and Minority Religious Symbols in the Public Sphere, in Ungureanu C. and Zucca L. (eds), *Law, State and Religion in the New Europe*, Cambridge University Press, Cambridge, 2012.

45 Law of June 1, 2011.

46 *Dahlab v. Switzerland* (App. no. 42393/98).

47 *Dogru v. France* (App. no. 27085/05); *Kervanci v. France* (App. no. 11645/04); *Sahin v. Turkey* (App. no. 44774/98).

48 *S.A.S. v. France* (App. no. 43835/11).

French republicanism.[49] Other rationales can be found in other countries and in the decisions of the ECtHR.[50]

In Italy, no similar ban has been adopted. The right to use the veil in public schools has been recognized by the ECtHR as the first example of Italy's benevolent approach towards religious minorities.[51] The Ministry of Internal Affairs has even allowed the Muslim veil in ID photos, provided that it does not obscure the view of the person's face.[52] When some Italian politicians and scholars attempted to limit and outlaw the use of veils to cover women's faces,[53] arguing that Muslim veils should be outlawed as promoting gender inequality and conflicting with a desirable open society, foreign commentators and scholars such as Martha Nussbaum directed screeds against the adopting of any such legislation. The attempt was aborted.

A more interesting legal battle in Italy is waged by forces attempting to limit the use of the Muslim veil by taking advantage of pre-existing legal provisions (rather than promulgating new ones) that had purposes other than enhancing secularism and opposing gender discrimination. Provisions passed in Italy in 1931[54] under fascism and 1975[55] to combat public demonstrations of violent groups that were rioting across the country prohibited the use of garments or helmets that disguise the identity of the wearer in public places.[56] Despite the fact that controversial Muslim veils (the *niqab* and the *burqa*) are hardly found in Italy, some officials used these provisions to prohibit the use of such

---

49 See the dossier at the French national assembly, http://www.assemblee-nationale.fr/13/pdf/rap-info/i2262.pdf, 203: "[C]ondamnant le port du voile integral comme contraire aux valeurs de la République, affirmant le soutien de la représentation nationale aux efforts engagés par les acteurs de terrain pour combattrecettepratique, condamnant les discriminations et les violences faites aux femmes et affirmant la solidarité de la France à l'égard des femmes qui en sont victimes de par le monde."

50 See *Sahin v. Turkey* (Grand Chamber decision, November 10, 2005, par. no. 116): "it was the principle of secularism which was the paramount consideration underlying the ban on the wearing of religious symbols in universities"; or *S.A.S. v. France* (Grand Chamber decision, July 1, 2014, par. 141) "the Court is able to accept that a State may find it essential to give particular weight in this connection to the interaction between individuals and may consider this to be adversely affected by the fact that some conceal their faces in public places."

51 See *Lautsi v. Italy*, cit., par. 74.

52 See Fiorita N., Libertà religiosa e società multiculturali: il caso del velo islamico, http://www.statoechiese.it/images/stories/2008.6/fiorita_libert.pdf,10.

53 Nussbaum M., *La nuova intolleranza*, Laterza, Rome-Bari, 2012.

54 Royal Decree no. 733, 1931, Art. 85.

55 Law no. 152, 1975, Art. 5.

56 On the modification of such laws, see Fiorita, Libertà religiosa e società multiculturali: il caso del velo islamico, 10.

garments for public safety.[57] The Italian judiciary reacted against these officials and held that the Muslim veil was legitimate, since it was a religious garment characterized by religious significance.[58] Further, it is clear that the pre-existing Italian provisions on hand could not be used to effect such a change. The 1931 and 1975 provisions were aimed at individuals who were consciously trying to modify or disguise their identity; the purpose of their passage did not allow the Muslim veil to be brought under their ambit. This decision highlighted the likely intention of the officials, who were not trying to protect public safety so much as they were trying to fight strands of Muslim religiosity that they found dangerous to Italian society.[59]

A Diverse Mosaic

Ritual slaughter and the wearing of the Muslim veil are but two examples of the issues that the Muslim presence raises in Italy. The issues that the Italian state must address with regard to Islam are wide-ranging and the potential legal issues are diverse. Authorities must analyze and endorse or reject issues that have already been decided with regard to other religions.

There are other Islamic practices that may be deemed acceptable by virtue of their similarity to practices of other denominations that have already been made legal. For example, the legality of Islam's day of worship and the status of mosques, religious leaders or the celebration of religious marriages could be acceptable by reference to state–religion agreements already in existence. Italy granted to the Jewish and Adventist communities the right to make Saturday their holy day, with the various exemptions that such a designation brings. It is thus reasonable to expect that the state would allow the Islamic community to establish Friday as their holy day in concert with Islamic practice. Similarly, as certain state–religion agreements provide exemptions that cater to basic tenets of the religion *qua* religion, Italy might similarly provide recognition to Islam's religious pillars and prerogatives (including exemptions for mosques, religious leaders and religious weddings). But other facts run against such allowances.

57 The power to take the necessary decisions to preserve public safety is given to mayors by the legislative Decree no. 267, 2000, Art. 54, par. 4.

58 Council of State (Sixth Section), judgment no. 3076, 2008. See also the Superior Council of Judiciary deliberation of February 22, 2012 on the duty to accommodate the religious prescriptions to wear hats and other garments that cover the head with the duty of attend judiciary hearings with the head uncovered, available at: http://www.csm.it/circolari/120222b_6.pdf.

59 http://www.interno.gov.it/mininterno/export/sites/default/it/assets/files/19/00036_Comitato_Islam_-_relazione_Burqa_07_10.pdf.

Since Friday is a work day, the effects of recognizing it as a holy day are much more significant than recognizing Saturday as a holy day. Mosques and religious leaders play a political role that has become highly scrutinized by Western democracies in the last 10 years, with the increase of the Muslim population and of terrorist threats. Further, religious marriages can hide polygamy and domestic inequalities. These issues must be squared in order to accommodate Muslims' needs, otherwise skepticism of the possibility of folding Islam into Italian society will halt any initiative.

In order to consider the various aspects of the integration of Islam into Italian law, we must ponder the methods and tools needed to build such an achievement. The main tool used to date is the state–religion agreement. Its importance is augmented by the difficulty of passing a generally applicable law on religious freedom, as we will see. The next chapter will focus on the established practice of implementing Art. 8 of the Italian Constitution in order to highlight the means through which religious freedom have been enforced and aligned to the needs of other religious denominations. I will then draw conclusions and will contrast them with the attempts to draft a state–religion agreement with the Islamic community, which requires that one or more bodies formally represent Islamic interests. The presence of a reliable and credible interlocutor and a platform of shared interests are vital components in the successful promulgation of a state–religion agreement. As will be seen in Chapter 2, however, the system of state–religion agreements has so far failed in this endeavor.

Chapter 2
The Role of State–Religion Agreements in Italy: An Imperfect Pluralism

Expanding Religious Freedom: Tension from the Presence of Muslims

Due to increased globalization and immigration, Italian and European societies have experienced an increasing cultural and religious pluralism. Whereas this pluralism has fueled social and political tension throughout the continent, some thinkers have seen it as a positive kind of Babelesque diaspora—a blessing rather than a curse.[1]

Examining the distinctive nature of religious and cultural pluralism creates an inroad for understanding the ability of government to deal with the phenomenon. The past few decades were characterized by the rise and affirmation of movements that tried to uniformly eliminate distinctions between social and racial communities, and create equality between religions. More recently, there has been a bifurcated but contemporaneous dynamic: on the one hand, each community exchanges practices and takes inspiration from one another[2] (hybridization);[3] on the other hand, each community highlights its own unique aspects and emphasizes how it is distinct from the others.[4] Notwithstanding the strong hybridization movement, the latter has become a trademark of a community's self-understanding and identity at an individual, communitarian and legal level.

There are reasons for emphasizing group identities. Legal acceptance of a religious or cultural community helps construct (rather than merely affirm or promote) a community's identity.[5] Understandably, these communities are not

---

1 Weiler J.H.H., *La Costituzione dell'Europa*, il Mulino, Bologna, 2003, 197.

2 See Galli C. (ed.), *Multiculturalismo. Ideologie e sfide*, il Mulino, Bologna, 2006, 23.

3 See Laplantine F., *Je, Nous et Les Autres. Etre Humains au dela des appartaneances*, Gallimard, Paris, 1999; Laplantine F. and Nouss A., *Le Métissage*, L'Harmattan, Paris, 2011; Scola A., *Una nuova laicità. Temi per una società plurale*, Marsilio, Venice, 2007.

4 Kymlicka W., *Multicultural Citizenship: A Liberal Theory of Minority Rights*, Clarendon Press, Oxford, 1995.

5 Scola, *Una nuova laicità*.

interested in obscuring their collective identities and practicing only in private. Rather, public acceptance generally furthers the goals of their religious or cultural mission and bolsters their internal solidarity.

Legal recognition of non-standard religions has been problematic. Contemporary legal regimes have centered on prevailing European conceptions of personhood, the good and other traditional values more so than many scholars and political leaders expected.[6] As such, many non-traditional cultures spent the last century blending into a relatively homogenous Judeo-Christian environment,[7] which served as common ground for them to develop their national policies.[8] In the last few decades, however, these and other emerging non-traditional cultures have imposed themselves on a national level and demanded social and political recognition.[9] By challenging the fundamentals of the European legal and social order, the legal integration of these cultures has become more complicated.

European and North American legal orders have responded dynamically to increasing pluralism through continuous legal adaptation, often—but not always—making room for new religious identities. Systems founded on new religious exceptions have increased in number to accompany older isolated religious exceptions that were originally conceived to accommodate limited religious practices. See, for example, the motorcycle helmet exception afforded to the Sikh population in the UK[10] or the efforts of the Italian Constitutional Court to eliminate discrimination for religious minorities by intervening on procedural laws regulating taking an oath before domestic courts.[11] These exception regimes are affected by the globalized character of immigrations and by the transnational dimensions of religious denominations. After the British Sikhs were given the helmet exemption, the Canadian Sikh community raised the same request for the first time in their history.[12]

While religious exemptions have increased over time, awareness that they cannot be unlimited in expansion has also increased. As the nineteenth-century *Reynolds v. United States*[13] decision affirmed the prohibition on polygamy

6 Galli C., Introduction, in Galli (ed.), *Multiculturalismo. Ideologie e sfide*, 14.

7 De Sousa Santos B., La debolezza dei diritti umani tra globalizzazioni rivali e la turbolenza nel rapporto sacro/profano, in *Democrazia e diritto*, 2006, 2, 58.

8 See Taylor C., *La modernità della religione*, Molteni, Rome, 2004, 119; and Taylor C., *A Secular Age*, Harvard University Press, Cambridge, MA, 2007, 454 and 459.

9 Ferrari S., Il diritto ecclesiastico e le stagioni della giurisprudenza costituzionale, available at www.statoechiese.it, 3.

10 *Road Traffic Act* 1988, Art. 16 par. 2.

11 Decision no. 334, 1996.

12 See the Canadian Supreme Courts' decision in *Multani v. Commission scolaire Marguerite-Burgeoys* (2006).

13 *Reynolds v. United States*, 98 US 145 (1878).

to Mormons who wanted it in the name of religious freedom, many recent decisions also deny the right to do everything that a specific religion permits. Similarly, the European Court of Human Rights affirmed that in order to effectively regulate our society, religious liberty needs to be limited.[14]

The Islamic community has likely experienced more difficulties than other minorities in the West attempting to legitimize its own regime of religious exceptions.[15] In fact, doubt has been cast on the practicality of integrating religious minorities, like Muslims, that historically have not been part of the European religious environment. These doubts derive both from the historical cultural exclusion of non-Western religions from the West and contemporary difficulties that have beset relations between the two.

Will it be possible to smoothly integrate Islam into legal and social European culture? Some believe that a sort of "siege syndrome,"[16] coupled with an insistence on traditional European identity values and millennial sensibilities, have possessed European societies. Anxiety over Islamic religious integration also stems from the perception that certain Islamic sects are pursuing demographic and cultural destruction. See, for example, anti-Jewish riots perpetrated by Muslims, which some scholars link to the relationship between Middle Eastern and Nazi leaders.[17] In addition, an increasingly visible Islamic presence in terms of certain Islamic cultural practices has fueled political conflict. These include genital mutilation, polygamy and gender discrimination, and receive social reprobation from virtually all Western societies. These and other practices have been grouped under the concept of "constitutional evils,"[18] a term that has been coined to reflect religious practices that are theoretically allowed under a religious freedom clause, but are realistically degrading and contrary to human dignity. Scholars have noted that Islamic religious integration has the potential to contribute to the increase of constitutional evils.

---

14 See *Kokkinakis v. Greece* (App. no. 14307/88, May 25, 1993), par. 33: "in democratic societies, in which several religions coexist within one and the same population, it may be necessary to place restrictions on this freedom in order to reconcile the interests of the various groups and ensure that everyone's beliefs are respected." See also Evans M.D., *Religious Liberty and International Law in Europe*, Cambridge University Press, Cambridge, 1997, 298.

15 Weller P., "Human Rights," "Religion" and the "Secular": Variant Configurations of Religion(s), State(s) and Society(ies), in *Religion and Human Rights*, 2006, no. 1, 31.

16 Casuscelli G., Le laicità e le democrazie: la laicità della "Repubblica democratica" secondo la Costituzione italiana, in *Quaderni di diritto e politica ecclesiastica*, 2007, 1, 174.

17 Ye'or B., *Eurabia. The Euro-Arab Axis,* Associated University Presses, Plainsboro, NJ, 2005.

18 Graber M.A., Constitutional Democracy, Human Dignity, and Entrenched Evil, in *Pepperdine Law Review*, 2011, no. 38, 893. See also Casuscelli G., La libertà religiosa alla prova dell'Islam: la peste dell'intolleranza, available at: www.statoechiese.it, 13.

The appearance of Islam in Europe has increased religious worries and has affected long-standing religious equilibriums. For example, the 2004 ban[19] on the wearing of the headscarf at public schools in France was crafted in a way that affected other religious minorities as much as it affected Muslims. Along with the loss of the right for Muslim women to wear a headscarf, Jewish students lost the right to wear the *kippah* in public schools. More generally, the enforcement of such laws aimed at Muslims has modified the legal relationship between state and religion in France that was initiated in 1905 and had changed little since then.[20]

Islamophobia and broader concerns that practices that are contrary to human rights could sneak into Western democracies through religious freedom claims also abound outside Europe. An example can be found in the repealing of the Arbitration Act in Ontario, Canada. The Act was signed into law in 1991 and had allowed the Jewish population significant religious exemptions, including the ability to address family and commercial disputes within rabbinical tribunals that could apply Jewish law. However, because the Muslim community in the province expressed the desire to have its own religious tribunals,[21] the Ontario legislature passed a law abolishing them for all religious communities.[22] Even more recently, the US saw confrontations on Islamic law between the state legislatures and federal judiciary. In 2010, the Oklahoma State legislature passed a constitutional amendment famously known as the "Save Our State" amendment.[23] The proposed amendment banned state courts from using or considering Islamic law in their judgments; the federal courts[24] struck down

19 Law of October 11, 2010.

20 Cavana P., *Interpretazioni della laicità. Esperienza francese ed esperienza italiana a confronto*, A.V.E., Rome, 1998.

21 See Saris A.-Potvin J.M., Canadian Muslim Women and Resolution of Family Conflicts: An Empirical Qualitative Study (2005–2007), in Ferrari S. and Cristofori R. (eds), *Law and Religion in the 21st Century. Relations between States and Religious Communities*, Ashgate, Farnham, 2010, 359.

22 Bill 27/06, amending the Arbitration Act (Art. 32) and the Family Statute Act (1990, Art. 51). The Arbitration Act mandated that: "In deciding a dispute, an arbitral tribunal shall apply the rules of law designated by the parties or, if none are designated, the rules of law it considers appropriate in the circumstances." After the amendment, a new paragraph states that: "In a family arbitration, the arbitral tribunal shall apply the substantive law of Ontario, unless the parties expressly designate the substantive law of another Canadian jurisdiction, in which case that substantive law shall be applied." After the amendment, the Family Statute Act says that "family agreement … is conducted exclusively in accordance with the law of Ontario or of another Canadian jurisdiction."

23 Or Oklahoma State Question 755 (2010).

24 *Awad v. Ziriax*, 670 F.3d 1111 (10th Circ. 2012), *aff. g.* 754 F.Supp. 2d 1298 (W.D. Okla. 2010); *Awad v. Ziriax*, Case no. CIV-10–1186-M (W.D. Okla. August 15, 2013).

the ban because it discriminated between Islam and other religions by explicitly excluding only Islamic law from courtrooms.[25] Following this, more states implemented or tried to implement laws that prohibited courts from quoting foreign laws as an indirect measure that would still lock Islamic law out of courtrooms, but would survive judicial scrutiny.[26]

Some scholars have expressed an interest in fashioning religious exemptions for Muslims to accommodate their needs. Informal religious arbitrations held according to Muslim law arose in the UK in the 1980s and flourished without any formal recognition.[27] The Anglican Archbishop of Westminster, Rowan Williams, has recently advocated working the informal arbitrations into the British legal system.[28] Further, 40 percent of British Muslims have recently stated that they would be willing to have such religious tribunals formally recognized by British law.[29]

These examples confirm the wide variety of understandings of religious liberty across countries that, however, share a common sensitivity for such liberty. Cultural differences and political reasons affect the understanding of this fundamental freedom and influence the responses of states to new religious phenomena. The use of instruments provided by the Italian Constitution for the protection of religious freedom reflects the recent dynamization of the religious landscape as well as the struggle to address the needs of the Muslim community in Italy. This chapter focuses on Italian policies in the field of religious freedom. It serves as a background against which I will reflect on the specific problems that arise when Muslims constitute a significant presence in a given country and reasons why the relationship between Islam and the European states tends to be problematic.

---

25 See Baig M.R.K., Operating Islamic Jurisprudence in Non-Muslim Jurisdictions: Traditional Islamic Precepts and Contemporary Controversies in the United States, in *Chicago-Kent Law Review*, 2015, no. 90(1), 79.

26 Ibid. See also Grunert J., How Do You Solve a Problem Like Sharia? Awad v. Ziriax and the Question of Sharia Law in America, in *Pepperdine Law Review*, 40(3), 699.

27 Borrmans M., Nota riguardante l'obiezione di coscienza e i problemi relativi alla pluralità di culture e all'unicità dell'ordinamento giuridico degli Stati moderni, in ambiente islamico o in relazione con la fede musulmana, in Perrone B. (ed.), *Realtà e prospettive dell'obiezione di coscienza. I conflitti degli ordinamenti*, Giuffrè, Milan, 2002, 239. See also Colaianni N., *Eguaglianza e diversità culturali e religiose. Un percorso costituzionale*, il Mulino, Bologna, 2006, 145.

28 Williams R., Foundation Lecture at the Royal Courts of Justice, Civil Rights and Religious Law in England: A Religious Perspective, February 7, 2008, available at www.rowanwilliams.archbishopofcanterbury.org. Shortly afterwards, the Lord Chief Justice of England and Wales, gave a lecture, "Equality before the Law," at the East London Muslim Centre, available at: www.judiciary.gov.uk.

29 Ye'or, who draws statistics from the *Sunday Telegraph*.

Lights and Shadows of State–Religion Agreements in Italy

In the last 30 years, religion has consistently attracted the attention of Italian legislators. During this period, old legal devices have been renovated, while others have been used for the first time. Two positive aspects of Italian policies in this matter are of note: the reform of the Concordat and the creation of several agreements with different religious denominations, some of which are deeply rooted in Italian society.

The New Concordat and its Consequences

The Concordat that Italy and the Holy See signed in 1929 (as part of the broader Lateran Pacts that ended the decades-old conflict between church and state) was dramatically modified in 1984.[30] Whereas the 1929 agreement reaffirmed the long-standing notion that Catholicism was the official religion of the Italian state, the 1984 Concordat declared that such a principle was no longer in force.[31] This ended the debate over religion's legal place in Italian society.

The 1948 Italian Constitution mentioned the Lateran Pact as the means by which the state and the Catholic Church collaborated in one section, while invoking equality and religious freedom in other sections. This formal, but ambiguous conjunction of religious preference of Catholicism in a constitution that also affirmed religious equality justified a state policy that was explicitly preferential to Catholics. As a result, the Constitutional Court perpetuated differences in terms of the treatment of Catholicism and other religions. The 1984 modifications to the Lateran Pacts, which literally supplanted the 1929 regime with a new pact, giving birth to a new agreement, pushed legislators and the Court towards finding a new religious liberty in constitutional interpretations that quash the discriminatory aspects of legislation created on the basis of the older religious inequality.[32] A few years later, the Constitutional Court affirmed that Italy is a non-establishment state ("laico," in the words of decision no. 293, 1989). Although the Court based its ruling on the religious equality provisions of the Constitution, it is clear that the 1984 modifications were what made such a ruling possible. The Court mentioned the 1984 pacts, framing it as a mere example of the enforcement of the new constitutional non-establishment principle in the context of the specific agreement between the state and the

30 Agreements were signed on the February 18 and November 15, 1984; the first was executed with the law of March 25, 1985, no. 121, and the second with the law of May 20, 1985, no. 206.

31 Additional Protocol no. 1.

32 See judgements no. 14 of 1973, 925 of 1988, 440 of 1995.

Catholic Church. That said, it was actually the 1984 pact that made a non-establishment principle possible in Italian law.

Non-Catholic State–Religion Agreements Flourish

The agreements system has substantially proliferated in the last 30 years. From 1948 (when the Italian Constitution was promulgated) to 1984, no agreement with non-Catholic denominations had been signed, notwithstanding Art. 8, par. 3 of the Constitution,[33] which contemplates such agreements as the normal way for the state to regulate its relationships with non-Catholic religions. Conversely, from 1984 to 2012, 18 state–religion agreements have been signed and executed into law by the Italian Parliament (although seven of these merely modified previous state–religion agreements), with one more on the way.

Until 2000, the religious groups which had crafted state–religion agreements belonged to the Judeo-Christian mainstream, although some of them were not deeply rooted in Italian society. In 2000, agreements with the Jehovah's Witnesses and the Italian Buddhist Union changed this. The Buddhists' agreement demonstrated that it is possible to use such legal instruments to regulate the relationship with religious groups that do not share Italian cultural roots.[34] The agreement was also relevant because of the debate surrounding whether or not Buddhism would legally qualify as a religion. Some scholars maintained that Italian Buddhists did not have the necessary characteristics to identify it as religious as opposed to merely cultural or philosophical. However, in part due to the gradual development of the concept of a "religious denomination," thanks to Italian judges,[35] the domestic legal culture has developed a broader understanding of the concept that now includes religions that do not presuppose the existence of a Supreme Being or a direct relationship between man and divinity.[36]

Treatment of religious minorities has also progressed with regard to Jehovah's Witnesses, which, despite having its roots in the Judeo-Christian tradition,[37] has created a lot of resistance to acceptance in the Italian legal community. The Jehovah's Witnesses' disapproval of the right and duty to vote, to health treatments such as blood transfusions and to military service has

33 "Their relations [of religions] with the State shall be regulated by law on the basis of agreements with their respective representatives."

34 Colaianni N., L'intesa con i buddhisti, available at www.olir.it, 2.

35 Council of State, brief no. 2158 of 1989; Court of Cassazione, decision no. 1329 of 1997, VI Penal Section.

36 Angeletti S., L'intesa tra lo Stato italiano e l'Unione Buddhista Italiana, available at www.olir.it, 3. See also Colaianni, L'intesa con i buddhisti, 2–3.

37 Long G., Le nuove intese: una naturale tendenza espansiva?, in *Quaderni costituzionali*, 2000, 2, 402.

created obstacles which have been difficult to overcome.[38] The acceptance of their state–religion agreement should therefore be considered a partial success in overcoming the doubts about the possibility of fully integrating a relatively non-traditional religion into the Italian social order.

However, the success of these state–religion agreements has proven to be at least partially illusory. For example, the agreements with the Buddhists and Jehovah's Witnesses took an excessively long time to complete. They were signed for the first time in 2000 and the pact with the Buddhists was finally legally executed in 2012, whereas the execution of the Jehovah's Witesses' one is still wanting. And, while their 2000 agreements were pending at the parliamentary level, the state signed several other agreements with more traditional religious denominations. Since the 2000 agreements with the Buddhists and Jehovah's Witnesses had not been executed, they were re-signed in 2007 with almost identical paperwork, highlighting the paradoxical disposition of denominations that had reached an agreement, but could not force the state to promulgate it.[39] Many critics believed that such agreements were little more than political tools that the Parliament was able to use and dismiss at its convenience.[40]

Between 2000 and 2007, several other religious denominations took advantage of the agreement system as a means to integrate themselves into the Italian legal and social environment. Unfortunately, all of them became equally mired in the process of putting their agreement into law, having to wait until 2012 before the Italian government formally processed their requests and blessed them with law execution[41] (with the Jehovah's Witnesses still waiting for official recognition).

The state–religion agreements of various religions are also defective in their provisions. Because the provisions in each agreement are largely identical to one another, their practical effect is extending the same protection to different

38 Ibid., 402.

39 See Pacillo V., L'intesa con la Chiesa di Gesù Cristo dei Santi degli Ultimi Giorni: prime considerazioni; Benigni R., L'intesa con l'Unione Induista Italiana Sanatana Dharma Samgha; Graziano L., Andando oltre la "standardizzazione" delle intese: la Chiesa apostolica in Italia e l'articolo 8.3 della Costituzione; Mori G., Ortodossia e intesa con lo Stato italiano: il caso della Sacra Arcidiocesi Ortodossa d'Italia ed Esarcato per l'Europa meridionale, all in *Quaderni di diritto e politica ecclesiastica*, 2007, 2.

40 Guazzarotti A., Nuove intese con le minoranze religiose e abuso della normazione simbolica, in *Quaderni costituzionali*, 2007, 4, 845. See also Angeletti S., La nuova intesa con l'Unione Buddista Italiana: una doppia conforme per il Sangha italiano, available at www.statoechiese.it.

41 With the Orthodox Archdiocese (Law no. 126, July 30, 2012); the Church of the Latter Day Saints (Law no. 127, July 30, 2012); the Apostolic Church in Italy (Law no. 128, July 30, 2012); the Buddhist Union (Law no. 245, December 31, 2012); and the Hindu Union (Law no. 246, December 31, 2012).

religions with little or no adaptation to the specificities of each religion.[42] The religions that have not been formally blessed with a state–religion agreement by the Italian Parliament are left to be ruled by the remains of the Law of Allowed Religions, no. 1159, issued in 1929 ("Legge sui culti ammessi") and its by-law, no. 289 issued in 1930, passed into law during the fascist period. While not all of these provisions do not conflict with religious liberty (for example, the by-law allows pupils from religious minorities to receive catechism at public schools in the absence of an applicable religious facility of their own), some are clearly outdated and inconsistent with constitutional provisions. For instance, Art. 1 of the Law of Allowed Religions admits non-Catholic denominations only as long as they refuse to profess principles or perform rites that are contrary to "public order" or to the "public morality." On the contrary, Art. 19 of the more recently promulgated Constitution contemplate limitations to *practices*—not *principles*—that are contrary to public morality. As such, one of the most common features of contemporary state–religion agreements consists in nullifying the application of the 1929–30 legislation for the relevant religion. The exit from the fascist regime is therefore a means for religious groups to receive greater liberty and is amongst the most powerful reasons to reach an agreement with the state.[43]

The opportunity to replace the older Law of Allowed Religions with constitutionally sound legislation on religious liberty has received attention from scholars and politicians alike, but it has not resulted in any new laws. New legislation on this matter, enforcing constitutional provisions, would be expected to increase the protection of the same individuals and religions that are lobbying for an agreement. This would also decrease the number of religions that are seeking an agreement only in order to achieve the broad liberty granted by the Constitution. As we will see, there are some doubts that the creation of such a law would actually result in a decrease of the number of agreements needed.

Copycat State–Religion Agreements

The enforcement of Italian constitutional provisions in the field of religious liberty diverges from the Constitution's text. The framers conceived of Art. 8

42 Ceccanti S., Le nuove intese: quando il simbolico conta più dello specifico, in *Quaderni costituzionali*, 2000, 399. But see Colombo S., I rapporti tra lo Stato e l'Unione Cristiana Evangelica Battista d'Italia: l'Intesa del 1995, available at: www.olir.it, 27.

43 All agreements have a provision that declares the 1929 legislation on allowed religions as no longer applicable to the relevant confessions: see the Agreement with the Waldensians (Art. 1); the Adventists (Art. 1); God's Assemblies (Art. 1); the Jewish communities (Art. 33); the Baptists (Art. 1); the Lutherans (Art. 1); the Orthodox Church (Art. 25); the Latter Day Saints (Art. 27); the Hindus (Art. 28); and the Buddhists (Art. 26).

as a flexible tool that allowed the state and each religion to find an agreement according to the religion's specificities. Unfortunately, the state–religion agreements that have been crafted up to this point are largely identical in their provisions, text and structure. This is contrary to both the needs of the Constitution and the needs of the religion.

The state–religion agreements are identical with regard to issues like religious assistance to the military or to convicts, the relationship between civil procedures and religious wedding ceremonies, and access to mass-media (the only state–religion agreement bucking this duplicative trend is the one signed with the Union of Jewish Communities).[44] Moreover, the identical provisions are largely pleonasms, merely repeating constitutional provisions that could have been avoided in the framing process.[45]

This repetition has had two relevant effects: first, it has created a body of norms that uniformly regulates some aspects of the relationships (such as spiritual counseling, religious teaching and the funding of religious bodies) between the state and religions across all the state–religion agreements,[46] creating a set of "copycat agreements."[47] See, for example, the Hindu and Buddhist state–religion agreements, which are largely identical to each other and previous agreements, despite being very different from each other and the Italian cultural environment.[48] Second, this phenomenon has acted to homogenize rather than cultivate the differences between the religions, as the Constitution called for. The religions that want to initiate a state–religion agreement have accepted that they must compromise on specific changes and amendments to the agreements that will accommodate their needs *qua* religion in order to have it easily passed through the government. The more similar their state–religion agreement is to a previous one, the more likely it is that the government would promulgate it expediently and without complaint.[49] For example, some central tenets of the Buddhist tradition were forcibly translated into terms and expressions that are common in Italian legal culture. The Jehovah's Witnesses' state–religion

44 Colombo, *I rapporti tra lo Stato e l'Unione Cristiana Evangelica Battista d'Italia: l'Intesa del 1995*, 27.

45 See Botta R., L'intesa con gli israeliti, in *Quaderni di diritto e politica ecclesiastica*, 1987, 99; or Long G., Le intese con l'Unione avventista e con le assemblee di Dio in Italia, in *Quaderni di diritto e politica ecclesiastica*, 1987, 124; Colaianni N., A vent'anni dalla prima intesa. Un'analisi economica, in *Quaderni di diritto e politica ecclesiastica*, 2004, 237.

46 Ferrari S., Libertà religiosa individuale ed uguaglianza delle comunità religiose nella giurisprudenza della Corte costituzionale, in *Giurisprudenza costituzionale*, 1997, 3097.

47 Ricca M., *Legge e intesa con le confessioni religiose. Sul dualismo tipicità/atipicità nella dinamica delle fonti*, Giappichelli, Turin, 1996, 200.

48 Angeletti, L'intesa tra lo Stato italiano e l'Unione Buddhista Italiana, 15.

49 Colaianni, Le intese con i Buddhisti e i Testimoni di Geova, 489–90.

agreement failed to address the most sensitive issues pertaining to that religious tradition, namely blood transfusions and conscientious objections.

The Constitutional Court's case law confirms the fact that the Italian Constitution was not designed to promote this repetitious praxis.[50] It has stated that: "The agreements enshrined in Art. No. 8, third paragraph, are … the instrument that the Constitution offers to regulate the relationships between religious denominations and the State on aspects that are related to single denominations' specificities or that need special regimes."[51] This language is clearly meant to suggest that state–religion agreements are intended to orient Italian law to the specificities of each religion or allow them the necessary exemptions to function harmoniously. In addition, state–religion agreements are not the only way in which the legislature can regulate religious freedom.

Thanks to bilateral agreements, the standard protection of religious freedom has increased in Italy. But this protection is not full, comprehensive and coherent if compared with the ideas that the framers of the Constitution intended to implement.

The Outcome and New Perspectives of Italian Religious Freedom Policy

Notwithstanding all the issues with state–religion agreements, they have provided denominations with various relevant advantages.[52] We will review some of them in order to highlight why religions would agree to state–religion agreements that do not respect their identities as religions.

A Share of the Revenue from Personal Income Tax

The clearest advantage in signing a state–religion agreement is the possibility of receiving public funding. Most of the state–religion agreements have provisions allowing taxpayers to divest 0.8 percent of their income tax revenue to go towards the religion of their choice (providing the religion had stipulated

50 Vitale A., *Corso di diritto ecclesiastico. Ordinamento giuridico e interessi religiosi*, Giuffrè, Milan, 1998, 192. Parisi M., Il sistema europeo di relazioni tra gli Stati e le organizzazioni religiose: conservazione o innovazione nella prospettiva della Costituzione dell'Unione Europea?, available at: www.olir.it, 12.

51 Decision no. 346 of 2002. See Parolin G.P., Edilizia di culto e legislazione regionale nella giurisprudenza costituzionale: dalla sentenza 195/1993 alla sentenza 346/2002, in *Giurisprudenza italiana*, 2003, 351–53.

52 Parisi M., Promozione della persona umana e pluralismo partecipativo: riflessioni sulla legislazione negoziata con le confessioni religiose nella strategia costituzionale di integrazione delle differenze, in *Il Diritto ecclesiastico*, 2004, 409.

to such a concept in its state–religion agreement). Only the state–religion agreements with the Jehovah's Witnesses, the Apostolic Church and (until recently) the Baptists lack such a provision, for reasons that are deeply rooted in their theological background.

A distinction can be drawn between the religions that have opted to receive a share of various citizens' income tax. Some elect to receive money only from taxpayers who expressly choose to give some of their taxes;[53] others (following the example set by the Catholic Church's state–religion agreement) receive tax money from both those who expressly choose to give and those who take no action whatsoever.[54] Pursuant to various state–religion agreements, the money from taxpayers who fail to tick the appropriate box is collected and split among the religions that have implemented the provision in their agreement. The total is allocated according to the percentage of the Italian community that has indicated a preference on their tax form for one religion or another. For example, if, of all Italian taxpayers who have chosen to give money to their religion through their taxes, 70 percent of them are giving to the Catholic Church, then the Catholic Church will receive 70 percent of the money taken from taxpayers who select no preference for giving to a religion on their tax form.[55] Moreover, religions that have passed their state–religion agreement usually get tax deductions for their donors, providing another advantage over religions that have not.[56]

Other Benefits

Of the other advantages, the foremost is being out from under the yoke of the Law of Allowed Religions of 1929. Beyond the backwards appellation of non-Catholic denominations as "allowed" and the "public order or public morality" limits to rituals imposed on such religions, there are still more improvements to being freed from the 1929 Law, much of which is still technically in force. For

53 See the Agreement with the God's Assemblies (Art. 23).

54 This has been disciplined in the Agreements with the Adventists (Art. 30), the Jewish communities (Art. 2 l, no. 638/96, which modified the Agreement's law), the Lutherans (Art. 27), the Orthodox Christians (Art. 21), the Apostolic Church (Art. 25), the Buddhists (Art. 20) and the Hindus (Art. 21). As for the Agreement with the Waldensians, see the amendments to the Agreement (law no. 68 of 2009).

55 For a critical approach, see Cardia C., *Stato e confessioni religiose. Il regime pattizio*, il Mulino, Bologna, 1992, 278–79.

56 See Art. 3, law no. 409 of 1993 of the agreement with the Waldensians; Art. 29 of the agreement with the Adventists; Art. 21 of the agreement with God's Assemblies; Art. 26 of the agreement with the Lutherans; Art. 16 of the agreement with the Baptists; Art. 20 of the agreement with the Apostolic Church; Art. 24 of the agreement with the Latter Day Saints; Art. 19 of the agreement with the Buddhists; Art. 20 of the agreement with the Hindus.

example, religious officials of non-Catholic denominations must receive official approval from the government to perform religious acts to which the state attaches public effects.[57] In striking contrast, modern state–religion agreements affirm that the state has no say in the choice of religious officials.[58]

State–religion agreements provided a means through which non-Catholic religions could leave the "Allowed Religion" umbrella and acquire full standing under Art. 7 of the Italian Constitution. It is not by chance that every state–religion agreement specifically provides for the nullification of the 1929 Law.[59]

The general effect of this elevation of non-Catholic religions to full standing is paradoxical. Remember that while the Italian constitutionalism that has been celebrating and vindicating cultural diversity by elevating non-Catholic religions out of the "Allowed Religions" era, theorizing that individuals and groups have the same freedom to be different,[60] the state–religion agreements produced by this process are nearly identical and fail to reflect the differences between the religions. The facility of achieving a standardized agreement with the state, along with the symbolic significance of the agreement itself, has prevailed over the possibility of obtaining a state–religion agreement catered to the specificities of the religion.[61]

A New Religious Freedom Law and its Implications for the State–Religion Agreement

The state's interest in promulgating state–religion agreements with identical provisions, coupled with the religion's interest in reaching an agreement quickly and easily, has produced an effect called "imperfect pluralism."[62] According to

57 Art. 3, law no. 1159, June 24, 1929.

58 Art. 2 of the agreement with the Waldensians; Art. 2 of the agreement with the Adventists; Art. 2 of the agreement with God's Assemblies; Art. 2 of the agreement with the Jewish communities; Art. 2 of the agreement with the Baptists; Art. 3 of the agreement with the Lutherans; Art. 2 of the agreement with the Orthodox Christians; Art. 3 of the agreement with the Latter Day Saints; Art. 3 of the the agreement with Apostolic Church; Art. 2 of the agreement with the Buddhists; Art. 2 of the agreement with the Hindus.

59 But see Casuscelli, Le laicità e le democrazie. On the analogies between the Italian and the American constitutional provisions on religious freedom, see Cardia C., Concordato, intese, laicità dello Stato. Bilancio di una riforma, in *Quaderni di diritto e politica ecclesiastica*, 2004, 25.

60 D'Arienzo M., Attualità della tolleranza, in *Il Diritto ecclesiastico*, 2004, 507.

61 Botta R., La condizione dei gruppi religiosi di più recente insediamento in Italia, in *Il diritto ecclesiastico*, 2000, 364.

62 Bouchard G., Concordato e Intese, ovvero un pluralismo imperfetto, in *Quaderni di diritto e politica ecclesiastica*, 2004, 70–71.

this, the religions have been ranked along the following lines: first, the Catholic Church, whose religious liberty is covered by Art. 7 of the Constitution; second, religions that have been accorded a state–religion agreement and thus have largely been given the same privileges that the Catholic Church enjoys; third, religions that are still formally under the fascist legislation of 1929 and 1930. This last category can be further subdivided into religions that have been formally recognized under this legislation and religions that do not enjoy any formal recognition.[63]

This ranking—which obscures the actual level of liberty of each religion, since the state–religion agreements are standardized—is complicated by those religions that have reached an agreement with the state, but have not seen those agreements executed. Although this problem afflicts only the Jehovah's Witnesses at the moment, it was shared by many other religions until recently, and will probably be shared by many others in the future. Legal scholars and judges share the view that these religions exist in a state of limbo. They have formal recognition from the government, but lack the ability to put the agreement into practice, waiting for Parliament to complete the process.[64]

Certain scholars have proposed a solution to the problem: a new law that would accord basic rights to any religion regardless of the presence of a state–religion agreement. A first glance at the relationship between a generally applicable law and the state–religion agreement sees both aimed at protecting religious freedom as one of the most fundamental liberties that characterize the elevation of human dignity, which lies at the core of the Italian Constitution. A state–religion agreement standing alone does not seem enough to fulfill the protection promised by the Constitution.

This new legislation would do away with the problematic existence of identical state–religion agreements into which various denominations' needs have been shoehorned. Further, a new law would also ideally officially abolish the outdated and outmoded fascist legislation on the subject.[65] It would orient itself to the standards already set forth in the Italian Constitution and to other contemporary conventions or international treaties on human rights, thus allowing religions broader liberties. Religions would be discouraged from requesting a state–religion agreement unless there was something truly distinctive about their religion which brought it out of the ambit of a generally applicable law on religious freedom. Issues such as marriage, spiritual assistance

63 Ibid., 70; Parisi, Il sistema europeo di relazioni tra gli Stati e le organizzazioni religiose.

64 See the judgment no. 6083, November 18, 2011, by the Council of State, Fifth Section. See, on this, Cianitto C. and Tirabassi M., Consiglio di Stato 6083/2011, in *Oxford Journal of Law and Religion*, 2013, 1, 226.

65 Finocchiaro F., *Diritto ecclesiastico*, Zanichelli, Bologna, 2003, 80.

in jails and hospitals, and money collection would be deferred to the generally applicable law.

This idea is not novel—it was originally proposed in the 1980s, when the new Concordat and the first state–religion agreements were signed.[66] In fact, the Concordat and the state–religion agreement with the Waldensians were intended to be the first pieces of a complete transformation of Italian ecclesiastical law.[67] A new generally applicable law would be the fulfillment of this promise. In addition, it would align the Italian government with contemporary international trends, which have seen a growing number of ex-totalitarian regimes enforcing generally applicable legislation on this subject.[68]

The distillation of constitutional values in specific legislation would not likely be pleonastic. It is widely acknowledged that the Constitution needs to be legislatively implemented in order to become effective. The four constitutional articles on religious liberty (Arts. 7, 8, 19 and 20) would find stronger application if they were actuated by a generally applicable law. It would not be satisfactory to a broad enforcement of religious liberty to simply abrogate the Fascist legislation.[69]

Nonetheless, projecting the effects of a generally applicable law on state–religion agreements cannot be done easily. Such a law would not necessarily lead to a decrease in requests for state–religion agreements or a decrease in the number of provisions within any given agreement. Further, state–religion agreements might still be placed at the core of Italian religious freedom policies instead of being shuffled to the periphery. This is because of the highly political role that is attached to a state–religion agreement compared to a general applicable law on religious freedom. A compact between a religion and the state bears a social recognition that would be still appealing, even in the presence of religious freedom legislation.

It will be useful here to review Spain's experience with this issue. Notwithstanding the enforcement of a generally applicable law, the state–religion agreements in Spain still suffered from the same defects we have seen within the Italian context: namely, that they were repetitive and largely unnecessary.

Religious freedom scholars are divided between those who support Spain's way of administrating their generally applicable law and those who think that

---

66 Long, Le nuove intese: una naturale tendenza espansiva?, 403.

67 Cardia, Concordato, intese, laicità dello Stato. Bilancio di una riforma, 29; Parisi, Promozione della persona umana e pluralismo partecipativo, 413–14. But see Casuscelli G. and Domianello S., *Intese con le confessioni religiose diverse dalla cattolica*, in *Digesto-Discipline pubblicistiche*, UTET, Turin, 1993, 522.

68 Cardia, Concordato, intese, laicità dello Stato. Bilancio di una riforma, 30.

69 Casuscelli G., Appunti sulle recenti proposte di legge in tema di libertà religiosa, in *Diritto ecclesiastico*, 2007, 1–2, 67.

state–religion agreements should be repealed.[70] As such, it will be useful to sketch the aspects that Spanish and Italian constitutionalism share in order to analyze how constitutional provisions have been actuated and consider the outcome of such policies.

Protecting Religious Freedom in Spain: A Comparison

The fundamentals of Spanish constitutionalism on religious liberty are found in four elements: religious freedom; separation of church and state, which unambiguously requires state impartiality towards all religious affiliations; the prohibition of religious discrimination; and the principle of cooperation between church and state, which maintains that, since both church and state address themselves to the same society, they are given the power to negotiate an agreement.[71]

These tenets of the constitutional relationship between church and state have led to the creation of a generally applicable law along with more particularized state–religion agreements. The generally applicable law came in the form of the *Law on Religious Freedom*, which was passed shortly after the new Spanish Constitution of 1978 was disseminated and which implemented the constitutional provisions on religious liberty.[72] The Law was also intended to align domestic legislation with the European Convention on Human Rights.[73]

The Spanish Model of State–Religion Agreements

Spain has introduced general religious liberty legislation as well as a Concordat with the Catholic Church. Three state–religion agreements have been signed:

70 See Martínez-Torrón J., La contribución del la Ley Orgánica de Libertad Religiosa a la transición democrática en España, available at: www.olir.it, 1; Fernandez-Coronado Gonzales A., Valoración jurídica del sistema de cooperación con las confesiones minoritarias en España, available at: www.olir.it, 12.

71 Bloss L., European Law of Religion—Organizational and Institutional Analysis of National Systems and Their Implications for the Future European Integration Process, Jean Monnet Working Paper no. 13/03, available at: http://www.jeanmonnetprogram.org/papers, 31.

72 Organic Law, July 5, 1980, no. 7.

73 See Art. 3 of the Organic Law, which, along the lines of Art. 9 of the European Convention on Human Rights, says that "El ejercicio de los derechos dimanantes de la Libertad Religiosa y de Culto tiene como único límite la protección del derecho de los demás al ejercicio de sus libertades públicas y derechos fundamentales, así como la salvaguardia de la seguridad, de la salud y de la moralidad pública, elementos constitutivos del orden público protegido por la Ley en el ámbito de una sociedad democrática."

one with the Evangelical Church,[74] one with the Jewish community[75] and one with the Muslim community,[76] all of which were signed in 1992. Because the regulations they establish are largely identical, many have considered these agreements to be far from what the framers of the 1978 Constitution considered ideal.[77] See, for example, the fact that the Evangelical Church's state–religion agreement subsumes the rights of the Orthodox Church along with it. The agreement is general enough to purport to cover both religions, even though they diverge significantly in terms of their doctrine and structure. In addition, the hasty rule-making involved in the Muslim state–religion agreement[78] is characterized by analogous shortcomings.[79]

The presence of a generally applicable law has done nothing to deter this undesirable homogeneity between the state–religion agreements of different religions. While the homogeneity of the agreements has decreased their importance,[80] it has also decreased the importance of the principle of cooperation between church and state. If the principle of cooperation fails to provide room for true negotiation between the two (which ideally should provide the narrowly tailored state–religion agreements that are preferable), what is left is mere general protection of religious freedom, which should not require a specific pact to be enforced. As such, Spanish legal scholars have criticized Spanish policies on religious liberty, believing it to be excessively narrow in comparison with constitutional provisions that contemplate broader bilateral agreements.

One positive aspect of the Spanish agreements compared to Italian agreements involves the fact that they allow the parties to break them with six

---

74 This agreement was executed with Law no. 24 of November 10, 1992. Two Christian Orthodox Associations (the Orthodox Confessional Association of the Greek Church in Spain and the Orthodox Greek Church) joined the Protestant Federation and therefore enjoyed the effects of the agreement.

75 Agreement executed with Law no. 25 of November 10, 1992.

76 Agreement executed with Law no. 26 of November 10, 1992.

77 Motilla A., L'accordo di cooperazione tra la Spagna e la Commissione islamica. Bilancio e prospettive, in Ferrari S. (ed.), *Musulmani in Italia La condizione giuridica delle comunità islamiche*, il Mulino, Bologna, 2000, 247; Barrero Ortega A., Cuestiones pendientes tras 25 años de libertad religiosa en España, available at: http://www.estig.ipbeja.pt/~ac_direito/AbrahamBarrero.pdf, 14–16.

78 This agreement came to pass in the early part of contemporary Spanish republican history, a few decades after the arrival of the first Muslim group to inhabit Spain since the Reconquista in the fifteenth century.

79 Martínez-Torrón J., Lo statuto giuridico dell'islam in Spagna, in *Quaderni di diritto e politica ecclesiastica*, 1996, 1, 56.

80 Ibid. See also Motilla A., Religious Pluralism in Spain: Striking the Balance between Religious Freedom and Constitutional Rights, in *Brigham Young University Law Review*, 2004, 585.

months' notice. Italian agreements fail to provide agreeing parties with the right to withdraw, forcing them to go through the same negotiation process with the state when they want to leave the agreement.[81] Because of the exit option, Spanish agreements are much more formally flexible and allow the parties to be more daring in their provisions. Despite this fact, no religion to date has crafted innovative clauses in their agreements which might be more tailored to their religion's specificities.

The Common Features of the Spanish and Italian Systems

The Spanish and Italian systems share the same shortcomings: each country's Constitution contemplated narrowly tailored agreements between the state[82] and the religion, and both have room for a generally applicable law.[83] However, the Spanish experience offers an interesting caveat to Italy's problems. It proves that the existence of a generally applicable law is not enough to decrease the recourse to generic and homogenous state–religion agreements. In fact, the generally applicable law can have the opposite effect of what it was intended for and may encourage religions to push for these generic state–religion agreements.

Spain's generic state–religion agreement problem stems from two related issues. First, the generally applicable law is largely redundant, as it is lofty and iterative of the relevant constitutional provisions. We can therefore conclude that a general, vague or iterative applicable law can cause recourse to generic state–religion agreements. It can only be counteracted with a specific and detailed law. Without it, religions will resort to a generic state–religion agreement.[84]

---

81 See the second additional provision of each agreement: "El presente Acuerdo podrá ser denunciado por cualquiera de las partes que lo suscriben, notificándolo a la otra, con seis meses de antelación."

82 Fernandez-Coronado Gonzales, Valoración jurídica del sistema de cooperación con las confesiones minoritarias en España, 8.

83 De La Hera A., Relations with Religious Minorities: The Spanish Model, in *Brigham Young University Law Review*, 1998, 395: "the three agreements could have been replaced by State law … If the three agreements had to say the same thing, with each one even including the subject matter from the articles in the same order, with very few differences, i.e., conservation of cultural heritage, holidays, some aspects of matrimony, then a state law common to all the eligible religious organizations would in fact have created the same legal requirements for all of them, which as a practical matter is the result attained by the existing agreements."

84 See Barrero Ortega, Cuestiones pendientes tras 25 años de libertad religiosa en España, 13; Torres Gutierrez A., El derecho fundamental de Libertad religiosa en España: un balance critico, available at: http://www.estig.ipbeja.pt/~ac_direito/AlejandroTorres.pdf, 31–32.

Second, religions in Spain tend to insist on generic state–religion agreements because it produces more popular support and visibility on a statewide level than merely insisting on a generally applicable law.[85] Arbitrating a state–religion agreement purports to place the religion and the state on the same level, dealing at the same negotiating table.[86] On the other hand, a generally applicable law is a passive agent of instilling rights which does not formally or substantially put the two on an equal footing. With a state–religion agreement, the state ostensibly takes account of each religion's wants and desires individually; with a generally applicable law, all the religions' wants and desires commingle and are generally blended and absorbed into the rationales of the legislation itself. From a symbolic standpoint, negotiating a state–religion agreement places each religion on the level of the Catholic Church, whereas a generally applicable law has the appearance of an unequal relationship.[87]

As such, a generally applicable Italian law on religious liberty has the benefits of bringing non-Catholic religions out from under the yoke of fascist legislation, aligning them to what is provided for them in the Italian Constitution and diminishing the problems associated with generic state–religion agreements. That said, a standard generally applicable law will not *sua sponte* create these positive effects. What Italy needs is detailed legislation in the domain of religious liberty that recognizes the religions' need for the visibility and popularity that comes from bargaining with the state. As they are at the moment, state–religion agreements conclusively reflect and even promote the ambiguous nature of our contemporary legal culture in that they elevate equality at the expense of cultural identity, and therefore minimally reflect the claims of social recognition that arise from the increasing religious pluralism.

---

85 "The texts of the agreements are so similar that it is surprising that each Federation [that is, the body that each confession has created to negotiate and to sign the agreement] was willing to accept a model of relations with the State with so few differences among them": De La Hera, Relations with Religious Minorities: The Spanish Model, 394.

86 Mantecon J., Islam in Spain, in Aluffi Beck-Peccoz R. and Zincone G. (eds), *The Legal Treatment of Islamic Minorities in Europe*, Peeters, Leuven, 2004, 216.

87 The constitutional text mentions only the Catholic confession. See Art. 16, third paragraph: "Ninguna confesión tendrá carácter estatal. Los poderes públicos tendrán en cuenta las creencias religiosas de la sociedad española y mantendrán las consiguientes relaciones de cooperación con la Iglesia Católica y las demás confesiones."

Chapter 3
Islam and the State: Tradition and Modernization

The Make-up of the Muslim Presence in Italy: Obstacles to a Unitary Representative Body

Italian political institutions must confront many complications with regards to founding a representative body for the Islamic community that would satisfy the standards of Art. 8 of the Italian Constitution. The benefits of such an organization are myriad: in addition to according Muslims political rights, it would also address non-political issues that arise in the religious context.

While these complications are common throughout Europe, each country addresses them differently. Looking through the lens of these differences, I will highlight reasons that make political representation of Islam so problematic. I will first consider relevant tenets of Islam and analyze their development through the centuries. I will then give a detailed portrait of how two European states with large Muslim populations have regulated the religion and addressed their internal disagreements. My goal in this chapter is to illustrate the difficulties of political representation of Islam arising from the problematic nature of its relationship between religion and state. As we will see, Muslim states often shape Islam to fit political needs rather than the needs that religious doctrine calls for. Finally, I will give an overview of attempts that were made to regulate Islam in a non-Islamic environment.

Islamic Tradition and its Regulation in Muslim Countries

The internal structure of Islam *qua* religion is a major obstacle to the unification of several independent organizations in Italy (which would be needed for a state–religion agreement). Sunni-form Islam,[1] for example, lacks an internal mandate or requirement for an organization that would represent the Sunni community in relationships with outside parties.

---

1 On Shi'a, see Fregosi F., Islam, una religione senza clero? Una riflessione comparata, in *Daimon*, 2003, 3, 106.

Unlike other religions, Islam does not have a built-in leadership structure (imposed by the Qur'an or otherwise). A particular sect or community can be and often is guided by individuals who are not formally vested with an official role. Although believers are given an extremely detailed guide to their ordinary lives (including matters commonly seen as non-religious), Islamic texts fail to conceive of the existence of a church or other hierarchical organization with officials given sacramental roles. As such, there is no definitive or uniform dictate with regards to dogma, rites or organization (as is so often seen in other religions like Christianity). According to Sunni doctrine, any kind of "Muslim priesthood" is actually just an unordained body of individuals in charge of running mosques.[2]

What we find instead is a body of legal scholars (or *'ulama*) and theologians (*fuqaha*) who patrol the orthodoxy and who enforce *Shari'a* law. This corpus of religious quasi-professionals has functioned in a religious and legal sphere for the majority of Muslim history.[3] Because of this intrinsic linking of law and religion, Islamic leadership (often provided by these scholars or theologians) has been intractably coupled with more generalized political leadership. The Prophet Muhammad himself exercised religious and political authority, both of which derived from his role as an indispensable medium between the people and the divine. After his death, this dual authority descended to his successors and has fanned out into all forms and variations on Islam.[4] Political fights have often been vested as religious fights, with no clear separation between them.

Political and Religious Power in the Classical Period

Classical Islamic doctrine (the dominant mode of thought from 800 AD to 1200 AD) had a critical impact on contemporary Muslim self-understanding. How this period of thought influenced the relationship between religion, law and politics has been deeply criticized. There are multiple and diverging narratives comprehending both the theory and development of Classical Islamic doctrine. Although it has been widely criticized for being oversimplified and reconstructed by Western colonizers of Islamic territories, I will only consider

2 Castro F., Diritto musulmano, in *Digesto—Discipline civilistiche*, UTET, Turin, 1994, 289. See also Ferrari S., *Lo spirito dei diritti religiosi*, il Mulino, Bologna, 2002, 229–31.

3 Fregosi, Islam, una religione senza clero?, 107–08.

4 It is meaningful to recall the first episode in which apostasy was sanctioned according to doctrine: after the death of Muhammad, the Islamic community believed that the obligation to pay religious taxes was over. Abu Bakr, the successor of the Prophet, affirmed that religious and political authorities were still connected and warned that sanctions would be imposed on non-taxpayers. See Lewis B., *Il linguaggio politico dell'islam*, Laterza, Rome-Bari, 98.

the prevailing, standardized narrative in order to explore Islamic understanding of the relationship between religion and power. This narrative largely shapes Western perceptions of Islam and is still relevant within Muslim communities: many difficulties that both Western and Muslim societies meet in articulating a fruitful and respectful relationship can be derived from this reading. Western as well as Islamic legal cultures alike are still affected by the legacy of this way of reading Classical Islamic doctrine.

Classical Islamic doctrine teaches that the link between religion and state can be traced through the word *Khalif*, which means "successor" and refers specifically to the person who became the main religious official after Muhammad's death.[5] In the Sunni context, the Khalif grew more political in short order: the successor of Muhammad, Khalif Abu Bakr, was called the "Khalif of the Prophet"; the successor to Khalif Abu Bakr, Khalif Othman, was called "Khalif of God."[6] This transition imbued the Khalifate with a major theocratic aspect.[7] Initially, this theocracy was somewhat democratic, since community members were involved in the selection of the Khalif.[8] This democratic aspect has subsided, and the Khalif has been functionally combined with the *imam* (who traditionally only led prayers) into one political and religious figure.[9]

In liturgical terms, the Khalif played a central role: he led the common prayer and said the *khutba* (the ritual sermon performed on the holy day). Further, he managed religious practice among believers and oversaw religious doctrine, either directly or through delegation.[10] But the political meaning of his position cannot be overestimated. Khalifs who were reluctant to play an active role in religious practices were criticized as anathema to the Khalifate.[11] Fights for political power took religious forms: adversaries were delegitimized through accusations of heresy and heterodoxy, if not apostasy. This phenomenon, among others, has conveyed the unitary theory of Khalifate as both religious and political leadership.[12]

---

5 Ibid., 54–55.

6 Modern scholars have demonstrated that this distinction was built during the Classical period for apologetic reasons, but did not have any practical implications.

7 Tyan E., *Institutions du droit public musulman*, Cedroma, Beirut, 1999, 165.

8 Ibid., 166–68.

9 Ibid., 169.

10 Predieri A., *Shari'a e Costituzione*, Laterza, Rome-Bari, 2006, 164.

11 On the stigmatization of the *mulk* regime, which would disregard religious interests as politically irrelevant, see Tyan, *Institutions du droit public musulman*, 676.

12 Predieri, *Shari'a e Costituzione*, 233 notices that the Italian fascist government, at the end of the Lybian war of 1911–12, allowed Muslims to mention the name of the Khalif during the communal Friday prayer, as tradition commanded, without realizing that that prayer affirmed a political rather than a merely religious leadership.

The unitary nature of the Khalif can be viewed from an institutional, popular and legal perspective. From an institutional perspective, the strong connection between religion and politics placed the functions of the Khalif at odds with each other. On the one hand, the Khalif was a religious figure required to promote observation of religion as the primary interest of the Khalifate; on the other hand, he was a political figure expected to enforce the religious doctrine without the flexibility of being able to introduce new laws.[13] From a popular perspective, this dual role put the Khalif in the awkward position of needing to be faithful (in fact, an example to the Khalifate) to religious doctrine, while taking into account the political realism needed to lead and manage a community.[14] The legal perspective understood the Khalif and other political institutions as tools in the hands of God. Such institutions were necessary and providentially provided by God for the sake of humanity.[15]

This doctrine has survived substantially unaltered for centuries.[16] Some scholars believe that its enduring influence can be explained by the fact that the political philosophy was scarcely relevant and as such never received much development and attention by Islamic legal and political culture; others believe that those with political power wanted to preserve their religious legitimacy and thus failed to push for a separation of political from the religious power.[17] Whatever the reason, for centuries, Khalifs surrounded themselves with primarily religious figures that kept the people pacified and kept the Khalif in touch with mores and culture of society.[18]

The role of the Khalif was maintained notwithstanding large shifts and transformations in Muslim political and social structures. The conquest of new territories and the rise of autonomous centers of powers undoubtedly decreased the powers of the Khalif, but Muslim officials preferred to maintain the formal leadership in these new contexts in order to preserve the cohesion

---

13 Some Islamic countries qualify their normative power as mere administrative power, enforcing Islamic law. See Castro F., Diritto musulmano e dei Paesi islamici, in *Enciclopedia giuridica*, Treccani, Rome, 1989.

14 Lewis, *Il linguaggio politico dell'islam*, 37.

15 Ibid., 34.

16 Lambton A.K.S., *State and Government in Medieval Islam. An Introduction to the Study of Islamic Political Theory: The Jurists*, Oxford University Press, Oxford, 1981, 13.

17 Khatami S.M., *La religion et la pensée prises au piège de l'autocratie*, Peeters, Louvain, 2005, 325: "Après Ibn Khaldun, que l'on peut citer comme le dernier penseur musulman dans le domaine politique – et dont la pensée était influencée par la réalité ambiante – on n'exagérera pas en affirmat qu'aucun discours nouveau n'est apparu dans le champ de la pensée politique musulmane."

18 Ibid., 256.

of the Islamic community (*'Umma*) rather than recognize any sort of dissolution of an aspect of the Muslim politico-religious hierarchy.[19]

Despite this reticence to change, a new political figure (the *Sultan*) began to appear and displace the functional authority of the Khalif while preserving the strong connections between religious and political affairs.[20] The Sultan, one of which eventually led the entire Ottoman Empire, was originally conceived as a deputy of the Khalif with authority in the religious domain. He could lead prayer, administrate activities within the mosque, collect the religious tax and enforce religious orthodoxy.[21] His role in religious life was a powerful tool of legitimacy, and there are occasions in which the Sultan took over leadership from the Khalif. On these occasions, the Khalifate did not see the usurpation as a profanation.

Thus, according to the prevailing Sunni narrative, the relationship between religion and politics has characterized Islamic understanding of political power. Religious legitimacy operated to provide more political power; political power had the power to preserve religious practice. This deep connection is informed by a radical reading of the Islamic god's omnipotence and its relationship to morality.[22] Islamic law teaches that humanity must rely on the Qur'an and other existing codes in order to establish what is moral. But what is moral to human eyes is uniquely human; because the omnipotence of the Islamic god and its responsibility for natural events can make it appear unjust, Islamic law teaches that its god plays by a different set of moral rules. God's morality and human morality are incommensurable.[23] The role of a religious-political figure like the Khalif is to know God's will; in order to know God's will, the Khalif must consult religious law. The intertwining of morality, politics and religion inherent to Islamic law thus incentivizes Islamic officials with political power to maintain strong ties with religion; the former would not survive without the latter.

Modern Trends: Muslim Institutions in Contemporary Legal Regimes

The transformation of Islamic political institutions through the centuries has generally preserved religion as an important source of legitimacy for political authorities. Albeit present within Islamic doctrine, the separation of religion and

19 Ibid., 268–69.

20 The religious legitimacy of the Sultan has inverted: the Sultan chose the Khalif depending on political interest, and then he swore the religious oath before him. See Lewis B., *Il Medio Oriente. Duemila anni di storia*, Mondadori, Milan, 1999, 144.

21 Tyan, *Institutions du droit public musulman*, 494.

22 Daga R., Loi et droit naturel en islam?, in *Communio*, 1991, 5–6, 58.

23 Ben Achour Y., L'idea di giustizia naturale nel pensiero giuridico sunnita, in *Daimon*, 2004, 4, 229.

state is a concept that is largely foreign to the Islamic state. When discussed, the doctrine has been thought of as contrary to the teachings of Islam, as a negative foreign influence borrowed from European culture or as a sort of Trojan horse introduced by colonial regimes to weaken Islamic identity.[24] The integration of church and state has impacted various other aspects of Islamic society.

The transformation of the role of a lawyer is a useful example. Historically, lawyers in society operated in a wide variety of fields straddling the line between religion and state, including the enforcement of religious orthodoxy. During the occupation by colonial powers in the nineteenth and first half of the twentieth centuries, lawyers were largely restricted to niche areas like family law. The contemporary transformation of Islamic regimes into twenty-first-century states has heralded the return of lawyers to the role of "Islamic watchmen" appointed by the state. Political officials have integrated lawyers into state administration for the purposes of more effectively controlling citizens by enforcing religious orthodoxy. Lawyers also have been utilized to legitimize socio-economic policies and criticize politico-religious opponents.[25]

In short, Islamic countries have adopted a system that takes advantage of the traditional integration of church and state. By establishing Islam as the state's official religion and by using political and legal forces to regulate and control its message, political leaders have been able to monitor and moderate cultural forces, isolating extremist and revolutionary tendencies.[26] The few countries that did not use Islam to this effect (like Pakistan and Afghanistan) became centers for extremist movements that received popular support.[27]

The positive influence of the integration of church and state is notable for several reasons. Often, it has played a key role in the realignment of the Islamic legal tradition and state laws along the lines of international human rights standards. Political officials have manipulated religion to persuade citizens that reforms were in accordance with Islamic belief. Two examples effectively illustrate this point.

In 1996, the Egyptian Constitutional Court upheld a law that banned use of the *niqab* (a veil which hides the whole face) in public schools.[28] The Court

24 See, among many others, Zakariya F., *Laïcité ou islamisme les arabes à l'heure du choix*, La Découverte, Paris/Le Caire, 1991. See also Roy O., *La laïcité face à l'islam*, Stock, Paris, 2005, 73–74.

25 Fregosi, Islam, una religione senza clero?, 107–08.

26 Pacini A., I musulmani in Italia, available at: www.centroedoardoagnelli.it, 7–8.

27 Roy O., *L'islam mondialisé*, Seuil, Paris, 2002, 46.

28 Lombardi C.B. and Brown N.J., Do Constitutions Requiring Adherence to Shari'a Threaten Human Rights? How Egypt's Constitutional Court Reconciles Islamic Law with the Liberal Rule of Law, in *American University International Law Review*, 2006, 21, 428.

grounded its decision in classical Islamic doctrine, stating that the Qur'an and other applicable Islamic law deigned to mandate the use of the *niqab*. This move was critical—the Egyptian Constitution, at that time, stated that *Shari'a* law is the primary source of Egyptian legislation.[29] Without glossing Islamic law, the Court might not have been able to create a cultural consensus on the topic. The other example occurred in 2003 in Morocco, when the government reformed the *Mudawwana* (personal status legislation) into a distinctly modern example of private law. Like the Egyptian Constitutional Court, the King of Morocco spearheaded this reform using rationales based on Classical Islamic Law.

Modern Islamic states have utilized their influence over religious leaders to influence cultural beliefs and practices. Islamic leadership does exist in these states, but political leadership appoints (and removes) its denizens. Any sort of religious body that purports to represent the religious lives of its members is more responsive to government control than to the desires of its members.[30]

The integration of church and state described above can be viewed in every Muslim country on the eastern and southern coast of the Mediterranean Sea, with the exception of Israel and Lebanon. This integration is operative in Turkey as well, despite the fact that Turkey's constitution proclaims the separation of church and state.[31]

Two Muslim countries with varying approaches to the integration of church and state will provide a useful case study illustrating some of the principles above: Tunisia (whose people immigrate mostly to Spain, France and Italy) and Turkey (whose people mostly immigrate to Germany). Both countries have a very modern and Westernized constitution and social structure. Tunisia is an Arab state, while Turkey is not. Moreover, Turkey, as we will see, has formally endorsed a rigid separation of church and state. I will limit the discussion of these states to the current structure of their government and society. Contemporary political movements in Turkey and the impact of the Arab Spring in Tunisia, while very relevant, are too new and fluctuant to accurately measure their effects on the integration of religion and state and the impact on the Islamic doctrine of the state.

The post-Arab Spring constitutional frameworks, however, do not depart from the long-established balance of powers, which prizes state institutions over religious autonomy. For example, the 2014 Tunisian Constitution, also

29 See also Luther J., Il velo scoperto della legge: profili di giurisprudenza costituzionale comparata, in Ferrari S. (ed.), *Islam ed Europa*, Carocci, Rome, 2006, 70.

30 Martínez-Torrón J., L'État confessionnel, in *Conscience et liberté*, 1999, 38.

31 Art. 2: "The Republic of Turkey is a democratic, secular and social state governed by the rule of law; bearing in mind the concepts of public peace, national solidarity and justice; respecting human rights; loyal to the nationalism of Atatürk, and based on the fundamental tenets set forth in the Preamble."

with the purpose of preventing extremism and religious violence, establishes the state as the protector of religion (Art. 6) and the President of the Republic as the appointer of the Tunisian Republic's *Mufti* (Art. 78); in the 2014 Egyptian Constitution, the Grand Sheikh of Al-Azhar Mosque is appointed according to the state law (Art. 7); and, according to the 2011 Constitution of Morocco, the Superior Council of the Ulema delivers its advisory legal opinions on Islamic law under the supervision of the King—who operates here in his capacity of Commander of (Muslim) Believers—and is appointed by royal decree (Art. 41).[32]

Islam in Tunisia

Tunisian constitutional history is characterized by intense efforts at decolonization. The attempts to gain independence from France—which the political movement of Arabism fueled during the first half of the twentieth century—won a partial victory in 1954, when the country achieved administrative autonomy, and complete victory in 1956, when independence was finally achieved.

The 1959 Constitution that followed shortly thereafter was strongly influenced by French legal culture. Republicanism was preferred over the monarchy, and a strong presidential figure was installed. A strong head of state is more typical of Arabic constitutionalism; true to form, the pivotal role that Habib Bourguiba played during the early years of Tunisian independence caused the constitutional committee to accord the President broad powers. Bourguiba transitioned from a tenured President after the initial constitution and became a lifelong President through constitutional amendment.[33]

Although Bourguiba's successor, Zine el Abidine Ben Ali, formally restored the term limit of the presidency, he never truly departed from the strong presidential model of government envisioned by the 1959 Constitution. In fact, he was re-elected at the end of every term limit from his accession in 1987 until 2011, when he stepped down after the controversy caused by the death of Mohamed Bouazizi, 26-year-old street vendor. Throughout this 23-year period, he maintained a very executive-focused mode of governing.

From a legal standpoint, the 1959 Constitution operated to transform and modernize existing codes, even within conservative areas of the law (like family and personal status law)[34] that typically resist conforming to international

32 The English version of such constitutional texts can be found at: www.constituteproject.org.

33 Oliviero M., *Il costituzionalismo dei Paesi arabi, I Le Costituzioni del Maghreb*, Giuffrè, Milan, 2003, 139–42.

34 See Aluffi Beck-Peccoz R., *La modernizzazione del diritto di famiglia nei paesi arabi*, Turin, Fondazione Agnelli, 2000; or Aluffi Beck-Peccoz R., *Le leggi del diritto di famiglia negli stati arabi del Nord-Africa*, Turin, Fondazione Agnelli, 1997.

standards of human rights. The political regime attempted this process of modernization without openly disavowing the traditionally conservative Muslim majority. Nonetheless, there has been significant resistance to this modernization by the judiciary and tensions between the innovative and conservative visions of national laws.

In concert with the principles described above, Tunisian officials tried to ground their political changes in religious orthodoxy. The Tunisian integration of church and state descended from its French occupancy, when the primary Tunisian political figure, the *Bey*, was simultaneously the primary religious representative.[35] The 1959 Constitution continued this tradition by affirming that Islam was the official religion of the state[36] and required the head of state to be Muslim.[37] While Bourguiba attempted to secularize certain areas of the laws (by outlawing polygamy and religious courts and otherwise liberalizing civil, penal and constitutional law) and implement socio-economic reforms, he concurrently ingrained Islam in various state institutions.[38]

Early in his tenure, Bourguiba created the Grand *Mufti* of the Republic, which was meant to be an Islamic legal expert in charge of counseling the government on Islamic orthodoxy. Further, he mandated that Islamic officials (to the extent that any were created) must be nominated through state decree. This trend of increasing integration of religion in the political order continued throughout Bourguiba's term and through to the end of Ben Ali's term as well.

The nature of this integration is twofold: on the one hand, Islam was highly valued and was accorded important institutional and administrative standing; on the other hand, it was tightly controlled and managed by political parties. For example, political officials commandeered *imams*, providing them with education and a salary. The government also created the High Islamic Council of the Republic in order to regulate the preservation of morals and religion. This organization included intellectual and religious leaders such as the Dean of the School of Theology of *Az-Zaytuna*, a famous religious university and mosque and the Grand *Mufti*.[39]

---

35 Decree of October 4, 1888; see Darmon R., *La situations des cultes en Tunisie*, Rousseau, Paris, 1930, 48–49.

36 Art. 1: "Tunisia is a free State, independent and sovereign; its religion is the Islam, its language is Arabic, and its form is the Republic."

37 Art. 38: "The President of the Republic is the Head of the State. His religion is Islam."

38 Samandi Z., Autorité religieuse et pouvoir politique: tradition et mutations. Le cas de la Tunisie, in *Pluralisme social, pluralism politique et démocratie*, *Cahiers du Ceres*, 1991, 19, 81.

39 Decree of April 22, 1987.

Political control of Islam intensified during the Ben Ali's presidency. The government passed laws that gave a legal definition to mosques, effectively bringing them under political control, and conditioned the creation of new mosques on the obtaining of a royal decree. Ben Ali also began exercising control over the activities and leaders of *Az-Zaytuna*, unilaterally replacing the Director of Religious Affairs of the mosque (formally a quasi-independent official of a ministry of religion) with a more directly controlled Secretary of State for Religious Affairs. Through this new position, the government promulgated a formal hierarchy of state control of religion, including religious recruitment, supervision of orthodoxy abroad, and the organization of pilgrimages to Mecca.[40]

Islam in Turkey

The Ottoman Empire was the main Sunni political player between the sixteenth century and the beginning of the twentieth century. Starting in the seventeeth century, through a series of military defeats that exposed the country as being technologically and culturally behind its Western counterparts, it began to transition into a modern state.[41]

One aspect of this transition into modernity was a reformation of its legal culture. Several Sultans attempted to stop the socio-economic decline prevalent in the nineteenth century through the enforcement of legal reforms that were inspired by Western legal culture. These *tanzimat* introduced social and civil equality and new powerful civil and penal codes drawn from French laws. While the civil code maintained strong ties with the Islamic legal tradition, it simultaneously empowered political institutions to create new non-Islamic legal jurisdictions. In practice, this designated state courts rather than Islamic courts as the enforcers of Islamic orthodoxy.

The end of the Ottoman Empire saw a gradual homogenization of the Turkish ethnicity. What had once been a variety of different Arab ethnicities coalesced into a Turkish nationalism that began to dominate in terms of culture and religion. A major aspect of this nationalism originated in historiographic tendencies that saw the Turks as descendants of Genghis Khan and as the core of global civilization.[42]

---

40 Bras J.P., L'islam administré: illustrations tunisiennes, in Kerrou M. (ed.), *Public et privé en Islam*, Maisonneuve & Larose, Paris, 2002.

41 The Ottoman Empire was also a multireligious nation: more than 40 percent of its population was not Muslim. Carducci M. and Bernardini D'Arnesano B., *Turchia*, il Mulino, Bologna, 2008, 32.

42 Introvigne M., *La Turchia e l'Europa. Religione e politica nell'islam turco*, Sugarco, Milan, 2006, 11.

The leader of this movement was Mustafa Kemal, nicknamed "Atatürk" or "father of Turks" for his contributions to society. Atatürk spearheaded Turkey's transition from a religion-centered social order to a Westernized constitutional state, culminating in 1923 with the birth of the Turkish Republic. The initial efforts to establish a republic hinged on grounding its legitimacy in religion (like similar efforts in Tunisia).[43] Through Atatürk's influence, however, these efforts were abandoned and the republic eschewed religious legitimacy in favor of a secular balancing of priorities.[44] Despite the role that Islam played under the Ottoman Empire, it was greatly diminished in the Turkish Republic. The first version of the Turkish Constitution declared Islam as the official religion; this clause was eliminated in 1928, and the official separation of church and state was declared in 1937.

The Turkish authorities took the separation of church and state very seriously.[45] Its Constitutional Court repeatedly declared *ultra vires* political parties that violated separation of church and state principles.[46] Further, the Turkish military has repeatedly threatened to overthrow parties in power through coups d'état on this basis.

Breaking with Turkey's Islamic past required more than constitutional reforms. On May 3, 1924, the Turkish Republic abolished the offices of the Khalifate, the Islamic Law Commissariat and other political-religious positions. Later that year the *Shari'a* law tribunals were dismantled. In 1926, the Republic promulgated a penal code based on the Italian legal system and a civil code based on Swiss law that prohibited polygamy and other controversial religious practices. Other symbolic measures were taken, such as requiring oaths of office to be sworn on one's honor rather than the Qur'an.

These measures unequivocally liberated the Turkish government from control by Islamic officials, but rather than a subsequent privatization of religion, as has occurred in much of the Western world, there has instead

43 An-Na'im A.A., *Islam and the Secular State*, Harvard University Press, Cambridge, MA, 2008, 199.

44 Kucukian T., State, Islam and Religious Liberty in Modern Turkey: Reconfiguration of Religion in the Public Sphere, in *Brigham Young University Law Review*, 2003, 486.

45 Interestingly, Mustafà Kemal's military education took place at the Artillery School of Toulouse in France, where the separation between religion and state was strongly enforced. See the dossier Charte de la laicité dans les services publics et autres avis, *Haute Conseil à l'integration*, 192.

46 The European Court of Human Rights dealt with the outlawing of a Turkish party that took place in mid-1990s and upheld the decision of the Turkish institutions (*Refah Partisi v. Turkey* (App. nos. 41340/98, 41342/98, 41343/98 and 41344/98)). See also Pin A., Democrazia, diritti fondamentali e islam, in Cartabia M. (ed.), *I Diritti in azione. Universalità e pluralismo dei diritti fondamentali nelle Corti europee*, il Mulino, Bologna, 2007.

been a *nationalization* of Islam.[47] The Turkish government (with Atatürk at its head) was as involved in Islam functionally as was the Ottoman Empire. This involvement has been reversed, however, with Turkish government officials controlling Islam instead of the other way around. Both the Ottomans and the Kemalists were very attuned to protecting their regime from criticisms on the basis of religion that could have undermined their legitimacy. Ottoman Empire officials established a hierarchical structure for Islam with a *Mufti* at its head.[48] The Turkish Republic, while purporting to be secular, has maintained similar structures, with new and different officials. Turkish government officials direct religious affairs, recruit *imams* and provide salaries, open new mosques and decide which Islamic doctrine should be adopted and followed.

The extent to which the Turkish government has imposed certain Islamic doctrines has fluctuated over the years. Certain regimes have preferred a more nationalistic and patriotic approach (seeing the establishment of the Turkish language as the official language used in mosques in 1932), while others have seen a return to more Islamo-centric policies (Arabic was restored as the official language used in mosques in the 1950s).[49] Throughout this process, however, the Turkish government has exercised unwavering control over Islam *qua* religion. While simultaneously distancing itself from the religion, the administration exerted greater control over it.

Pursuant to this mindset and to insulate Islam from external influences and align it with Turkish and other Western republican institutions, Turkish officials began to administrate Islam as a part of its bureaucracy. Further, the government encouraged Islam to conform to contemporary and nationalistic policies.[50] Turkey's Constitutional Court in 1972 validated this treatment of Islam and maintained that it would need to be administered and regulated in this manner to satisfy the strictures of state–religion separation that the Constitution commanded.[51]

The relationship between church and state in Turkey does not necessarily align with the view of the European Court of Human Rights (ECtHR). In its 2001 and 2003 decisions in *Refah Partisi v. Turkey*,[52] the Court stated:

---

47 Sakalloglu U.C., Parameters and Strategies of Islam-State Interaction in Republican Turkey, in *International Journal of Middle East Studies*, 1996, 231–51; and An-Na'im, *Islam and the Secular State*, 197.

48 Lewis, *Il linguaggio politico dell'islam*, 35–36.

49 Jacob X., Islam et politique (Turquie), in *Religion et politique: un thème pour le dialogue islamo-chrétien*, Spoglio, Vatican City, 1999, 121 and 125.

50 Ayata S., Patronage, Party and State: The Politicization of Islam in Turkey, in *Middle East Journal*, 1996, 42.

51 Jacob, Islam et politique (Turquie), 143.

52 App. nos. 41340/98, 41342/98, 41343/98 and 41344/98.

> The Court further observes that there was already an Islamic theocratic regime under Ottoman law. When the former theocratic regime was dismantled and the republican regime was being set up, Turkey opted for a form of secularism which confined Islam and other religions to the sphere of private religious practice.[53]

This is not an entirely accurate picture of either historical or contemporary state–religion separation in Turkey. In a theocracy, religion is at the top of the political structure, providing legitimacy to and control over government officials. The Ottoman Empire was not a true theocracy—Islam exercised considerable influence over the government, but it was equally influenced, if not controlled, by the head government official, the Sultan. Turkey is not a true secular republic with privatized religion either. Rather, Islam has been incorporated into the government bureaucracy for the purposes of controlling it; this is an institutionalization of Islam, not a privatization.

Islam in Europe

History and recent practice demonstrate that in traditionally Islamic states, Islam *qua* religious institution is controlled and regulated by the government (with the exception of Albania, which has compelled a strict atheistic regime). Where there is no internal hierarchy mandated by the Qur'an, states like Turkey and Tunisia often create and manage a state-sponsored hierarchy within their government system. By establishing external structures and practices, these states sow political and social tensions within their Islamic population. So, when Muslims immigrate to Italy, they usually emigrate from countries with this background of tension and control.

Islamic religious tradition largely endorses this relationship between religion and state, for several reasons: first, because Islam is often the official religion of the state, the transition into state control of Islam is conceptually easy for both religious and political officials to tolerate; second, Islam has commonly played a strong role in shaping contemporary political regimes and is therefore conceived as a tool of political legitimization of the nationhood.

In Europe, both of these empirical phenomena are missing. Many European states have an official or de facto separation of church and state, and those states that do not have such separation commonly draw a distinction between the two. Political institutions are commonly grounded in representative, non-religious policies and find their legitimacy in democracy rather than religion. Demographically, most Europeans identify as Christians rather than Muslims. Therefore, it is no surprise that certain Muslim scholars have treated such

53 Grand Chamber decision, February 13, 2003, par. 17.

differences by urging the development of a specialized legal and religious syllabus (known as the *fiqh al-aqallyyat*) for Muslims living in a non-Islamic state.[54]

For these reasons, Muslims in Europe articulate their relationship with the government in ways that are sensibly different from those in Islamic states. These regimes of religious autonomy have provided nationalistic Islamic minorities in each state with the necessary conditions to want to self-organize for religious purposes. The result is a very diverse Islamic environment:[55] ethnic groups exist around and are empowered by small structural entities that cater to different religious preferences or geographic origins. These entities include small mosques headed by local leaders, prayer centers connected with their nations of origin or their consulates, or international Islamic organizations' bodies.

To address the rapid growth and increasing visibility of Islamic communities in European states, various attempts have been made to organize the scattered pods of individuals in each state. The problems inherent in these organizations often outweigh their benefits: grassroots groups that sprung up around single leaders are too ephemeral and scarcely representative; entities supported by international organizations reflect political priorities more than the Islamic populations' real needs; mosques created and managed by the governments of the mother states are usually disregarded by immigrants of different origins. This last entity experiences disparate support from Muslims that hail from the mother state creating and managing the mosque; these Muslims often resist what they feel to be arm's-length control by their mother states and the deprivation of their ability to manage their religious life.

European states favor unitary organization of Muslims in their territory, pushing them to federate or (at least) collaborate with each other in the service of a greater aggregation of believers. The Italian and Spanish governments have created an agreement-based system of relations between religion and state, and have tried to identify reliable and representative Islamic groups that can facilitate communications.

Before delving into the problems with the Italian treatment of Islam as a religious institution, we will focus on some early experimentation in other European states and analyze their results. In attempting to re-create the policies of traditionally Islamic states, these experiments created a political relationship that was at once intrusive and ill-fitting.

54 Macrì G., Islam, rappresentanza degli interessi religiosi e diritto comune europeo, available at: www.olir.it, 18–19. Some scholars maintain that Islam should go beyond the classical dichotomy between *dar al-islam* (Muslim territories) and *dar al-harb* (hostile territories, which with Islam can only make war or truce) to develop the category of *dar al-hiğra* (territories of emigration).

55 Maréchal B., Mosquées, Organisations et leadership, in Dassetto F., Maréchal B. and Nielsen J. (eds), *Convergences musulmanes*, L'Harmattan-Bruylet, Louvain, 2001.

Leaving aside for a moment the religious freedom issues that such attempts to forge a unitary representation of Islam may cause, it must be noted that societal changes make such initiatives increasingly difficult: this is a necessary premise to understand the gravity of this moment and why failures have been so frequent. Contemporary societies have seen the structures of religions change deeply. Alongside other religious traditions, Western Islam has also experienced a "process of deinstitutionalization." The institutional forms through which it is made visible, represented and socially active have changed. Islamic actors have increased over time, as happened before to other religious groups. Belonging to Islam now in Europe means something different from what it meant before and in Islamic countries.[56]

Belgium, Bulgaria, and Austria before Nationalized Islam

The Belgian government has played a very involved role with its Muslim community.[57] By the end of the 1980s,[58] political officials had created an Executive Committee of Belgian Muslims (*Executif ds Musulmans de Belgique*) designed to respond to community requests that Muslim students receive an education in Islam at school.[59] It was created through a referendum of Belgian Muslims and seats were reserved to each major Muslim group in the country (with the exception of extremist groups).[60] Fifty-one members were elected; they then chose 16 members from among themselves to serve as active members on the Committee.

The 16 members of the Committee eventually became embroiled in severe disagreements, leading to a political crisis in 2003. The larger 51-member assembly passed a vote of no confidence on the 16-member committee; as a

56 Göle N., Islam, European Public Space, and Civility, available at: http://www.eurozine.com/articles/2007-05-03-gole-en.html.

57 The Muslim community was officially recognized by the law of July 19, 1974. See Torfs R., State and Church in Belgium, in Robbers G. (ed.), *State and Church in the European Union*, 2nd edn, Nomos, Baden-Baden, 2005, 9 and 13.

58 *Arrêté Royal*, June 24, 1988.

59 Foblets M.C. and Overbeeke A., State Intervention in the Institutionalisation of Islam in Belgium, in Shadid W.A.R. and Van Koningsveld P.S. (eds), *Religious Freedom and the Neutrality of the State: The Position of Islam in the European Union*, Peeters, Leuven-Parigi, 2002, 119 and 120–21.

60 Ferrari S., Profili giuridici e valoriali dell'integrazione dell'islam nella società europea e italiana e modelli di rapporto tra confessione islamica e Stato in corso di elaborazione in Europa, speech given at the *L'islam in Italia. Appartenenze religiose plurali e strategie diversificate* Conference, Turin, December 2–3, 2004, available at: www.centroedoardoagnelli.it, 8–9.

result, the Belgian government provisionally[61] nominated 16 influential members of the Islamic community and set new elections. It then asked the Council of State (the Supreme Administrative Court of Belgium) for an advisory opinion; the Council declared the establishment of the Committee itself unconstitutional as unduly ruling over the life of a religion and its organizations.

Nonetheless, the government created a new commission that would ostensibly be representative of all Belgian Muslims. Certain Islamic organizations protested this decision as being against state neutrality and discriminatory towards Islam (as opposed to other religions that the state allows to self-organize), if not against the European Convention on Human Rights.

The Court of Arbitration (now renamed the Constitutional Council) declared the legislation to be consistent with constitutional provisions.[62] The measures taken by the Belgian government were considered as an exceptional and temporary solution that did not affect state neutrality. Further, Islam is structurally different from other religious groups: it lacks an internal hierarchy that functions to protect individual religious rights. This difference, the Court concluded, justified state intervention to protect religious rights for Muslims.[63] The success of state intervention in this case was delusive: only a minority of the electorate participated in the elections.[64]

Bulgaria has exercised even stronger influence over Islam.[65] The country has a large Muslim population deriving from significant immigration during the Ottoman period. After years of repression during its occupation by the Soviet Union, the Islamic community has returned to vibrancy.[66] In the years immediately following the collapse of the Soviet Union, the Bulgarian government attempted to organize the scattered Islamic community.[67] It felt

---

61 *Arrêté Royal*, July 18, 2003.

62 Decision no. 14/05, September 28, 2005.

63 Cavino M., Gli organi rappresentativi del culto islamico in Belgio: uno strappo al principio di neutralità dello Stato, in *Diritto pubblico comparato ed europeo*, 2005, no. IV, 1712–15.

64 Voyé L. and Dobbelaere K., La gestion publique de la diversité religieuse en Belgique. Pluralism religieus et pratiques d'accomodement, in Côté P. and Gunn J. (eds), *La nouvelle question religieuse. Régulation ou ingérence d'État?*, Peter Lang, Brussels, 2006, 175–76.

65 Kristeff A., An Attempt at Modernization: The New Bulgarian Legislation in the Field of Religious Freedom, in *Brigham Young University Law Review*, 2001, 602; Peteva J., Chiesa e Stato in Bulgaria, in Ferrari S., Cole Durham W., Jr. and Sewell E.A. (eds), *Diritto e religione nell'Europa post-comunista*, il Mulino, Bologna, 2004, 71–72.

66 Broun J., Bulgaria's Muslim Communities: Rehabilitation and Recovery, in *Religion, State and Society*, 2007, 134.

67 Cimbalo G., L'esperienza dell'Islam dell'Est Europa come contributo a una regolamentazione condivisa della libertà religiosa in Italia, available at: www.statoechiese.it.

justified in intruding in Islamic life in order to end inner religious conflicts, creating a unified Islamic representative body and promoting Islamic groups amicable to the Bulgarian state (even removing problematic Islamic leaders and replacing them with state-approved ones).[68] Several of these actions were challenged before the ECtHR on the basis of violations of the religious freedom clause of the European Convention.[69] The ECtHR ruled in favor of the Islamic groups, stating strongly that political institutions have a duty to protect pluralism and dialogue between and within religions and to grant a peaceful and tolerant environment without unduly controlling religious life.[70] Bulgaria's actions were impermissible, even if to preserve stability in its society.

Austria, like Belgium and Bulgaria, has exercised considerable influence in its Islamic community.[71] Unlike Belgium and Bulgaria, Austria's actions were better calculated to produce more positive results. The policies date back to how the Habsburg Empire regulated Islam during eighteenth and nineteenth centuries. When the Austrian government made the decision to recognize its growing Muslim population in 1979, it decided to enforce legislation that had been introduced during the "jurisdictionalist" period in 1912 and that drew from the Habsburg approach to religion.[72] The legislation officially recognized Islam as a valid religion in Austria, accorded it autonomy from the state in internal matters and included it in state administration as a public law corporation.[73]

This legislation was originally only applicable to Sunni Muslims and only the *Hanafi* legal tradition (one of the four classical Sunni legal traditions) within it. In 1979, the Austrian government passed further legislation recognizing

---

68 Fantelli P., Le minoranze islamiche nella Bulgaria post-comunista: ingerenze statali e libertà confessionale, available at: www.statoechiese.it.

69 *Hasan and Caush v. Bulgaria* (App. no. 30985/96); *Supreme Holy Council of the Muslim Community v. Bulgaria* (App. no. 39023/97).

70 *Supreme Holy Council of the Muslim Community v. Bulgaria* (App. no. 39023/97), December 16, 2004, par. 96: "The Court reiterates, however, that in democratic societies the State does not need in principle to take measures to ensure that religious communities remain or are brought under a unified leadership. The role of the authorities in a situation of conflict between or within religious groups is not to remove the cause of tension by eliminating pluralism, but to ensure that the competing groups tolerate each other."

71 Potz R., State and Church in Austria, in Robbers (ed.), *State and Church in the European Union.*

72 It was mainly after the assumption of control of the Bosnia-Herzegovinan territories (1878) that the Habsburgs systematically addressed the issue of the Islamic presence, although some Muslim communities had been present on the Imperial soil since the Middle Ages.

73 Testa Bappenheim S., Brevi cenni introduttivi sull'istituzionalizzazione dell'Islam nella felix Austria, available at: www.statoechiese.it, 4.

the other Sunni legal traditions as well as Shiite Muslims, endowing the entire Islamic universe in Austria with religious internal autonomy. The legislation further lent guidance on how the Muslim community should structure itself: Art. 29 of the decree suggested that local assemblies should nominate imams through a detailed process,[74] and that at the top of the Islamic community there should be a *Mufti* to represent the community in government processes.[75]

Austria is unique in that it relied on earlier "jurisdictionalist" legislation to inform[76] its control over its Islamic community.[77] The legality of this approach under the Austrian Constitution and ECtHR dictates is unclear. The treatment of the Bulgarian attempts to regulate Islam by the ECtHR implies that Austria's actions may be similarly condemned, although the success of Austria's efforts may indicate otherwise.[78]

The teachings of these state–religion experiments in Belgium, Bulgaria and Austria can and will inform future efforts by Italy to create a political hierarchy for Islam and a policy of religious freedom that is consistent with human rights protection. Italy should also look to the methods by which traditionally Muslim states administer their relationship with Islam as a religious institution; it should avoid creating a nationalized Islam like Tunisia and Turkey, but should be aware that Muslim immigrants are familiar with having their religious life and practice heavily influenced, if not controlled, by the state. Italy does not have internal policies that give an indication as to how to address religious freedom for Muslims. As discussed in Chapter 2, Italy also has a history of promulgating heavily generic and homogenous state–religion agreements that gloss over important distinctions in the needs of religions.

Chapter 4 will focus on those distinctions in the Islamic community in Italy and will sketch different attempts that Italy has made to address their needs.

---

74 Ibid., 13.

75 Art. 35 of the decree.

76 In Austria, Muslim communities have faced tensions, mainly due to the conflicts between the majoritarian Turkish Muslim population and the Arab countries that try to control Austrian Islam through the financing of religious institutions. See Heine S., Islam in Austria: Between Integration Politics and Persisting Prejudices, in Shadid W.A.R. and Van Koningsveld P.S. (eds), *Intercultural Relations and Religious Authorities: Muslims in the European Union*, Peeters, Leuven, 2002, 34.

77 A unified Islamic representative body enforced total control of Islamic law schools in the country. The Islamic Academy for religious education was established in 1997.

78 The legislation of other European countries was scrutinized by the European Court of Human Rights on the same grounds. See *Serif v. Greece* (App. no. 38178/97) and *Metropolitan Church of Bessarabia and others v. Moldova* (App. no. 45701/99).

Chapter 4
Islam and Relations with the Italian State

Islam in Italy: Negotiations and Precedents

Given their scattered origins, Muslims in Italy tend to fall into several different associations and organizations. This prevents the state from classifying them together into a unified representative Muslim body. Since there is no reliable state classification of a unified Muslim association, there can be no agreement under Art. 8 of the Constitution.

The passage of time has not made a potential agreement between Italy and Italian Muslims a reality. Through the years, the number of Muslims in Italy has increased because of both immigration and conversion.[1] The population increase has created a greater number of unique and individual Muslim religious factions, each with its own representative leader.[2]

There are two main kinds of Muslim groups. The first group is immigrant associations. These associations are composed of people emigrating from the same Muslim country. The intention of these associations is not to integrate Islam into Italian society, but instead to preserve its members' traditions and links with their country of origin. Members of these groups tend to practice Islam privately, avoid proselytizing and seldom speak publically as Muslims. This first group is largely irrelevant to our discussion.[3]

The second group consists of the four mainly Sunnite groups and is much more relevant to the Italian public sphere. The first sizable association of this kind is the Union of Islamic Communities and Organizations in Italy (UCOII), which was established in 1990 by a group of Muslim students from the Middle East. Its structure is comparable to that of similar organizations in

---

1 Pacini A., I musulmani in Italia. Dinamiche organizzative e processi di interazione con la società e le istituzioni italiane, in Ferrari S. (ed.), *Musulmani in Italia. La condizione giuridica delle comunità islamiche*, il Mulino, Bologna, 2000, 11.

2 This is a common feature amongst religious groups increasing in size because of immigration. See Ferrari S., *Lo spirito dei diritti religiosi*, il Mulino, Bologna, 2002, 237–38.

3 Senegalese brotherhoods are characterized by such dynamics: Guolo R., La rappresentanza dell'Islam italiano e la questione delle intese, in Ferrari (ed.), *Musulmani in Italia*, 79–80. See also Pacini, I musulmani in Italia, 15.

France or Belgium.[4] It is rumored to be related to the Muslim Brotherhood,[5] a fundamentalist Islamic organization that fosters a communitarian vision in Islam where virtue and religious practice are extremely important.[6] Among UCOII's objectives has been the creation of a pure Islamic society within a non-Islamic framework. Consequently, it advocates for an Islamic separation from the rest of Italian society and wants to negotiate a special status for Muslims through which its members could live according to Islamic law.[7] It initially attempted to represent the Muslim community as a whole and, shortly after its creation, it proposed an agreement to the Italian state and submitted a draft with this purpose in mind.[8]

The second group is the Islamic Cultural Center of Italy. To this day, it is the only Muslim body that has been officially recognized by a President of the Republic's decree; namely, by a presidential act that acknowledges its religious status.[9] The Center established and now runs the grand Mosque of Rome.[10] It claims to express the interests of the most economically and politically influential Muslim states, namely Saudi Arabia and Morocco,[11] both of which have a global impact on the economy and immigration through the Muslim World League. Its governing body is composed of ambassadors from Muslim states. It has expressed a desire to reach an agreement with the state, but has failed to submit a draft to this end. This delay could be because of two main obstacles. First, the Center is run by elements of various Muslim states, so Muslim immigrants end up feeling that they are still being controlled by the state they emigrated from. Second, the Muslim states do not always agree on how the

4 Fouad Allam K., L'Islam contemporaneo in Europa e in Italia fra affermazione identitaria e nuova religione minoritaria, in Zincone G. (ed.), *Secondo Rapporto sull'Integrazione degli Immigrati in Italia*, il Mulino, Bologna, 2001, 604.

5 Guolo R., La rappresentanza dell'Islam italiano e la questione delle intese, in Ferrari S. (ed.), *Musulmani in Italia La condizione giuridica delle comunità islamiche*, il Mulino, Bologna, 2000, 71; Allievi S., *I musulmani in Italia: chi sono e come ci vedono*, in *Limes*, 2004, 3, 100.

6 Fouad Allam, L'Islam contemporaneo in Europa e in Italia fra affermazione identitaria e nuova religione minoritaria, 605.

7 Guolo, La rappresentanza dell'Islam italiano e la questione delle intese, 71.

8 Allievi, I musulmani in Italia: chi sono e come ci vedono, 100.

9 Decree of the President of the Republic, December 21, 1974, n. 712.

10 As to the establishment of this mosque, see Allievi, I musulmani in Italia: chi sono e come ci vedono, 101. Its Imam is nominated on an annual basis by the Islamic university of Al Azhar, Egypt.

11 Guolo, La rappresentanza dell'Islam italiano e la questione delle intese, 72. The political conflict has a religious intonation because the Saudi King is the "Protector of the Two Mosques" (in Mecca and Medina), while the Moroccan King has the title of "Leaders of the Believers."

Center should be run. Saudi Arabia, which is extremely influential because of its wealth, and Morocco, whose emigrants represent a large proportion of Italian Muslim society, are rivals and each has its own independent view on the Center and its role in Italian Islamic life.

The third Muslim group is the Italian Islamic Religious Community (COREIS),[12] which is the antithesis of UCOII. It consists of Italians who have converted to Islam. It is a sizable group, but is smaller and with less political power than UCOII. However, it has established itself as a player in Islam–Italian relations largely because of its connections with the Vatican and major Islamic states. It adheres to Sufi spirituality and follows French philosopher and Islamic convert Rene Guenon in his belief that an understanding of Islam will peacefully and successfully satisfy Muslims' religious needs and Italian state religious policy needs.[13] Because of this belief, its draft agreement does not explicitly aim to negotiate a specific status for Muslims, but instead attempts to achieve the full integration of Muslims into Italian society.[14]

The final group is the Italian Muslim Association (AMI), which has gathered together a number of Italian converts to Islam. After attracting attention thanks to a draft agreement that it proposed to the state, it almost disappeared from the Italian public environment. It advocates a full integration of Islam into the Italian legal system, and thus distances itself from more fundamentalist thinking and UCOII.[15] However, it also distinguishes itself from COREIS by being less esoteric and more of a religiously Islamic organization.

Each of these rival organizations claims to be the only reliable representative of Muslims in Italy. Each of them has its own highlighted and unique attribute: UCOII boasts of its popularity; COREIS claims to be compatible with the Italian legal system; and both COREIS and AMI advertise that many of their members are Italian citizens. A group's desire to distinguish itself from its rival groups was probably a motivating if not the sole factor in its drafting of Italian–Muslim agreements.

The Convenience of State–Religion Agreements

It will be difficult for the Italian state to reach an agreement with the Muslim community in large part because none of the groups represents a significant

---

12 The acronym is reminiscent of the Quraysh, the Prophet Muhammad's Arab tribe.

13 On the theories that underpin the existence of this group, see Pallavicini A.A.W., *L'islam interiore*, Mondadori, Milan, 1991.

14 Guolo, La rappresentanza dell'Islam italiano e la questione delle intese, 76.

15 Allievi, I musulmani in Italia: chi sono e come ci vedono, 102.

portion of Muslims in Italy.[16] Even UCOII, which claims to control 90 percent of the mosques in Italy,[17] cannot definitively show that it represents a large proportion of the Italian-Muslim population. In fact, only a minority of Muslims belong to any of these groups. Many Muslims simply worship in a conveniently located mosque and do not join any of the four main Muslim groups. In addition, many Muslims do not practice Islam or do not feel attached to any kind of Muslim association or league.[18]

It is unlikely that such associations could merge into one group in order to reach an agreement with the state. Many prominent Muslim figures are reluctant to share their political power and fame with other Muslim figures.[19] In 1998, UCOII, the Islamic World League and the Islamic Cultural Center of Italy joined forces to create the Islamic Council of Italy.[20] The organizations not included in the Council opposed this initiative, probably because they were aware that the Council had a good chance of finally reaching an agreement with Italy.[21] However, rivalries in the Council were so strong that the board members could not even agree as to when their meetings would be held.

There is nothing Italy can do to force Italian Muslims into a single organization.[22] Even if a religious group requested it, the Italian state is forbidden by its own Constitution to force all Italian Muslims into a single organization because the Italian state has no powers in the religious domain and therefore cannot create religious institutions. The Italian Constitution states in Art. 8 that "religious confessions other than Catholicism have the right to organize themselves in accordance with their own statutes, to the extent that these are not in conflict with the Italian legal system."

Even if the Italian Constitution did permit forcing Muslims into a single group, the European Court of Human Rights, which polices the respect and the implementation of the European Convention on Human Rights that Italy has signed and enforced, also prohibits governments from imposing a certain structure on religion. In *Supreme Holy Council of the Muslim Community v. Bulgaria*, the Court stated that "in democratic societies the State does not need in principle to take measures to ensure that religious communities remain or are brought under a unified leadership. The role of the authorities in a situation of conflict between

---

16 Ibid., 102–03.

17 Guolo, La rappresentanza dell'Islam italiano e la questione delle intese, 73.

18 Allievi, I musulmani in Italia: chi sono e come ci vedono, 103.

19 Macrí G., Islam, rappresentanza degli interessi religiosi e diritto comune europeo, available at: www.olir.it, 17.

20 Guolo, La rappresentanza dell'Islam italiano e la questione delle intese, 74–75.

21 Ibid., 75.

22 Finocchiaro A., Art. 8, in Branca G. (ed.), *Commentario alla Costituzione*, Zanichelli, Bologna-Rome, 1975–76, 407.

or within religious groups is not to remove the cause of tension by eliminating pluralism, but to ensure that the competing groups tolerate each other."[23]

At the very same time, it would be inappropriate, and even unconstitutional, for the state to reach an agreement with only one of the Islamic associations.

The last paragraph of Art. 8 presupposes that the state will reach an agreement with a religion, not with a part of it. This implies that the agreement should endow Muslims with more rights *as Muslims*, not as *adherents to a given Islamic organization.*

Moreover, each Islamic party claims the full representation of the Islamic community, at least prospectively, and not just of its adherents. If an agreement was signed with only one association, this would draw the attention of Muslims and affect the autonomous life of each organization, as well as influence how Muslims gather together.

Finally, as we will see, agreement proposals provided by Islamic groups vary significantly. This discourages any agreement with merely a sector of the Muslim community, since the rights they would be granted are debated within the Islamic community and are not necessarily the rights that Muslims need to enjoy greater religious freedom.

Without a state–religion agreement, the Islamic community falls within the scope of the old 1929 provisions on allowed religions,[24] and within the package of rights that the Italian Constitutional Court has elaborated after its inception. Although this endows them with full freedom of worship, they are not given a sizable set of rights, such as the right to receive spiritual counseling in hospitals and prisons, nor do they enjoy the special protection of their properties and organizations. All these features are regulated by agreements and, without them, Muslims are excluded from such rights. In order to meet Islamic needs, scattered accomodation have been put in place in several public institutions, but they are piecemeal and ephemeral, since they can be taken away at the discretion of each institution.

The Government's Endeavors

After failing to forge Italian Islam into a single organization to satisfy the requirements of Art. 8 of the Constitution, the Italian government has established a number of consultative bodies in order to obtain Islamic feedback on topics relevant to Islam in Italy. Less was expected of this milder approach and, indeed, it ended up reviving the very conflicts that had destroyed the possibility of an initial unified agreement. As such, this approach accomplished minimal results.

While forcing Islamic organizations into a shared agreement is prohibited, other Italian state initiatives do not conflict with the Constitution when they

23 App. no. 39023/97, December 16, 2004.

24 Law no. 1159, June 24, 1929.

respect Muslims' right to freely associate.[25] For instance, in 2005, the then Minister for Domestic Affairs created an Islamic Consulting Body, which was set up to explore the needs of Muslims.[26] Such an initiative paralleled those that were undertaken in other countries with different constitutional backgrounds (for example, in France, the *Conseil Francaise du Culte Musulman* was created by the state,[27] while in the UK, the *British Muslim Council* was established). In the Italian initiative, the government nominated members of the Islamic Consulting Body, but did not create this as part of an aim to establish an "official" Islam. In fact, the Minister created this Body in order to facilitate discussions and dialogue with experts and Islamic public figures, and to propose concrete legal accommodations for Muslims.[28] The state hoped to receive advice and observations from the Body during the drafting of bills and other legislation or decisions that could have an impact on Italian Muslims.[29]

The Body's task was not easy. Some of its members opposed one another to the extent that they prevented the Body from seeking a resolution on how Muslims should be integrated into Italian society. These conflicting views arose because of religious as well as political issues, and the differing views of Islamic doctrine and the Israeli–Lebanese war of 2006 were especially strong dividing factors.

This conflict within the Body persuaded the next Minister for Domestic Affairs to introduce a new Scientific Council,[30] whose purpose consisted of shaping a clear conception of citizenship and finding a correct approach to cultural integration. While formally the Scientific Council's mission was to form an integration framework that would fit the needs of any immigrant, the Council focused on aiding the social integration of Muslim immigrants in particular.[31]

---

25 See the talk of the Minister for Domestic Affairs Giuseppe Pisanu at the Commission for Constitutional Affairs, Chamber of Deputies, November 23, 2004, about the bill on *Libertà religiosa e culti ammessi*, available at: www.camera.it.

26 The Body was established on September 10, 2005. The members' formal appointment followed on November 30, 2005.

27 The French Council's life faced similar difficulties. It was initiated in 1989, but only assumed authority in 2003.

28 Macrì, Islam, rappresentanza degli interessi religiosi e diritto comune europeo, 27. See also Sileoni S., Partecipazione e tutela del pluralismo: la tavola transculturale per la questione dell'emergenza in Canada e la consulta per l'Islam in Italia, available at: www.associazionedeicostituzionalisti.it.

29 See the talk of the Minister for Domestic Affairs Giuseppe Pisanu at the Commission for Constitutional Affairs, Chamber of Deputies, November 23, 2004, about the bill on *Libertà religiosa e culti ammessi*, available at www.camera.it.

30 See the Decree of the Minister for Domestic Affairs, April 13, 2007.

31 See Colaianni N., Una "carta" post-costituzionale?, available at: www.statoechiese.it, 1.

It drafted a document entitled the *Charter of Values of Citizenship and Integration*,[32] which was meant to portray the basic features of Italian culture and traditions. It was designed to be handed to immigrants and proposed as a shared understanding of what constitutes Italy and its values. In order to gather a broad level of approval for this document, it was later submitted to the Islamic Consulting Body for its approval, but some of the Body's members refused to sign it, which demonstrated that the attempt to give a shared overview of the Italian identity was not without controversy.

After this refusal, the Italian government attempted other initiatives to gather different Islamic voices around a table and have them debate on specific issues, such as visible Islamic signs or Islamic burials, but with no significant results. In 2010, the *Committee of Italian Islam* was established by the Ministry for the Domestic Affairs.[33] This gathered Islamic believers and intellectuals together, but did not attempt to undertake the state–Islamic agreement issues. In 2012, with the *Committee for Religions, Culture and Integration*, the Italian government focused more on the issue of immigration and social policies than of religious law reform, detaching itself even more substantially from the problems arising from the Islamic presence.

The Islamic communities themselves have apparently dropped the project of a state agreement. In 2008, some long-standing Islamic organizations drafted a *Declaration of Intents*,[34] which aimed at federating Italian Islamic groups that believe in the values of the Italian Constitution and in the *Charter of Values of Citizenship and Integration.* Among its aims, the *Declaration* did not mention the state–Islam agreement following Art. 8 of the Constitution; instead, it focused on specific issues, such as Mosque regulations and Imams' training, which could, however, form part of an agreement. The potential for an agreement within Art. 8 does not appear to be on the horizon.

The problems encountered in signing and enforcing an agreement between Italy and Italian Muslims are not unprecedented. Some relevant Italian and foreign experiences show that similar state religious agreements were also initially problematic, but eventually successful. Italy, for example, has already had to face the religious integration of the Waldensians, the Jewish communities and the Pentecostal groups, all of, and was eventually able to unite each group in order to create a state–religious agreement. I will first highlight each of these situations and then reflect on their applicability to Islamic communities in Italy.

32 Decree of the Minister for Domestic Affairs, April 23, 2007.

33 Established on February 10, 2010.

34 The initiative was taken by: the Azad review, the Ismailite community of Italy, Coreis, the Islamic Cultural Center of Italy, the National Association "Oltre le Frontiere," the Moroccan Women in Italy Association and the Dar Ah-Hikma Cultural Center.

Previous Experiences: The Waldensian Church State–Religion Agreement

The 1984 agreement between the Waldensian Church and Italy ("Intesa tra il Governo della Repubblica italiana c la Tavola valdese")[35] is valuable and analogous to the Italian–Muslim conflict.

The Waldensians are structured on a local basis. They are composed of a hierarchy of assemblies, and such a hierarchy ensures that the fundamental resolutions are taken at the central level.[36] Local churches compose a Synod, which is in charge of the fundamental decisions for the religion. When the Italian state inaugurated a new season in state–religion relationships in 1984, with a new Concordat with the Holy See, the Waldensians were able to reach the first state–religion agreement, which addressed several relevant aspects of religious life—from spiritual counselling, to a special treatment for the clergy and for religious bodies, to religious education—which tailored the state agreements that the state would sign with other religions later. Interestingly, the state–Waldensians agreement also applies to the Methodists. This is because, in 1975, the Waldensian Church Synod and the Methodist Church in Italy had signed a pact of integration. Since then, some decisions taken by a unified body, comprised of representatives of both religions, have binding effects on each religion, but in other aspects the two religions remain separate. This pact of integration made it possible to have the state agreement with the Waldensians also applied to the Methodists. In short, it was the integration between the two religions that made it possible for the state to have the same rules applicable for both. As with the Islamic groups, here we see different groups remaining distinct for religious purposes, but under the same regime before the state.[37] Nonetheless, this was made possible because of the religious integration of the Methodists and the Waldensians, which is exactly the point that Muslims failed to achieve due to mutual rivalries.

The Union of the Jewish Communities–State Agreement

The 1987 Jewish agreement ("Intesa tra il Governo della Repubblica italiana e l'Unione delle Comunità ebraiche italiane")[38] is an example of how to reach an agreement with a community that does not have an established hierarchy endowed with the power to preserve the doctrine or rule over a group of believers. The Jewish population in Italy gathers around its local communities,

35 Signed for the first time on February 21, 1984; executed by law on August 11, 1994, no. 449.

36 Long G., *Le confessioni religiose "diverse dalla cattolica." Ordinamenti interni e rapporti con lo Stato*, il Mulino, Bologna, 1991, 108.

37 Ibid., 111.

38 Signed on February 27, 1988; executed by law on March 8, 1989, no. 101.

which the agreement qualifies as "traditional institutions of Italian Judaism" and "original social bodies."

Some preconditions for the Jewish community–Italian state agreement were paradoxically prepared during the fascist regime. Under Mussolini, the Jewish communities had been regulated by the state.[39] One of these regulations required each Jewish believer to be affiliated with the local Jewish community.[40] At the head of the Jewish organization was the Union of the Israelite (later Jewish) Communities, which was composed of all Jewish Italians. Such strong ties facilitated the mutual recognition between the Union and the believers, and probably helped in reaching an agreement between Italian Jews and the Italian state.[41]

When the provisions of the Italian–Jewish agreement were discussed, the Constitutional Court struck down a piece of legislation mandating that every Jewish individual in Italy be affiliated to a local Jewish community.[42] This was found to violate several constitutional provisions, most importantly one on equality (Art, 3 of the Constitution), which prohibited discriminatory treatments based on race and religion (only Jews were compulsorily grouped); and another of freedom of association (Art. 18 of the Constitution)—which prohibited compulsory affiliation to religious associations. This judgment made it so that the Union of Jewish Communities could not legally represent all Jews in Italy.

However, even after the Constitutional Court's decision, the Union was still very rooted in the Italian Jewish life and represented an overwhelming majority of the Italian Jewish population. Its democratic internal structure,[43] through which local Communities elected members to the central body of the Union,[44] increased the Union's representation of Jewish Italians. It was able to negotiate and sign an agreement with the state in representation of the overwhelming majority of the Jewish-Italian population.

The Pentecostal Experience of Agreements with the State

The dynamics of the Pentecostal spiritualism in Italy is similar to that of Muslims in Italy. Both communities gather locally and both oppose merging into a unified national body.

39 Royal Decree of October 30, 1930, no. 1731: "Norme sulle comunità israelitiche e sull'Unione delle comunità medesime."

40 Art. 4 of the Royal Decree.

41 Long, *Le confessioni religiose "diverse dalla cattolica." Ordinamenti interni e rapporti con lo Stato*, 149 and 151–52.

42 Judgment no. 239, 1984.

43 For details, see Dazzetti S., *L'autonomia delle comunità ebraiche italiane nel Novecento*, Giappichelli, Turin, 2008, *passim.*

44 As to the Rabbis' role, see ibid., 163–64.

This typically Pentecostal localism can be traced both in Assemblies of God's life[45] as well as Baptist communities,[46] two Christian denominations that have flourished in the United States (respectively, "Intesa tra il Governo della Repubblica Italiana e le Assemblee di Dio in Italia"[47] and "Intesa tra la Repubblica italiana e l'Unione Cristiana Evangelica Battista d'Italia").[48] Both were able to sign agreements with the Italian state. The negotiations gathered scattered religious communities around unitary representative bodies according to Art. 8 of the Constitution. Only some Assemblies that fiercely opposed any kind of hierarchization refused to join their co-believers in a unitary body and sign an agreement.

Assemblies of God's congregationalism[49] imposed some changes to the standardized pact that is usually signed under Art. 8. Agreements between a religious group and Italy often list a number of religious organizations that are officially recognized by the state while allowing the religious group in question the right to create new religious institutions.[50] In contrast, the Assemblies of God's agreement does not contain such provisions and so precludes the possibility of subsets of Assemblies of God not already recognized in the agreement from joining the agreement.[51]

This aberration from the norm of an Italian religious agreement was requested by the representative body of the Assemblies of God itself.[52] The Assemblies wanted to have a closed number of religious bodies both because of the small number of Assemblies of God believers in Italy and because they feared that an increase in the number of institutions would lead to difficulty in maintaining a unified religion. Given the strong autonomist and separatist spirit of this religion, the creation of new state-recognized bodies could easily provoke internal religious conflicts. Such division would have necessarily increased internal conflicts and weakened the significance of the agreement with the Italian state.

45 Long, *Le confessioni religiose "diverse dalla cattolica." Ordinamenti interni e rapporti con lo Stato*, 136–37.

46 Ibid., 231–35.

47 Signed on December 29, 1986; executed by law on November 22, 1988, no. 517.

48 Signed on March 29, 1993; executed by law on April 12, 1995, no. 116.

49 Long, *Le confessioni religiose "diverse dalla cattolica." Ordinamenti interni e rapporti con lo Stato*, 251.

50 Art. 12 of the Agreement with the Waldensians; Art. 20 of the Agreement with the Adventists; Arts. 17 and 20 of the Agreement with the Jewish communities; Art. 11 of the Agreement with the Baptists; Art. 18 of the Agreement with the Lutherans. See also Arts. 10–11 of the Agreement with the Buddhists and Arts. 10 and 14 of the Agreement with the Jehovah's Witnesses.

51 Cardia C., *Stato e confessioni religiose. Il regime pattizio*, il Mulino, Bologna, 1992, 226.

52 Ibid.

Despite the fact that a faction of the religion opposed an Italian agreement, the state signed and implemented the agreement because the dissenters were not significant in number.[53] The majority of the Assemblies of God believers wanted the agreement to be signed. Had the agreement been more equally divisive among the believers, the state would not have agreed on a pact that was so selective and favorable to the signing faction to the extreme that other institutions of the Assemblies of God could not be recognized by the state. What persuaded Italy to sign the agreement was the fact that the central body of the Assemblies of God had the actual capacity to represent the vast majority of other Assemblies.

The very conditions that made the state agreements with the Waldensians, the Methodists, the Union of the Jewish Communities, and the Pentecostals possible are the very conditions that make a state agreement with Islam unlikely. Italian Islamic communities are mostly centralized and are reluctant to gather around unified and representative bodies, as do the Waldensians, the Methodists, the Jewish communities and the Pentecostals. The initiatives aimed at unifying Islam also have a hidden purpose of monopolizing the Muslim constituency. There is no unified majority within the Muslim community and the understandings of Islam are so diverse among Muslims that religious needs are not uniform.

It is also not possible to limit the number of officially recognized Islamic organizations as the agreement with God's Assemblies did. Since the Islamic groups are so divisive, the creation of a selected list of officially recognized Islamic organizations would necessarily be arbitrarily selective and partial.

The Spanish agreement between the state and Islam has suffered from this very problem and the partisan regulation of state–religion relations has increased internal conflict among Islamic groups.

The Muslim Community in Spain's State–Religion Agreement

Spain encountered several difficulties when attempting to sign an agreement with Spanish Muslims. Notwithstanding the territorial and social fragmentation of Muslims in Spain, since the 1980s, the state has worked to reach a pact with Spanish Muslims, or at least a significant proportion of them. Similar attitudes were manifested during negotiations with the Protestants and the Jews in Spain. The state of Spain pushed for an agreement with each of these religious organizations, but insisted that the agreement had to be concluded with a single

53 Long, Le confessioni religiose "diverse dalla cattolica." Ordinamenti interni e rapporti con lo Stato, 241.

religious interlocutor.[54] Therefore, non-hierarchical religions were forced to unify for the purpose of the agreement.[55]

Islam rose to prominence in Spain in the late 1960s when some students from Islamic studies came to Spain to study. In the 1970s, some prominent leftist intellectuals converted to Islam and established themselves in Andalusia in order to deepen their understanding of Spain's Islamic roots.[56] But it was only in the 1980s and 1990s that the Muslim population in Spain truly began to grow thanks in part to the more favorable terms of the democratic constitution established in late 1978.

The two largest Spanish Islamic groups were founded in the late 1980s and early 1990s. The first group is the Spanish Federation of Islamic Religious Entities (FSERI), which was created in 1989. This group consisted of 11 mostly Sunnite communities.[57] In 1991, the second predominantly Sunnite organization was established, the Union of Islamic Communities in Spain (UCIDE), whose ideology was similar to that of the Islamic fundamentalism of the Muslim Brotherhood.[58] UCIDE's peaceful attitude persuaded Spain's state's institutions to trust the group.

FSERI and UCIDE opposed each other and attempted to negotiate separately with the state, while the Spanish government clarified that it would only sign an agreement with a single unified group. The two groups then created one unified body which was to represent Spanish Muslims for the purposes of a religious state agreement,[59] calling itself the Islamic Commission of Spain. Muslims as well as scholars understood this organization to be a broker that intended to work together on behalf of Spanish Muslims only in order to form an agreement with the state.[60] It worked, and Spain signed an agreement with the Commission—the "Acuerdo de Cooperación entre el Estado Español y la Comisión Islámica de España" ("Agreement of Cooperation between the Spanish State and the Islamic Commission of Spain") in 1992.[61]

The results of this process were not fully satisfactory. The Commission's flaws were soon apparent. The disagreements between FSERI and UCIDE eventually caused a deadlock in the Commission and the proposals brought

54 Motilla A., L'accordo di cooperazione tra la Spagna e la Commissione islamica. Bilancio e prospettive, in Ferrari (ed.), *Musulmani in Italia*, 248.

55 Ibid., 249.

56 Mantecon J., Islam in Spain, in Aluffi Beck-Peccoz R. and Zincone G. (eds), *The Legal Treatment of Islamic Minorities in Europe*, Peeters, Leuven, 2004, 213.

57 Motilla, L'accordo di cooperazione tra la Spagna e la Commissione islamica, 2000, 249.

58 Ibid., 250.

59 Ibid., 251.

60 Mantecon, Islam in Spain, 216.

61 Signed on April 28, 1992; enforced by law on November 10, 1992, no. 26.

before the Commission were blocked by either party. This prevented the enactment of the Spain–Islam agreement. The insistence of the state in pushing for the quick conclusion of a unitary agreement proved to be counterproductive at the time of its factual enforcement.

The veto policy not only operated to prevent internal progress, but also outwardly. The agreement's provisions permitted new Islamic groups to join the Commission, but the admittance of any group is conditional on the approval of FSERI and UCIDE, which reserve the right to refuse new memberships. FSERI and UCIDE have been very selective and reluctant to allow other Islamic groups to join the Commission. In addition, they have boycotted territorial agreements between local governments and local Islamic communities.[62] This deadlock created by the Commission has led to a general criticism of Spain's attempt to provide Muslims with religious freedom. To combat this, Spain has intervened with by-laws in an attempt to correct this gridlock. In 2011, Spain issued a Royal Decree commanding that all Islamic organizations that are officially recognized by the state have a right to be included in the Spain–Islamic agreement unless the Commission explains why it refused the admittance of a particular group.[63]

Difficulties

The previous examples show the difficulty of reaching an agreement between Muslims in Italy and the Italian state. The Waldensians integrated quite easily with the Methodists. Italy's successful agreement with the Union of Jewish Communities derives from the stable historical roots of Italian Judaism. The Union of Jewish Communities has proven to be a reliable organization, both for the state and for Jewish believers, as seen by the fact that the Communities and the Union survived fascism and entered the Republican era intact. And creating an Italian–Pentecostal agreement was easy because the majority of Pentecostals wanted an agreement with the state.

In contrast, Islam in Italy is characterized by multiple organizations, each striving to prove its own legitimacy and disprove the other's authority. The Islamic Council of Italy is a prime example of Italian Muslims' resistance to forming a unified organization. More recent steps to integrate Muslims into Italian society have faced the same difficulties and it seems impossible that an agreement under Art. 8 of the Italian Constitution will be reached.

The Spanish experiment, while an example of when it was possible to reach an agreement, shows that even after an agreement is reached, minimal progress

62 Motilla, L'accordo di cooperazione tra la Spagna e la Commissione islamica, 251–52.

63 Royal Decree of October 14, 2011, 1384.

may be achieved when the two main factions involved cannot reach any conclusions. The Spanish government would have liked to have the agreement signed in 1992 to commemorate the 500-year anniversary of the Reconquista, and pushed for a fast and successful conclusion of the negotiations. But this agreement did not end internal Islamic conflicts, nor did it provide for full religious freedom for Muslims or garner support for a Spanish–Muslim agreement. Any initiative attempted by the Commission was impeded by internal conflict, and large parts of the agreement's provisions did not take effect for almost 20 years, while religious groups wanting to take part in the agreement were forbidden from doing so by FSERI and UCIDE.[64]

The Spanish model of an open agreement that would be initially signed by some Islamic organizations but later made accessible to more organizations as they wished to join has been considered in Italy. The Italian Buddhist Union and Italy have signed such an agreement ("Intesa tra la Repubblica Italiana e l'Unione Buddhista Italiana").[65] According to their agreement, more Buddhist groups may join the Union and be protected by the provisions of the agreement, or they can leave the Italian Buddhist Union and therefore leave the agreement.[66] The Union retains the right to approve or deny the admittance of new organizations into the agreement.

However, this solution, which was so effective for Italian Buddhists, would probably not work for Italian Muslims for two reasons. First, even in the Buddhist context, other Buddhist associations have attempted to create their own agreement with Italy subsequent to the original Italian–Buddhist agreement.[67] Open agreements do not rule out the possibility of more organizations of the same religion attempting to form a unique agreement with the state. Moreover, having separate agreements is hardly consistent with the constitutional provisions and might be counterproductive for the internal affairs of the Islamic community. It is likely that separate agreements would not be just constitutionally problematic for Italian law, but also detrimental to the Islamic community, since they could prompt disaggregation instead of integration among Muslim groups.

The second reason why an open agreement would not work with Italian Muslims is that the parties to the agreement would probably reserve the right to approve or deny admittance of other organizations to the agreement. This

64 Bonetti P., La laicità dello Stato di fronte alle proposte di intesa con la confessione islamica, in Bin R., Brunelli G., Pugiotto A. and Veronesi P. (eds), *La laicità crocifissa? Il nodo costituzionale dei simboli religiosi nei luoghi pubblici*, Giappichelli, Turin, 2004, 44.

65 Signed on April 4, 2007; executed by law on December 31, 2012, no. 245.

66 Art. 25 of the Agreement.

67 Angeletti S., *L'intesa tra lo Stato italiano e l'Unione Buddhista Italiana*, available at: www.olir.it, 5.

clause could prevent the admittance of other Muslim groups to a Muslim–Italian agreement.[68]

In short, the relationship between Italian Muslims and Italy is a difficult one, in large part because Islam is a religion traditionally led by the state in Muslim countries, the rival Italian Muslim political and religious leaders in Italy make it hard to find common ground, and there is a long-standing tradition of boilerplate state–religion agreements. The needs of Italian Muslims can only be met if Italian institutions go beyond the surface of the standard state–religion agreement and instead reflect closely on the needs of Italian Muslims. These needs will be the subject of Chapter 5.

68 See Art. 12 of the Agreement with the Waldensians; Arts. 17 and 20 of the Agreement with the Jewish communities; Art. 11 of the Agreement with the Baptists; Art. 18 of the Agreement with the Lutherans; Art. 20 of the Agreement with the Adventists.

Chapter 5
Making Sense of Religious Freedom for Italian Muslims

The Deadlock of Religious Freedom for Muslims

Italy's current political and religious climate will not allow for a smooth accommodation of Muslims' needs. The process that has led other traditional religious groups (such as the Jews or the Waldensians) and more exotic religions (such as Buddhism) into a peaceful agreement with the Italian state will not work for Italian Muslims.

As discussed in Chapter 4, the preliminary obstacles stem from the historical structure of Islam as well as its current manifestation in Italy. Traditionally, Islam has no hierarchy and, pursuant to that, no hierarchical structure has appeared in Italy. While many individuals and organizations claim to be representative of the Italian Islamic community, this is hardly confirmed by the religious practices and attitudes of a Muslim community that is deeply divided based on nationality and personal religious inclinations.

An Italian–Muslim agreement is not the only way to bring religious freedom to Muslims; an alternative could be to advocate for religious freedom through general legislation. Such legislation could not endow Muslims in Italy with the rights they could have claimed through a religion–state agreement, but it could give Muslims in Italy some protections such as a Friday holy day, the civil acceptance of Muslim marriages or the sanction of Muslim religious activities in public schools.

However, like the possibility of a religious state agreement, any legislative proposals for Islamic religious freedom have been unsuccessful. Attempts to enforce generally applicable legislation that would meet the needs of Muslims in Italy have been unsuccessful. In this, Italy bears full responsibility for its inability to enact crucial legislation that would be fundamental to recognizing Islamic rights. The presence of Muslims in Italy has politically discouraged the implementation of religious freedom legislation: a section of Italian public opinion is concerned that there will be no limit to what Muslims ask for or how they could exploit the possibilities opened up by new legislation. Some Islamic requests and practices are perceived as obstacles to a Muslim's full integration into Italian society. Some of these practices are even perceived as violating Italian constitutional values. Political pressures affect religious freedom policies for Muslims, and make the issue both urgent to address and extremely sensitive to social perceptions and misrepresentations.

In this chapter, I will first explore where Muslim practices are or are perceived to be problematic, then I will reflect on the reasons for the Italy's failure to objectively address the needs of Italian Muslims. I will then contrast this Italian state–religion approach with some notes of attitudes towards multiculturalism. Finally, I will urge a reconsideration of the constitutional tools that could be used to meet the needs of Islamic Muslims.

Italian Policies on Religious Freedom and the Muslim Community: An Initial Assessment

On the surface, much of what Italian Muslims demand is similar to those made by similar religions that have successfully signed an agreement with the state. In fact, though, the inner divisions within the Islamic community, and the different interpretations of Islam and of its integration to non-Muslims contexts make Muslim demands more complicated than those of other religions. In order to understand the Islamic struggle, it is important to fully understand the theological and religious concerns behind the importance of a particular right.

Muslims are advocating in particular for the following rights and requests:

- The assignation of estate properties to construct mosques.
- Accommodation of working hours during Ramadan and the five daily prayers.
- Weekly vacation days on Fridays.
- The right to spiritual counseling for Muslims in penitentiaries or hospitals.
- Official appointments of religious personnel.
- Civil acknowledgement of Islamic marriages.
- The instruction of Islam in public schools.
- The right to open private schools.[1]

These formalized requests are only some of the demands made by Italian Muslims. For instance, 10 years ago, around 41.3 percent of Italian Muslims advocated for the legality of polygamy.[2] Even requests that have been formalized in the agreement drafts are more problematic than they initially appear. There

1 Fouad Allam K., L'Islam contemporaneo in Europa e in Italia fra affermazione identitaria e nuova religione minoritaria, in Zincone G. (ed.), *Secondo Rapporto sull'Integrazione degli Immigrati in Italia*, il Mulino, Bologna, 2001, 606–07.

2 Stefanini M., *Le forme degli islam nostrani*, in *Limes*, 2004, 3, 116.

are several perspectives that make these requests unique and different from similar requests made by other religions in Italy.[3]

An example of this is the push toward making Friday a holy day.[4] COREIS still includes this right in its proposed agreement, while UCOII has changed its position over time.[5] Such a right is subject to the condition that such a request may be accommodated without undue disruption to the company's business practices. This request, if satisfied, would have sizable ramifications on the Italian economy and business management. Jews and Adventists already have the right to abstain from work and school on Saturday, but on Saturday many working activities are already suspended and many schools are closed. In addition, the population of Muslims in Italy is much higher than the Jewish or Adventist population. This means that any Muslim work-day abstention would have a greater effect that any Jewish or Adventist abstention.

The instruction of Islam in public schools is likewise problematic.[6] So far, similar religious agreements have allowed a religion to intervene in public schools at the request of its representative institution. But such intervention would be episodic and only aimed at illustrating a religious tradition or experience in broad, non-denominational terms.[7] No agreement has yet included a provision about the instruction of religious doctrine, with the exception of the Agreement with the Catholic Church,[8] and this only included instruction of religious doctrine

3 Castro F., L'islam in Italia: profili giuridici, in *Quaderni di diritto e politica ecclesiastica*, 1996, 280; Tedeschi M., Cristianesimo e islamismo presupposti storico-giuridici, in *Quaderni della scuola di specializzazione in diritto ecclesiastico e canonico*, 4; Tedeschi M., *La presenza islamica nell'ordinamento giuridico italiano*, Jovene, Naples, 1996, 38.

4 Art. 15 of the COREIS Agreement draft, published in *Intesa tra la Repubblica Italiana e la Comunità Islamica in Italia*, Milan, 1998. The first paragraph states that Muslims that are public or private employees, or who run businesses, or who serve in the military or as civil servants have the right to enjoy, upon request, the religious festivities on Fridays. The last paragraph of the same article says holy days will be considered justified.

5 Art. 3, para. 2 of the UCOII Agreement draft, published in *Quaderni di diritto e politica ecclesiastica*, 1993, 2, which states that absences of Muslim students on Fridays are justified.

6 See Art. 10, third paragraph, of the AMI Agreement proposal, available at: http://www.google.com/url?sa=t&rct=j&q=&esrc=s&source=web&cd=1&ved=0CB4QFjAA&url=http%3A%2F%2Fwww.jus.unitn.it%2Fusers%2Fcamassa%2Fdirecc l%2Ftopics%2Fmateriale%2FBozza%2520A.M.I.doc&ei=P8glVKHrItaoyATmiYDYCw&usg=AFQjCNFdgapmjLGS3WAclVcNHNu22VJz9Q&bvm=bv.76247554,d.aWw. The relevant provision states that Muslim students who request it have the right to participate in Islamic lessons.

7 Art. 10 of the Agreement with the Jewish communities.

8 Art. 9, par. 2 of the Agreement of Revision of Concordat, executed with law no. 121, 1985, which states that the Republic should continue teaching the Catholic doctrine in consideration of the Catholic religious heritage and traditional value to Italian society.

in consideration with the specific role that Catholicism has played in Italian history.[9] Moreover, Catholic doctrine is taught only to students who request it; conversely, ideally Islamic doctrine would be taught to only Muslim students. This means that a student's religion would be tracked in order to single out those that have a right to receive Islamic education. Finally, the instruction of Islam in public schools could increase divisions within the Muslim community as factions attempt to agree on what Islamic doctrine should be taught and who should teach it.

The two examples of holy days and school instruction show that Muslims desire many of the same rights as other religions, but that these rights are more complex and difficult to obtain. *The goals of the pact are therefore ambiguous.* An Italian–Islam agreement would paradoxically provide them with equal religious rights in Italy, but would hardly allow Muslims to integrate into Italian society.

These demands are therefore highly symbolical. For some Muslim groups, the possibility of an agreement has become a political as well as a legal tool for them to legitimize themselves in the Italian state and society. Such emphasis on gaining political rights as well as religious rights likely derives from Islam's traditional lack of distinction between the religious and political spheres; therefore, every political success is a religious success and vice versa.[10] This blurring of religious and political lines also explains why an agreement is more desirable to many Muslims than religious reform legislation. An agreement has greater force and greater political implications.

The Need for Guidance

As we have seen, as in other European countries, many of the religious rights in Italy are gained through a separate agreement with each religious organization. While a European constitution will broadly protect religious rights, certain specific benefits such as respect for holy days or tax benefits can be obtained most effectively through a religion–state agreement.

However, an agreement with the state or religious legislation that could further recognize the rights of Muslims is difficult to obtain. The internal structure of Islam in Italy polarizes cultural trends and makes intra-religious negotiations extremely difficult. The absence of a hierarchy does not endow any religious figure with the capacity of signing a pact that could speak for all Muslims in Italy. Further, the different origins and understandings of the

9 Cardia C., *Stato e confessioni religiose. Il regime pattizio*, il Mulino, Bologna, 1992, 315.

10 Musselli L., *Islam e ordinamenti giuridici europei: momenti di contrasto e momenti di possibile integrazione*, *Quaderni della scuola di specializzazione in diritto ecclesiastico e canonico*, 4, *La presenza islamica nell'ordinamento giuridico italiano*, Jovene, Naples, 1996, 19.

Islamic faith among Muslim believers make it hard to define the scope and goals of the Muslim movement.[11] The fact that Muslim believers believe that both their political and religious rights are involved raises the stakes.

Currently, the issue of Islam in Italy is complicated by the social imagery and the political facets that are attached to Muslims and to their religious needs. Until now, the state has protected the rights of small religious minorities in Italy, even those that were previously persecuted. However, the current public and political affirmation of Islam, in an era that has seen the return of religious terrorism, is making it harder to find a smooth and politically acceptable solution to Islamic political and religious tensions.

Admittedly, the problem with Islam is not just a variable of the present condition of religious pluralism in Italy. Institutional and political skepticism pre-dates the current political climate. The Constituent Assembly, which drafted the 1948 Republican Constitution, saw the integration of Islam into Italy's public sphere as a challenge. While at that time the presence of Islam in Italy was only theoretical and culturally disconnected from any terrorist threats, one of the members of the Assembly alluded to the possibility that one day Italy would need to sign a pact with Muslims.

Skepticism about the full integration of Muslims to Italian society not only stems from the concern that Islamic religious practices are not consistent with the Italian Constitution, such as polygamy, or practices that are in use among some Muslim populations, such as female genital mutilation, which collide with basic constitutional principles such as the monogamous nature of marriage, gender equality or human health and body integrity, but there is also a concern that Islam tends to strongly identify with the state and with the political community at large. According to this view, a separation between politics, law and religion that is so customary in modern liberal-democratic regimes is incompatible with Islamic doctrine. Any attempt to assimilate Islam into modern democracies would result in a deformation of Islam.

But this focus on Islamic history and doctrine, in contrast with liberal democracies, cannot hide the problems that the Italian state has constantly encountered in addressing religious needs within the last few decades. The difficulties in finding a legal resolution between Italy and Islam derive not just from Islam, but also from the state. To assess the growth of religious minorities, Italy has developed an extremely standardized pact which fails to recognize the uniqueness of each religion.[12] As the pacts became more standardized, the

11 "If law is seen as part of culture, and culture as part of law, we can expect to find an irriducible continuum running between law and custom": Rosen L., *The Justice of Islam*, Oxford University Press, New York, 2000, 85.

12 Fumagalli Carulli O., Dai "culti ammessi" alla libertà religiosa: un cammino incompiuto, in *Iustitia*, 2004, 2–3, 178.

process became slower and many religions had to wait several years before the implementation of a pact protecting their religions rights. These problems are universal in Italy and show that the difficulties in establishing a Muslim–Italian pact are not solely the fault of Muslims.

The purely formalistic repetition of previous solutions, such as the granting of Fridays as a holy day because Jews and Adventists have been given free Saturdays, is not in the spirit of the Italian Constitution. Art. 8 of the Constitution commands that each religion be granted what is appropriate to its doctrine and its need, but not necessarily what has been provided for other religious groups. In fact, pursuant to Art. 3 of the Constitution, which contains the principle of equality, to treat different religious groups the same is as wrong as to discriminate against religions. This caveat is supposed to apply to the legal treatment of all religious groups.

Art. 8 can be successfully used to address the religious rights of Muslims without indulging in fears that the pact might be hijacked for becoming too politically powerful. If Art. 8 does not empower the government to tailor specific pacts to each individual religion, then there is no point in providing government guidance in the context of growing religious and cultural pluralism. As of now, Italy's legal system has practiced a strict equalitarianism, which does not endow religions with what they need, and enforces loose policies based on negotiations that arbitrarily concede or refuse demands for special regimes.[13] By treating all religions the same, religion–state relationships have suffered many of the shortcomings that are attached both to equalitarianism and multiculturalism.

The Agreement Method and its Implications: Neutrality, Multiculturalism and Beyond

The confused and fluctuating approaches to understanding religious needs are further complicated by the ideas and tactics of other nations in terms of how they choose to approach any religious problems.

A new understanding of cultural and religious diversities in Italy has emerged as theories of law and justice have evolved from equalitarian theories to pluralist theories. Drawing largely from North American experience, the Italian legal and philosophical culture has grown beyond the Rawlsian paradigm of equality and now conceptualizes diversity differently. Recent years have seen the increasing legal understanding that cultural diversity is not the same as social or economic

13 Ferrari S., Introduzione, in Ferrari S. (ed.), *Islam ed Europa*, Carocci, Rome, 2006, 28–30.

diversity. Social or economic diversity can be eliminated, while cultural diversity should be protected.

The Italian legal culture is split on how to protect cultural and religious diversity. Some embrace a sort of multiculturalism-based approach that uses the Constitution as a framework that enables the state to protect cultural traditions as goods in themselves. Proponents of multiculturalism argue that each tradition enriches the group that practices it, and therefore must be protected as a part of protecting the rights of religious believers. The other side, supporters of "laicità," the Italian understanding of neutralism, argue instead that cultural traditions must be cherished because they enrich the whole of society, whether they are practiced by a majority or a minority of Italians. I will first explore the first legal trend and show why it is an inadequate template to explain the protection of religious minorities. Then I will move on to the second trend and link it to the constitutional principle of "laicità."

Multiculturalism, as is often depicted according to Italian doctrine, believes that ideas on justice and good are incomparable and even cannot be evaluated, both in terms of their descriptive and prescriptive value.[14] Proponents of this doctrine believe that ideas of justice in each culture are incommensurable to each other and to public values. Multiculturalism accords virtually all practices the very same respect only because they are practiced, but maintains that their value cannot be understood.[15] This means that public discourse and public policies cannot give full consideration to cultural practices or ideals; their value is believed to reside in its cogency for the group that practices it, not in its validity.[16]

This idea of multiculturalism highlights cultural traditions, but not the culture's values or claims. This contradiction, which has also been detected in multiculturalist environments such as Canada, fails to respect minorities: multiculturalist constitutionalism focuses on protecting their rights, not on protecting their values as important for the whole society. In short, it respects minorities, but not what they believe in.[17]

These attitudes of multiculturalism have appeared in Italy. A recent idea is that Italy provides cultural and religious diversity simply by providing legislation

14 Benhabib S., *La rivendicazione dell'identità culturale. Eguaglianza e diversità nell'era globale*, il Mulino, Bologna, 2005, 54 and 59.

15 Donati P., *Oltre il multiculturalismo*, Laterza, Rome-Bari, 2008, 6–7; Prades J., *Occidente: l'ineludibile incontro*, Cantagalli, Siena, 2008, 6; Novak D., *Natural Law in Judaism*, Cambridge University Press, Cambridge, 1998, 190.

16 For a criticism of this reading of multiculturalism from a Western Muslim perspective, see Tibi B., *Euro-Islam. L'integrazione mancata*, Marsilio, Venice, 2003, 144 and 150.

17 See Botturi F., Riconoscimento e cultura. Per un modello delle soggettività interculturali, in Prades J. (ed.), *All'origine della diversità. Le sfide del multiculturalismo*, Guerini, Milan, 2008, 81.

that allows religious exemptions from normal state activity, such as work or school on holy days.[18] But this proposal does not allow conflicting interests to be balanced and resolved. It does not take into account how conflicting values should be addressed or how the state can accommodate different religions. This idea of multiculturalism does not take into consideration the importance and role that each tradition might have in a religion, and how it impacts the whole society.

Multiculturalism has not yet made its way to the heart of Italian legal culture. Cultural and religious claims have been addressed mainly through more political negotiations, which constititute a rather unstable and unsatisfactory alternative. Whether a consideration or allowance is granted to a religion depends on how rooted a cultural practice is, as well as on social and demographic power and the reputation of each religious group. This approach is exemplified with the standard religion–state agreements in Italy. Now, though, religions normally align their requests to what has been traditionally conceded, as opposed to what the religion actually values. Requests that differ from the norm are discouraged and are subject to deeper scrutiny.

This approach of a standardized agreement not only fails to address the needs of Italian religious factions, but it also fails to address the needs of the state. Through the standardized pact has grown the assumption that if the state has conceded a grant to one religion, it must concede that grant to all religions.[19] Once a right is ceded to one agreement, each religion believes it should also be entitled to that right, even though there are not strong reasons as to why that concession should be granted. While a religion's need varies based on the religion, each religion claims to have the same rights as those who have signed previous pacts, even though in reality, one right might be more important than another.[20] While pretending to grant further rights, in reality, these distortive practices end up forcing each religion into the same mold.

If we do not objectively scrutinize the needs and values of each religion, we cannot accommodate a religion's cultural and religious needs in conjunctions with Italy's Constitution. We cannot simply weigh general religious values against general constitutional values; instead, we must contrast each distinct constitutional value with its constitutional counterweight to see if we can find a solution.

18 Elia L., Introduzione ai problemi della laicità, in Pace A. (ed.), *Problemi pratici della laicità agli inizi del secolo XXI*, Cedam, Padua, 2008.

19 Casuscelli G., Libertà religiosa collettiva e nuove intese con le minoranze confessionali, available at: www.statoechiese.it, 12.

20 In general terms, see McConnell M.W., "God is Dead and We Have Killed Him!": Freedom of Religion in the Post-Modern Age, in *Brigham Young University Law Review*, 1993, 175.

To find a solution and provide adequate religious rights in Italy, we must leave behind the multicultural paradigm as well as practical, undertheorized negotiations. Traditions can and must be weighed against other public interests and accommodated in the context of a religion's social and moral values. These values should not be accommodated simply in order to protect the rights of minorities, but because an understanding of these religions' claims enrich all of Italian society:[21] these religious values are hypotheses on truth, morality and ethics.[22] Such values must be accommodated, not simply permitted, and a balance must be struck between these religious interests and the interests of the Italian state.[23]

In contrast to multiculturalism and to political compromises is the neutrality principle, as crafted by the Italian Constitutional Court and encapsulated in the word "laicità." The Italian version of the neutrality principle attempts to value religious beliefs and traditions as opposed to simply supporting the rights of individuals to follow those beliefs or values. "Laicità" can prompt a new understanding of religious and cultural pluralism and usher in a new era of religious rights in Italy. The Italian version of neutrality, as will be understood in the following chapter, can capture each religion's claims in order to understand fundamental truths.

Far from endorsing any vision of truths and morals, "laicità," as shaped by the primitive Constitutional Court's jurisprudence, recognizes cultural and religious claims. Cultural and religious traditions must be protected not just because they are followed by groups; they are to be protected because of their religious significance. In other words, they must be pondered precisely in order to best understand their value for the believer and their significance for the whole society.[24]

A Precondition: Religious Freedom and State Neutrality

The condition for a reconsideration of Art. 8 requires a re-evaluation of the relationship between political institutions and religious groups. Italy must reaffirm that its representative institutions are capable of understanding and responding to religious needs with legal reform.

---

21 Cardia C., *Stato e confessioni religiose. Il regime pattizio*, il Mulino, Bologna, 1992, 141; Ferrari S., *Lo spirito dei diritti religiosi*, il Mulino, Bologna, 2002, 59–60.

22 Waldron J., *Valori particolari e moralità critica*, in Ferrara A. (ed.), *Comunitarismo e liberalismo*, Editori riuniti, Rome, 1992, 312.

23 Dalla Torre G., *Europa, Quale laicità?*, San Paolo, Cinisello Balsamo, 2003, 91.

24 Selznick P., Dworkin's Unfinished Task, in *California Law Review*, 1989, 77(3), 513.

Public institutions do not have the power to control religions—they cannot manipulate religious beliefs as can be done in Muslim states or in Europe's past, where the monarch controlled the religion. Now Italy is forbidden from controlling a religion both by its own Constitution and the European Court of Human Rights, which forbids a state from attempting "to determine whether religious beliefs or the means used to control such beliefs are legitimate."[25]

State activism can either be directed to influence the life of religious organizations or to understand it. Understanding religions is a part of a state's task and one that consists in detecting religious identities in order to offer believers a state in which they can freely practice their faith. Each specific religion must be understood according to its individual characteristics. A religion's tenets and reasons for its practices must be understood by the state.

Legal doctrines of each religion can be tracked in order to understand what role that religion will play in state politics. Religious laws can be detected and their prescriptive character can be understood to an extent.

If Italian legal culture adheres to this conceptualization of the relationship between church, state and religious freedom, then it can understand Islam and meet its very needs. The needs of Muslim believers must be considered in order to integrate Islam with Italy. Once Italy understands Islam, it can form a pact to meet the needs of Muslims and provide them with the allowances they need, while not granting them allowances that are frivolous. The Italian Constitution itself can show Italy how to track and register the needs of Muslims.

The next chapter will explore the principle of "laicità" as it has been shaped by the Constitutional Court's case law as well by legal scholarship. This principle is the very constitutional pivot around which Italian religious freedom policies have been built over the past 25 years. "Laicità" is also a powerful tool that can be used as a compass by the state when dealing with different religious beliefs. The shifting attitude of this principle will be accurately described in order to capture its value in addressing contemporary religious needs.

Chapter 7 will deal with long-standing issues of religious freedom for Muslims that have occupied the legal and political debate in Italy. I will use them as case studies to give proof of the validity of a method that uses "laicità" as a compass to address religious needs and tailor specific pacts.

The constitutional principle of "laicità," as shaped by the Constitutional Court, can be fruitfully used in the process of negotiation between religion and state. It establishes a framework to address religious freedom needs and allows the state to detect and ponder real religious needs, therefore enabling it to balance these needs with competing state interests.

"Laicità" enables the state to single out religious fundamental needs and therefore to establish a set of priorities in religious freedom requests. At the

25 *Hasan and Chaush v. Bulgaria* (App. no. 30985/96), October 26, 2000, par. 78.

same time, it reinvigorates the state–religion agreement system, since it sets down the preconditions for the shaping of pacts that are truly tailored to each religion's specific needs. And the shaping of specific pacts is a political necessity as well as a constitutional duty of the state.

Chapter 6

The Italian Version of State Neutrality: "Laicità"

Introduction

The constitutional principles that govern the relationship between church, state and religious freedom are synthetically defined in Italian as "laicità": this word has much in common with the principle of neutrality, but with some distinctive features. If properly understood, "laicità" provides a device for understanding how to accommodate Muslims in Italy. Given its legal and political meaning,[1] it can successfully be used by courts as well as by political institutions. This principle offers guidance in assessing religious claims, pondering religious needs and indicating how the Italian government should approach these issues. Such relationship between state and religion, as shaped by the Italian Constitutional Court, allows for different legal regimes in an attempt to grant each religious group what it needs.[2]

Taken seriously, "laicità" can play a strong role either in negotiating a religion–state agreement or in drafting religious legislation. The use of the "laicità" principle can help to detect important religious claims and to balance these claims with constitutional principles. Exemptions or allowances are permitted without seeming to endanger the rights of other religious groups.[3] This same "laicità" principle that should apply to Italian Muslims should also be used when considering how to best accommodate other religions in Italy as well.

1 Fontana G., La tutela costituzionale della società democratica tra pluralismo, principio di laicità e garanzia dei diritti fondamentali. (La Corte europea dei diritti dell'uomo e lo scioglimento del Refah partisi), in *Giurisprudenza costizionale*, 2002, 379–94, 387.

2 Mirabelli C., Intervento alla Tavola Rotonda. Laicità dello Stato, confessioni religiose e multiculturalismo, in *Quaderni di diritto e politica ecclesiastica*, 2006, 354.

3 Dalla Torre G., *Europa, Quale Laicità?*, San Paolo, Milan, 2003, 96.

Neutrality and Separation of Church and State in Europe: Constitutions and Legal Studies

Before delving into Italian case law, it is necessary to briefly highlight the different understandings of the role of the European state in relation to different religious rights.[4]

Through the case law of the European Court of Human Rights, European states have for the most part affirmed the "neutrality" principle, both at the domestic as well at the supranational level. In fact, virtually all European countries are members of the Council of Europe and have signed the European Convention on Human Rights, a pan-European list of human rights that the states are committed to enforce and whose respect is policed by the European Court of Human Rights (ECtHR). The ECtHR reviews cases that are appealed after state domestic remedies are exhausted—its minimal purpose is to ascertain whether a state has violated any of the rights upheld in the European Convention on Human Rights. As the Convention is intended to protect individuals against violations by the state, the structure of this judicial remedy invariably sees individuals or groups challenge a state for having actively violated, or passively failed to respect, their rights under the Convention.

Usually, a case is first addressed by a section of the Court, which delivers a judgment. The losing party can appeal before the Grand Chamber, which will decide whether to address the case or declare the appeal inadmissible. If it does accept to take on the case, the judgment will be final. Winning applicants are provided with monetary compensation from the state.

The ECtHR has repeatedly stated that "neutrality" is one of the unmistakable features of democratic states.

Neutrality is surely an important part of the shared European legal heritage. However, each state understands neutrality in its own way when dealing with religious needs.[5] From the French model, which endorses a neutrality principle that involves a strict separation of church and state,[6] to the English model, in

---

4 Randazzo B., Laicità "positiva" e crocifisso nelle aule scolastiche: incostituzionalità dell'obbligo di esposizione e incostituzionalità dell'obbligo di rimozione, in *Quaderni costituzionali*, 2004, 842; Musselli L., Insegnamento della religione cattolica e tutela della libertà religiosa, in *Giurisprudenza costituzionale*, 1989, 909; Olivito E., Laicità e simboli religiosi nella sfera pubblica: esperienze a confronto, in *Diritto Pubblico*, 2004, 2, 550.

5 Spadaro A., Laicità e confessioni religiose: dalle etiche collettive (laiche e religiose) alla "meta-etica" pubblica (costituzionale), in Pace A. (ed.), *Problemi pratici della laicità agli inizi del secolo XXI*, Cedam, Padua, 2008.

6 Art. 1 of the Constitution: "France shall be an indivisible, secular, democratic and social Republic. It shall ensure the equality of all citizens before the law, without distinction of origin, race or religion. It shall respect all beliefs. It shall be organised on a decentralised basis."

which the monarch has been the "Defender of the [Anglican] Faith"[7] since 1544, to the Greek[8] model, which has an official state church, to the Irish model, which explicitly mentions God and a single religion in its Constitution[9]—all of these states, while different, fall under the same "neutrality umbrella" shaped by the ECtHR and all of these models are subject to continuous changes with domestic legal solutions that fluctuate and make it harder to understand the true meaning of "neutrality" in European legal culture.

These fluctuations are not just a matter of degree, nor do they correspond to a different level of religious freedom protection. In fact, neutrality and religious freedom do not necessarily go hand in hand, with the increase of one meaning the increase of the other. States with strict neutrality principles do not necessarily allow more religious freedom than other states with a more established religion, and states with an established church do not necessarily discriminate more against religious minorities. For example, British law has largely welcomed religious minorities even though it incorporates Anglicanism in its very institutional structure.

European legal scholarship generally acknowledges that neutrality must include a nation treating its citizens equally, must provide religious toleration, must provide autonomy from spiritual power and must grant the right to self-determination for all churches.[10] After this initial basis, though, opinions on how a nation should provide religious freedom for its citizens and autonomy

---

7 http://www.royal.gov.uk/MonarchUK/QueenandChurch/QueenandChurch.aspx.

8 Art. 3 of the Constitution: "1. The prevailing religion in Greece is that of the Eastern Orthodox Church of Christ. The Orthodox Church of Greece, acknowledging our Lord Jesus Christ as its head, is inseparably united in doctrine with the Great Church of Christ in Constantinople and with every other Church of Christ of the same doctrine, observing unwaveringly, as they do, the holy apostolic and syn- odal canons and sacred traditions. It is autocephalous and is administered by the Holy Synod of serving Bishops and the Permanent Holy Synod originating thereof and assembled as specified by the Statutory Charter of the Church in compliance with the provisions of the Patriarchal Tome of June 29, 1850 and the Synodal Act of September 4, 1928."

9 The Preamble of the Irish Constitution says: "In the Name of the Most Holy Trinity, from Whom is all authority and to Whom, as our final end, all actions both of men and States must be referred,

> We, the people of Éire,
> Humbly acknowledging all our obligations to our Divine Lord, Jesus Christ,
> Who sustained our fathers through centuries of trial."

10 Randazzo B., La Corte "apre" al giudizio di uguaglianza tra confessioni religiose?, in *Giurisprudenza costituzionale*, 1998, 1864; Martinelli C., Le necessarie conseguenze di una laicità "presa sul serio," in Bin G., Brunelli R., Pugiotto A. and Veronesi P. (eds), *La laicità crocifissa?*, Giappichelli, Turin, 211; Roca M.A., *La neutralidad del Estado: fundamento doctrinal y actual delimitación en la jurisprudencia*, in *Il diritto ecclesiastico*, 1997, 408.

for religions vary widely. In fact, the neutrality principle is normally understood only within a specific state's legal system and is referred to in reference to the state's version of the neutrality principle.[11] There is no single neutrality model that serves as a universal reference for all European states; instead, there is "French neutrality," "Irish neutrality," etc., depending on the state referenced.[12]

In other words, this principle of "neutrality" is susceptible to different interpretations and these models of neutrality take different shapes. The identity and implications of the *concept* of "neutrality" really depend on the *conception* of neutrality that a specific legal system embraces—or, in other words, on how the state sees the relationship between church and state.[13]

As to the Italian law, it was only after the Italian legal state had already familiarized itself with general church–state relationship theories that the Italian Constitutional Court developed different terms for understanding church–state relations. First came the term "laicità," then the Court began using the word "neutralità," meaning "neutrality," in its case law. And, as we will see, the shift was not only in the wording; it also affected the protection of religious freedom.

The Church–State Relationship in Italian Law

The European disagreement on the meaning of "laicità" has pervaded Italian law as well. It has been equally difficult for the Italian state to decide how this "laicità" principle should be applied, for two reasons.

First, the concept of religion–state reciprocal autonomy is ambiguous in itself. The constitutional law of the United States is a prime example of this concept.[14] The idea of a "wall of separation" between the two has shifted in US case law through the centuries.[15] This "wall" was erected initially through the Establishment Clause in the US Constitution, but the meaning of this clause has

11 Tega D., La libertà religiosa e il principio di laicità nella giurisprudenza della Corte di Strasburgo, in Bin et al. (eds), *La laicità crocifissa?*, 301.

12 Martinelli, Le necessarie conseguenze di una laicità "presa sul serio," 211. Also in the French context, some scholars maintain that "La signification du mot est devenue instable": Bottin M., La liberté religieuse en France. Ou les paradoxes de la laïcité, in *Quaderni di diritto e politica ecclesiastica*, 2005, 125–45, 144.

13 On the distinction between "concept" and "conception," see Dworkin R., *Taking Rights Seriously*, Harvard University Press, Cambridge, MA, 1978. See also Zagrebelsky G., *Manuale di Diritto costituzionale. Il sistema delle fonti del diritto*, UTET, Turin, 1998, 85–86.

14 Witte, Jr., J., That Serpentine Wall of Separation, in *Michigan Law Review*, 2003, 101, 1869.

15 McConnell M., Why is Religious Liberty the First Freedom?, in *Cardozo Law Review*, 1999, 21, 1243.

been heavily influenced by the changing legal and social mentalities over time.[16] To this day, there is still a debate on what the framers intended through the Establishment Clause; it has only been through the subsequent development of the relationship between religious and civil institutions that we have begun to understand or at least apply a meaning to it.

Second, the details of neutrality are also highly contested. In Italy, even textualists, who attempt to derive meaning and rights from a strictly literalist interpretation of the Italian Constitution, are divided in terms of how to provide a reciprocal autonomy between church and state. Some textualists argue that the text of the Italian Constitution strongly advocates separatism,[17] while other textualists claim that no derivation of separatism can be found in the Constitution.[18] Views on separatism also differ, with some scholars believing that Italy should attempt to become a separatist state,[19] while others believe that the current lack of separatism in Italy is positive for church–state relationships.[20]

Notwithstanding the existence of such debate, it is possible to affirm that strict separatism, which would entail mutual indifference and maybe even hostility between church and state, should have no place in the Italian legal system. This derives from a strict textualist interpretation of the Italian Constitution as well as by looking at the framers' intention when drafting it.

The framers,[21] who were extremely familiar with the French legal and political culture, were aware of the French model of "laicità." They knew it to be a traditional system of relations between church and state that was characterized by a mutual indifference between church and state and dominated by a high level of political hostility against any public role for religion. State institutions had to patrol the public sphere to keep it free from religious infiltrations. The Italian framers explicitly chose not to use the word "laicità" in the constitutional text in order to avoid the French constitutional tradition of a hostile understanding of

16 See the First Amendment of the US Constitution: "Congress shall make no law respecting an establishment of religion, or prohibiting the free exercise thereof; or abridging the freedom of speech, or of the press; or the right of the people peaceably to assemble, and to petition the Government for a redress of grievances."

17 See Lariccia S., *Coscienza e libertà. Profili costituzionali del diritto ecclesiastico italiano*, il Mulino, Bologna, 1989, 58 and 167.

18 See Parisi M., Il sistema europeo di relazioni tra gli Stati e le organizzazioni religiose: conservazione o innovazione nella prosettiva della Costituzione dell'Unione Europea?, available at: http://www.olir.it/areetematiche/83/documents/Parisi_Europa_e_fenomeno_religioso.pdf, 1.

19 Fusaro C., Pluralismo e laicità. Lo Stato non può ridurre la fede a cultura, né costruire sul fatto religioso identità partigiane, in Bin et al. (eds), *La laicità crocifissa?*, 153.

20 Cavana P., *Interpretazioni della laicità. Esperienza francese ed esperienza italiana a confronto*, A.V.E., Rome, 1998.

21 See Sale G., *Il Vaticano e la Costituzione*, Jaca Books, Milan, 2008.

the relationship between church and state.[22] They did not want to align Italian law with a strict separatist model that was based on political skepticism towards religion and religiosity.

But it is mostly from the text of the Constitution itself that we can see a deep relationship between religious and legal tradition in Italy. In fact, the first sentence of Art. 7 of the Italian Constitution establishes a fundamental pillar of church–state relations when it states that: "The State and the Catholic Church are independent and sovereign, each within its own sphere." This wording, which was so successful that it later inspired that Vatican Council II in its *Guadium et Spes* Constitution,[23] was agreed upon during the constitutional assembly and, more importantly, was clearly founded upon the Catholic doctrine of "two powers." During constitutional debates, the framers repeatedly quoted language from the Encyclical Letter *Immortale Dei* (1885), delivered by Pope Leo XIII, stating that:

> The Almighty, therefore, has given the charge of human race to two powers, the ecclesiastical and the civil, the one being set over divine, and the other over human, things. Each in its own kind is supreme, each has fixed limits within which it is contained, limits which are defined by the nature and special object of the province of each, so that there is, we may say, an orbit traced out within which the action of each is brought into play by its own native right.

The framers, when writing Italy's Constitution, knowingly drew from these Catholic teachings[24] and, in so doing, established a strong cultural connection between Italian constitutional law and religion.

The second sentence of Art. 7 also derives from language used in *Immortale Dei* when it states that:

> Their relations [between the state and the Catholic Church] are governed by the Lateran Pacts … Inasmuch as each of these powers has authority over the same subjects, and as it might come to pass one and the same thing … might belong

22 See the reports of the Constituent Assembly, November 21, 1948, 418, available at: http://legislature.camera.it/frameset.asp?content=%2Faltre%5Fsezionism%2F304%2F8964%2Fdocumentotesto%2Easp%3F.

23 See Sale, *Il Vaticano e la Costituzione.*

24 The first time *Immortale Dei* is mentioned is by Giuseppe Dossetti at the first Subcommission (November 21, 1946, 422). At the plenary, Hon. Riccio mentions it (March 13, 1947, 2057): "è ormai pacifico, e non solo negli scrittori cattolici, in quanto non è stato affermato soltanto da Leone XIII, soprattutto nella *Immortale Dei*, ma anche in altri scrittori cattolici e non cattolici, tra cui Santi Romano (*L'ordinamento giuridico*, Sansoni, 1946), Gismondi (*Il nuovo giurisdizionalismo italiano*, Giuffrè, Milan, 1946), De Luca (*Considerazioni sull'autonomia e la pubblicità della Chiesa nel diritto italiano*, Giuffrè, 1946)."

> to the jurisdiction and determination of both, therefore God … has marked out the course of each in right correlation to the other.

Since the debates and even the wording of the Constitution derive from the Catholic traditions, we can rule out the possibility that the framers intended to set up a new constitutional order that would be hostile to religion and religious tradition in Italy. No religious hostility can be found either in the text of the Constitution or in the sources that were relied upon when writing it. The Italian constitutional tradition and the Catholic tradition both rely upon a friendly church–state relationship where each side can collaborate with the other when feasible and necessary.

If the roots of the Constitution's wording are clear, the concept that stems from them remains quite ambiguous. The relations described in the Constitution involve a mutual respect and effort to collaborate between church and state; however, no clear concept is used to articulate these ideas. The Italian Constitution never directly mentions a constitutional model to adhere to, such as "neutrality" or "separatism."[25]

It has been up to the Italian Constitutional Court through case law to distill a constitutional concept that would be able to articulate constitutional precepts in this field.[26] The Court is empowered by the Italian Constitution to address issues of constitutional salience. This occurs most commonly when a domestic court has concerns about the constitutionality of a statute or legislation in question in a case. A judge can refer a case to the Constitutional Court and let it address the constitutional issue before remanding it back to the lower court to handle the other legal issues.

The Constitutional Court was repeatedly requested to address the constitutional articles pertaining to religious freedom, and to analyze them through an interpretation of the constitutional text. Therefore, it is only through following the path formed through the Constitutional Court's decisions that it is possible to understand how the Italian legal system has conceptualized the means to address the needs of religious groups.

The Constitutional Court "invented" the principle of "laicità" by imputing it from the constitutional framework as the constitutional principle that encapsulates the relationship between church and state. In order to describe the principle of "laicità" as it applies to Italy, it is necessary to summarize the

---

25 See Casuscelli G., Il crocifisso nelle scuole: neutralità dello Stato e "regola della precauzione," available at: www.olir.it, 18; or Guerzoni L., Considerazioni critiche sul "principio supremo" di laicità dello Stato alla luce dell'esperienza giuridica contemporanea, in *Il diritto ecclesiastico*, 1992, 94.

26 Sicardi S., Questioni aperte nella disciplina del fenomeno religioso: dalla laicità al sistema delle fonti, in *Quaderni di diritto e politica ecclesiastica*, 2005, 9.

Constitutional Court's case law and follow the nuances that it has taken over time. A handful of decisions that have focused on "laicità" will be singled out from those cases that merely referenced it. Further decisions not mentioning "laicità" will be analyzed to describe the broader picture of the church–state constitutional framework.

The analysis of how "laicità" was initially shaped and later reinterpreted needs to be detailed thoroughy here because it is a fluctuating concept. Its distinctive aspects emerge only piecemeal and sporadically through the legal practice of Italian courts, which incidentally are not *common law* courts, and therefore are comparatively both less committed to crafting sharp legal concepts and less authoritative. This is especially true for courts other than the Constitutional Court and the Court of Cassation: the first interprets the Constitution with the purpose of outlawing pieces of legislation that are incompatible with it, while the second secures a consistent interpretation of Italian law, but has no power to set a law aside. But, in addition, the Constitutional Court and the Court of Cassation do not have a strong and rigid *stare decisis* praxis, so their case law evolves over time, even implicitly or imperceptibly.

The last decade has been characterized by an intense debate around the display of the crucifix in public schools. This provision, which has been in place for more than 100 years now, has been challenged before domestic courts and later before the ECtHR, which tackled the issue of the crucifix, bearing in mind the theoretical and practical dispute around neutrality that characterizes contemporary legal and political philosophy.[27] This huge debate, which drew the attention of the whole European legal scholarship in the field of religious freedom and state neutrality, is therefore a good template to locate the Italian understanding of the transnational concept of neutrality and the most recent interpretation of "laicità" within the broader European framework on the correct place of religion in the public sphere.[28] I will consider the issue of the crucifix in public school in depth, then as a proxy to elucidate the contemporary understanding of "laicità."

The Constitutional Court and "Laicità"

The First Steps: A "Friendly" Separation (Late 1980s–Early 1990s)

The Constitutional Court's seminal decision in the field of church–state relationships is judgment no. 203, which was delivered in 1989. This is the first

27 Kyritsis D. and Tsakyrakis S., Neutrality in the Classroom, in *International Journal of Constitutional Law*, 2013, 11, 203.

28 Ibid., 200 .

decision that endorsed the principle of "laicità," albeit with an untraditional understanding of the concept.[29]

The Court was referred by a domestic judge in order to ascertain whether the teaching of Catholicism in public schools is compatible with the Constitution. The teaching of Catholicism is public schools is required under the Catholic Church–state agreement, although the fact that it is taught does not mean that all students are required to take the course.[30] The class in question was an elective, but opponents argued that it still affected the school's daily schedules and curriculum. The teaching of this class was challenged as discriminatory against those who did not want to participate in lessons of Catholic orthodoxy.

The Constitutional Court ruled in favor of the school and maintained that students were not discriminated against since they were under no obligation to take the class and so were not affected by the fact that a class on Catholicism was taught in the school. In fact, during the Catholicism class, they were not supposed to attend any alternative class. If these students were forced to take another subject, then they would have been discriminated against since they would have been required to attend lessons simply because they did not wish to learn Catholicism.

In its opinion, the Court said it was going to judge the case starting from the principle of "laicità," as embedded in the Constitution. Since the right of

---

29 See Floridia G. and Sicardi S., *Dall'uguaglianza dei cittadini alla laicità dello Stato*, in *Giurisprudenza costituzionale*, 1989, 1086.

30 The texts discussed in this case were:

a) Art. 9, no. 2 of the Agreement with the Catholic Church: "La Repubblica italiana, riconoscendo il valore della cultura religiosa e tenendo conto che i princìpi del cattolicesimo fanno parte del patrimonio storico del popolo italiano, continuerà ad assicurare, nel quadro delle finalità della scuola, l'insegnamento della religione cattolica nelle scuole pubbliche non universitarie di ogni ordine e grado.
Nel rispetto della libertà di coscienza e della responsabilità educativa dei genitori, è garantito a ciascuno il diritto di scegliere se avvalersi o non avvalersi di detto insegnamento.
All'atto dell'iscrizione gli studenti o i loro genitori eserciteranno tale diritto, su richiesta dell'autorità scolastica, senza che la loro scelta possa dar luogo ad alcuna forma di discriminazione."

b) No. 5 *b)* of the Protocol, at nos. 1 and 2: "Con successiva intesa tra le competenti autorità scolastiche e la Conferenza Episcopale Italiana verranno determinati:

1) i programmi dell'insegnamento della religione cattolica per i diversi ordini e gradi delle scuole pubbliche;
2) le modalità di organizzazione di tale insegnamento, anche in relazione alla collocazione nel quadro degli orari delle lezioni."

Catholic education was included in state–Catholic Church agreements which are protected by Art. 7 of the Constitution, the Court maintained that the teaching of Catholicism in schools enjoys a special constitutional protection. However, it stated that these agreements are still subject to judicial review to ensure that they do not conflict with the "supreme principles of the constitutional system." This Court decision stated that "laicità" was a constitutional principle and therefore could be used as a tool when judicially reviewing the agreements and their provisions, such as the teaching of Catholicism at schools. The principle of "laicità" was hierarchically superior to the agreement, so its provision could be subject to the Court's judgment.

The teaching of Catholicism was referred to the Court for violation of Art. 2 of the Constitution, which protects the fundamental rights and dignity of each person; Art. 3, which commands equality amongst its citizens; and Art. 19, which protects religious freedom. The Court blended these articles together with Art. 7, which governs the relationship between the state and the Catholic Church, Art. 8, which disciplines the state's relationship with other religions, and Art. 20, which provides freedom for religious organizations. The Court stated that Arts. 2, 3, 7, 8, 19 and 20 of the Constitution comprise the Italian principle of "laicità."

In the Court's wording, "laicità" "doesn't entail any state indifference towards religions but instead ensures the state commitment in granting religious freedom, in the context of a religiously and culturally pluralist regime."[31] The state attitude of "laicità" was, according to the Court's decision, a principle that served to firm up the needs of religion and conscience among its citizens and was not hostile towards religion.

The circumstances under which the principle of "laicità" was introduced prompted a unique formulation of it. "Laicità" was used to legitimize the religious teaching of Catholicism in public schools. Through "laicità," the Court explained that, as the state–Catholic Church agreements stated, religious teaching has a deep cultural value in a pluralist context and Catholic values are deeply rooted in Italian culture. To teach Catholicism in public schools, the Court wrote, was therefore a manifestation of the Italian understanding of "laicità" as a tool that connects state, religious and societal values.

With this portrayal of "laicità" which legitimized Catholic classes in public schools, the Constitutional Court differed from the indifferent, if not hostile, liberalism of the nineteenth century.[32] As we have seen, the framers avoid using

31 Section 4 of the judgment.

32 See Musselli, *Insegnamento della religione cattolica e tutela della libertà religiosa*, 909; Vitale A., *Corso di diritto ecclesiastico. Ordinamento giuridico e interessi religiosi*, Giuffrè, Milan, 1998, 29–31; Manco M., Esposizione del crocifisso e principio di laicità dello Stato, in *Quaderni di Diritto e Politica Ecclesiastica*, 2005, 35–40.

this word at the Constitutional Assembly precisely because they did not want to convey a sense of hostility towards religions. Eventually the use of "laicità" as a hostile principle abated and the term developed more neutral terminology, to the extent that the Court decided to use it.

This new understanding of "laicità" drew from a large spectrum of constitutional articles, in particular Arts. 2, 3, 7, 8, 19 and 20. From these articles, "laicità" is best understood as merely a synthetic description of church–state relations instead of a precise constitutional concept.[33] The Court clarified the religious-friendly attitude of Italian law and institutions, but, instead of crafting a new model for this concept, used the old word of "laicità" to describe these principles.

This depiction of "laicità" that the Court offered was clearly ambiguous and received widely different receptions.[34] The Court had decided to use a word that the framers had specifically avoided when writing the Constitution, and used it to describe a concept hitherto unrelated to the traditional understanding of "laicità." It is no surprise, therefore, that legal scholars were sharply divided over whether "laicità" should be used to describe this novel Italian concept or whether other terms should be used to describe the church–state relations for which the Court advocated.[35]

These reactions of the Court's use of "laicità" prove that the Court's holding in judgment no. 203 was puzzling both in its concrete implications (that the Church could teach Catholicism in public schools) and in its reasoning (that "laicità" could now be used in an unprecedented and unexpected way).

The Court re-addressed the principle of "laicità" two years later in judgment no. 13 in 1991. Once again, at issue was the teaching of Catholicism in school. This time, the case was about the hours during which the class was taught. The domestic judge that referred this case to the Court argued that students who did not take the Catholicism lessons were being discriminated against, since

33 See Guerzoni L., Considerazioni critiche sul "principio supremo" di laicità dello Stato alla luce dell'esperienza giuridica contemporanea, in *Il diritto ecclesiastico*, 1992, 91.

34 Barbera A., Il cammino della laicità, available at: http://www.forumcostituzionale.it/wordpress/images/stories/pdf/nuovi%20pdf/Paper/0036_barbera.pdf, 44. Ninatti S., Il rilievo dell'original intent nell'interpretazione dell'art. 7 della costituzione italiana, in Nicotra I.-Giuffrè F. (ed.), *Lavori preparatori ed original intent del legislatore nella giurisprudenza costituzionale*, Quaderni del Gruppo di Pisa, Giappichelli, Turin, 2008.

35 Randazzo, La Corte "apre" al giudizio di uguaglianza tra confessioni religiose?, 1998, 1843, 1865; Oddi A., Il principio di "laicità" nella giurisprudenza costituzionale, in Bin et al. (eds), *La laicità crocifissa?*, 247; Lariccia S., Diritti di libertà in materia religiosa e principi di imparzialità e di laicità delle istituzioni civili: la parola alla Corte costituzionale, in Bin et al. (eds), *La laicità crocifissa?*, 186–87; Guazzarotti A., *L'"inammissibile" eguaglianza. Diritto ecclesiastico e tecniche legislative di privilegio*, in *Giurisprudenza costituzionale*, 1996, 1648.

fewer hours of lessons were imparted to them, and they were forced to be at school. The judge referred the case to the Constitutional Court, enquiring whether the legislation in question discriminated against students not taking part in the Catholicism lessons.

The Constitutional Court cited the standard in case no. 203 in 1989 for its reasoning and found no violation of the Constitution. According to the Court, the teaching of Catholicism was not only a compatible of "laicità," it was also a manifestation of it. While in dicta, this language demonstrated the Constitutional Court's friendly attitude towards religion and understanding of "laicità." [36]

As of 1989 and 1991, the Court's attitude was distant from the traditional liberal understanding of church–state relations built on mutual indifference.

The Court interpreted the Constitution's guidance on church–state relations in a way that differed from the traditional notions of a liberal state and prescribed a close relationship between state and religions and a state embracing of religious needs.[37] In a nutshell, the Court used the French concept of "laicità" to frame a policy of friendly church–state relations that was closer to the US model.[38]

The Next Stage in the Evolution of Constitutional Interpretation: From Equidistant and Impartial Pluralism to "Neutrality" (Mid-1990s)

After these two initial decisions in 1989 and 1991, the Court's reasoning took a new direction. Through a meandering course, it largely reshaped "laicità" and its legal consequences. However, the departure from the initially friendly approach was slow, especially in the first decisions.

Judgment no. 440 in 1995 declared partially unconstitutional a statute that penalized offenses against the "Divinity, or the Symbols, or the Persons that are venerated by the official religion of the state." This provision of the Penal Code was censored because it violated the constitutional principles of equality regarding individuals (Art. 3) and religions (Art. 8).

The Court identified the "official religion" mentioned in the provision with Catholicism. It held that since the constitutional principle of equality required that the law should not discriminate against individuals on the basis or religion, the relevant article of the Penal Code could not pass judicial scrutiny.

Interestingly, this holding did not make the entire penal provision unconstitutional. Through a powerful reflection on the wording of this provision, the Court ruled out only the penal protection of "Symbols, or the Persons that are venerated by" Catholicism; meanwhile, the "Divinity" survived the Court's scrutiny.

36 Section 3 of the judgment.

37 De Ruggiero G., *Storia del liberalismo europeo*, Feltrinelli, Milan, 1977.

38 Barbera, Il cammino della laicità, 42.

The Court, basing its reasoning on the canon law tradition, singled out a part of the provision from the rest.[39] The word "veneration," the Court pointed out, strictly referred to the "symbols and persons," not to the "Divinity," who is, theologically, an object of "adoration." This distinction was important. Therefore, the Court maintained that the legislation criminalized two different acts separately: a) on the one hand, the offenses against "the Divinity," with no further religious specification; and, on the other hand, the offenses made against "the Symbols and the Persons venerated" by Catholicism. According to the Court, the provision criminalized any offence on the Divinity—of whatever creed; on the contrary, only symbols and persons venerated by Catholicism were protected.[40] The first part of the article, which prohibited any offence against any conception of Divinity, was not discriminatory and therefore remained in place. Only the reference to Catholic symbols and persons was discriminatory and therefore was outlawed.

In short, the Court left the penal protection of the Divinity untouched, while it declared unconstitutional the protection of Catholic traditional figures. In a sense, it disconnected the protection of the religiosity of Italians from its concrete manifestations. The sole Divinity was protected, but not the symbols and the persons that the vast majority of Italians connected to the Divinity.

This decision complicated the meaning and enforcement of the statute. Depending on one's religious heritage, the Divinity could be understood in different ways. Jesus has a divine nature for Christians and is therefore protected by the legislation, but he is only venerated by Muslims, and is therefore not protected by the statute. The interpretation of the penal rule, as amended by the Court, could be read differently, with consequences on its practical applicability.

In 1996 the Court further departed from its original interpretation of "laicità" in judgment no. 334. At issue in this judgment was trial oath. The law commanded that, before testifying, the judge should remind witnesses of the religious and moral value of the oath they were about to take, following which they would swear to tell the truth "before God and human beings." [41] A refusal to swear to this oath would entail penal consequences for the witnesses. At issue before the Court was whether such an oath respected religious freedom.

The Court found this law unconstitutional because it violated religious rights and ordered that the oath be changed to exclude the words "God and human

---

39 Venditti R., Reato di bestemmia e pluralità di religioni, in *Giurisprudenza costituzionale*, 1995, 4519.

40 Section 3.4 of the judgment: "la Divinità, indicata senza ulteriori specificazioni e con un termine astratto, ricomprendente sia le espressioni verbali sia i segni rappresentativi della Divinità stessa, il cui contenuto si presta a essere individuato in relazione alle concezioni delle diverse religioni."

41 Art. 238 of the Civil Procedure Code.

beings." The Court stated that not only were religious rights of atheists and agnostics violated when they had to take this oath, but even the obligation of swearing to this oath had religious consequences that were unconstitutional. It held that every manifestation of religious acts had to be completely free and not mandated by the state, regardless of the personal religion of the individual asked to perform the act. State institutions, the Court stated, could not interfere with the freedom of conscience of individuals. Whether the witness was religious, willing to take the oath or not was irrelevant to this purpose: the Italian law could not expect even religious people to perform an act with religious significance—namely, to swear before God. The Court's understanding of the "distinction" between the religious and civil order of the Constitution prevented the state law from forcing individuals to act religiously by swearing to a religious oath.[42]

The Court cited the principle of "laicità" in its reasoning and claimed that that principle prohibited the state from reinforcing its laws through religious obligations. The disestablishment of religion, the Court maintained, protected freedom of conscience by prohibiting the state from using religious means to secure its goals.

Despite this Court's affirmation, at work in the Court's decision is not simply disestablishment of religion; in reality, the Court underwent a complete change in its view of religious freedom and church–state relations. We see this most clearly when it justified the use of the word "oath" when swearing in witnesses. The judge that had referred the case to the Court suggested that the law be changed from using the word "oath" to the word "promise" because the word "oath" was burdened with more religious connotations.[43] Instead, the Court permitted the use of the word "oath," but outlawed any reference to "God" or to "human beings." In its judgment, it cited two reasons for removing a reference to "human beings." First, once "God" was erased from the phrasing, the prescription to swear "before human beings" could be understood as the replacement of God with a humanistic religion, based on the adoration of mankind. Second, and more importantly, the oath, without the reference to God, could be understood in a variety of secular meanings and could fit in with the religious pluralistic environment that the Court envisioned.[44]

According to the Court, the "oath" could remain in the law because it no longer had any religious connotation. The original religious foundation had adapted to the times. This now "religiously neutralized" oath could survive in the statute because, as the Court stated, the religious and moral implications of the word "oath" now depended solely on the "individual's conscience and vision of the world, from what each individual believes to be binding and worth observing." The word could

42 Section 3.2 of the judgment.

43 Section 5.1 of the judgment.

44 Section 6.1 of the judgment.

remain in the statute because, in current times, its meaning was ambiguous and neutralized. The meaning of the word "oath" now had no religious connotation and only depended on each person's individual moral values.

Here we have a hidden separation between religious pluralism and the law. While the 1989 and 1991 decisions welcomed religiosity to the point that the Court accepted religious teaching in schools, in the later decisions, religiosity became acceptable only as long as it had no legal implications. Since individuals disagree on the concept of an "oath," the word and use of an "oath" may survive only because it is religiously and politically neutral.

Soon, the Court would develop new terms to reflect its changing ideology. In its 1997 judgment no. 235, it used the term "neutrality" in reference to church–state relations. The case at stake concerned special legislation that exempted Catholic buildings' rentals used to cover Catholic priests' living expenses from a real estate tax.[45] Challengers of this law argued that other religious buildings could not enjoy this same exemption[46] and claimed that such special treatment towards Catholics was not in line with the constitutional principles of equality among individuals and religions (Arts. 3 and 8) and religious freedom (Art. 19), and requested to enlarge the exemption to the buildings of other religions.

Here, the Court held that only the Catholic Church–state agreement disciplined the tax exemption of religious buildings to cover priests' expenses. It could not extend the exemption to the buildings of other religions without straying from the purpose of the agreement provision,[47] which addressed the topic of the subsidies for the clergy. As such, the Court did not extend the scope of the legislation to other religions.[48]

The importance of this decision did not lie in its rationale, but in its wording. The Court affirmed that different treatments were allowed as long as these treatments satisfied the test of "neutrality" (*neutralità*). [49] However, it did

45 Under the Court's scrutiny were Art. 8, third paragraph, of law no. 904 of 1977, and Art. 45 of law no. 222 of 1985.

46 Art. 25, second paragraph, Decree of the President of the Republic no. 643 of 1972.

47 Section 4 of the judgment: "comprendono l'esercizio del culto, l'istruzione e l'educazione religiosa, la promozione della cultura ebraica, la tutela degli interessi collettivi degli ebrei in sede locale, l'assistenza degli appartenenti alle Comunità stesse, secondo la legge e la tradizione ebraiche."

48 Section 3 of the judgment: "rispetto o la violazione del principio di uguaglianza da parte delle norme tributarie statali devono, perciò, valutarsi tenendo necessariamente conto delle distinte discipline dei soggetti destinatari di quella normativa, dove la distinzione é conseguenza del sistema di regolamentazione dei rapporti tra lo Stato e le confessioni religiose voluto dalla Costituzione."

49 Randazzo, La Corte "apre" al giudizio di uguaglianza tra confessioni religiose?, 1851.

not explain what exactly "neutrality" was and did not explain the relationship between "neutrality" and "laicità." Actually, it did not mention the word "laicità."

This new understanding of church–state relations did not go unnoticed.[50] The use of this concept of "neutrality" in the Court's reasoning was seen as a move towards a more traditional, less accepting attitude of the state in relation to religion. The concept of "laicità" from the Court's earlier decisions had legitimized a deeper relationship between church and state; after this most recent decision, it seemed that the idea of pluralism was being pushed out of Italian law or, at least, was being strongly reconsidered.

Judgment no. 329 in 1997 further developed this trend of "laicità" which would bring a new understanding of legal pluralism in the government. This case concerned a Penal Code article that punished offences against the official religion of the state more heavily than it did offenses against other religions.[51] At issue in the case was the whether this different treatment was constitutional under the principle of equality in Art. 3 (equality amongst individual) and Art. 8 (equality amongst religions).

The Court held the provision to be unconstitutional on the grounds that the protection of religious beliefs is linked to the protection of religious freedom and that the beliefs of all individuals must be equally protected.[52] The religion that was offended was irrelevant;[53] the good that needed to be *equally* protected was the individual religious beliefs.

In this decision, the Court reframed the principle of "laicità." Under this opinion, now it meant "equidistance and impartiality of legislation." The Court stated that the connection between "laicità" and equidistance and impartiality had been affirmed in its previous decisions, and enlisted them explicitly: judgment nos. 203, 1989; 259, 1990; 195, 1993. However, in these same decisions, the Court had never described "laicità" as "equidistance and impartiality." It was only now, eight years after the first decision referencing "laicità" that it began to describe "laicità" in those terms.

50 Ibid.

51 Art. 404 of the Penal Code provides the sanction of one to three years in jail for those who, in a religious place, in public or in a place open to the public, offend the religion of the state through vilipend of items that pertain to the cult; Art. 406 of the Penal Code decreased the sanction if the religion that was offended was not Catholicism.

52 Section 2 of the judgment.

53 Section 2 of the judgment: "la protezione del sentimento religioso, quale aspetto del diritto costituzionale di libertà religiosa, non è divisibile. Ogni violazione della coscienza religiosa è sempre violazione di quel bene e di quel diritto nella loro interezza e tale dunque da riguardare tutti allo stesso modo, indipendentemente dalla confessione religiosa cui eventualmente si appartenga."

Defendants of the legislation argued that there were deep sociological concerns that prompted this legislation, such as the fact that Catholicism was the primary religion of Italy and that any offense against that religion could prompt a mass reaction. The Court ignored these concerns and stated that such concerns could not justify the penal statute. Instead, it held, the principle of equality had to be interpreted precisely in order to protect religious minorities, instead of being altered to permit preferential treatments for more popular religions. Through judgment no. 329, the Court changed its understanding of "laicità" from a concept that was understood as being open to social practices and customs to one that now became more protective of individuals against majoritarian social practices.

Overall, the Constitutional Court judgment no. 329 of 1997 was a landmark decision for several reasons. First, it molded a new concept of "laicità" that stressed the importance of "equidistance and impartiality." Second, it said that in the religious field, the legislation could not reflect the feelings of the majority of the population. In fact, the Court went so far as to state that equality required legislative indifference towards social trends and needs. The state, the Court held, must remain indifferent to features of Italian society and to its changes. The Court had finally managed to lay down a conceptual framework for the new wording of "laicità" as "neutralità" in the Italian legal system.

Finally, this judgment tied back the ideas that governed the relationship between church, state and religious freedom to concepts such as "equidistance" and "impartiality." While the Court's decision further explained some concepts, the connection between these idea, and the concepts of "neutralità" and "laicità" still remain largely or completely unexplained. The consequences of this ambiguity will be explained shortly.

A Broad Overview of the Constitutional Court's Rulings

"Neutrality," "impartiality," "equidistance" and "laicità" are not necessarily synonyms. The Court has used these words almost interchangeably without explaining their background or how these concepts relate to one another. In fact, the Court probably did not need to reference any of these concepts at all in its religious decisions as most of the legislation at issue could have been upheld or struck down based on the constitutional grounds of equality or religious freedom. Instead, the Court discussed these religious concepts using broad terms that leave its actual intention and meaning ambiguous.

The Court's conceptualization of church, state and religious freedom underwent a transformation starting in the late 1980s. Then, the Court imputed the existence of the principle of "laicità" despite the fact that the framers had deliberately refused to adopt this word in the Constitution. Further decisions referenced concepts such as "equidistance," "impartiality" and "neutralità" without any formal connections to the previous concepts. Clearly, there was a change in the way it articulated the role of public institutions towards religion: from a positive attitude towards religious groups and social needs (in the 1989 decision) to the protection of religious minorities and the indifference of the state towards social attitudes and demographics (in the latest judgments).

The conceptualization of the relationship between church, state and religious freedom was perhaps too complex to handle, absent any meaningful constitutional text's indications, and it was surely too nuanced when compared with what concrete cases brought before the Court actually needed to be addressed.

Below, we will examine the precedent this language set for other Italian domestic courts with a special reference to the most hotly debated case in recent years in the field of religious freedom: the display of the crucifix in public schools, which has proven to be one of the most sensitive issues around which concerns about state neutrality, religious freedom and protection of national traditions group together. Out of these several domestic court decisions, we will examine only those that have impacted the understanding of "laicità."

The Latest Debate: The Crucifix and Neutrality

The Crucifix in Election Rooms

In 2000, the Court of Cassazione, the highest court of appeal whose precedents all courts must follow, delivered an extremely important decision in the field of religious rights regarding the use of a crucifix in election rooms. This decision drew from the Constitutional Court's case law, but assembled the concepts in a new unique fashion.

Through an Italian by-law, crucifixes are required to hang in every classroom.[54] During election time, these public schools normally host the polling booths. In Italy, working the election ballots is a public duty, much like jury duty, and those who refuse to comply with their civil duty are subject to penal sanctions.[55] One of these individuals objected to being exposed to the crucifix during his shift. He refused to help work the ballots and cited religious reasons for his refusal to do so.

The Court of Cassazione did not punish the individual because it claimed that the individual's religious beliefs protected him from having to work in the

54 The relevant pieces of legislation are: Art. 118, Royal Decree of April 30, 1924, no. 965 and Art. 119, Royal Decree of April 26, 1928, no. 1297.

55 Following Art. 108 of the Decree of the President of the Republic no. 361 of 1957.

presence of a crucifix. This decision provided a powerful vindication of the separation of church and state and—implicitly—of the unconstitutionality of the crucifix.

In its reasoning, the Court claimed that the presence of the crucifix created an inner conflict between the "personal adhesion to the supreme principle of laicità embraced by the worker, and the obligation to comply with a public duty."[56] To further explain this conflict, the Court stated that, according to the principle of "laicità," as understood by the Constitutional Court, religious pluralism was protected and had to be understood as treating every religious and moral view equally.

As a part of that decision, the Court drew from the Constitutional Court decisions to hold that public places must be characterized by "laicità" and "neutralità."[57] This "neutrality" would prohibit a single belief from dominating the public sphere.[58]

This reference to the Constitutional Court's decisions inaccurately reflected the Constitutional Court's actual holdings. In judgment no. 235 in 1997, the Constitutional Court did not speak of "laicità," but only of "neutrality." It was the Court of Cassazione itself that established a link between these two concepts and, by doing so, conflated these two ideas into one meaning.

In the Court of Cassazione's reasoning, the respect for religious pluralism requires the state to foster a separation between public institutions and religions instead of welcoming religions. The Court also excluded the possibility that the crucifix could be understood as a cultural symbol with universal, non-religious values that would have no consequences on a worker's religious freedom. Understanding the crucifix in such way—the Court of Cassazione reasoned—would denigrate the crucifix from a symbol of religious values to a political instrument. For this purpose, the Court of Cassazione quotes the German Federal Constitutional Court which had used similar reasoning in its decision to prohibit the crucifix from being used as a state or political symbol.[59]

This concern that a public display of the Catholic crucifix could profane its religious value is an idea that is not typical in Italian legal scholarship. Likely because of Italy's strong Catholic background, which welcomes connections between the religious and secular realms, this argument of profaning a religious symbol by causing it to become a political one has seldom been utilized. In contrast, a fear that religious symbols could be illegitimately adopted by the state for its own political purposes was a concern that was typical of German Protestant political thought.

56 Section 9 of the judgment.

57 Section 5 of the judgment.

58 Section 6 of the judgment.

59 Section 7 of the judgment.

The German precedent is particularly revealing in terms of the clash between the Protestant and the Catholic understandings of religious symbols. Notably, Germany is predominantly Protestant, with the exception of the Bavarian region, which is largely Catholic, and experienced this tension between the two Christian cultures precisely in the context of the display of the crucifix. In Bavaria, a provision mandated the presence of the crucifix in schools, along the Italian lines. This provision was struck down by the German Federal Constitutional Court—a court that, like the Italian Constitutional Court, deals with constitutional issues—which mentioned the argument of profanation of religion. Bavaria then restored the provision that commanded the presence of the crucifix, even though in milder terms. The Italian Court of Cassazione inadvertently drew from Protestant thinking to criticize the Catholic tradition of displaying the crucifix.[60]

In broad terms, the Court of Cassazione referenced arguments used in the Constitutional Court's case law to mold a principle of "laicità." But instead of merely endorsing an individual's claim to be exempted from participating in a ballot based on his religious objection, the Court reinforced an understanding of "laicità" as a separation between church and state and a removal of religion from public institutions.[61]

The Crucifix in Public Schools: From Italian Courts to the European Court of Human Rights

The Crucifix in the Domestic Courts

It is hotly contested as to whether the crucifix can be displayed in public schools where lessons are held and students of different ages and religious traditions are exposed to this religious symbol.

The first court decision that examined this issue was in 2003, when a domestic judge of the central Italian town of L'Aquila decided to order a provisional removal of the crucifix in order to protect students as well as to enforce equality and "laicità."[62] The decision did not affect the legitimacy of the crucifix, but ignited a debate that would be long-lasting.

Judge Montanaro claimed the crucifix was a religious symbol, and that its public display implicitly affirmed Catholicism as the only true religious

60 Cavana P., La questione del crocifisso in Italia, available at: http://www.olir.it, 6; Patruno F., Crocifisso, giurisprudenza straniera e laicità, available at: http://www.olir.it/, 5.

61 Di Cosimo G., Simboli religiosi nei locali pubblici: le mobili frontiere dell'obiezione di coscienza, in *Giurisprudenza costituzionale*, 2000, 1130, 1135.

62 Order of October 23, 2003, available at: http://archivio.rivistaaic.it/cronache/file/crocifisso_ordinanza.html.

experience and Catholic values as the only unifying spiritual and moral factors of religious identity. Therefore, he concluded, the protection of religious minorities required the removal of this symbol.

Judge Montanaro not only criticized Catholicism for its prominence in Italian culture, he also referenced a frontal opposition between the Catholic Church and the Italian state that dated back to the era of the nineteenth-century unification of Italy, when the Pope had opposed the enlargement of the Italian state to include the Vatican and other church territories. Following the unification of the Peninsula, education became a major battlefield partly because, as Judge Montanaro pointed out, both the Italian state and the Catholic Church wanted to educate according to their own (either Catholic or Italian) values, which were often mutually exclusive. Judge Montanaro believed that this battle over education was still ongoing and the state still had an interest in pushing religious education out of public schools. Since the school was a public place where students were to be educated in civil Italian values, Judge Montanaro reasoned that schools should not be seen to endorse Catholicism through publicly displaying a crucifix. In his thinking, "laicità" would request the state to keep religion out of public schools precisely in order to prevent religious thinking from influencing students.

A few years later, the case of the crucifix in Italian classrooms gained international audience. Soile Lautsi, a Finnish mother of two children who attended public schools in Italy, asked her children's school board to remove the crucifix from their classroom. Since her request was rejected, she challenged the school's decision before the Administrative Regional Tribunal (TAR) of the Veneto Region in order to have the decision reversed and the crucifix removed.

The TAR upheld the public display of the crucifix as constitutionally permissible, but it did not cite cultural reasons for doing so.[63] It did not affirm that the crucifix could remain because of its cultural significance, as many expected, nor did it claim that the symbol had no religious meaning and so could not offend the beliefs of non-Christian students.[64] Instead, it held that the crucifix could remain in the school because it was religiously significant. To support this thesis, it indulged in dubious theological reflections that are inconsistent with the normal duties of a state judge.

---

63 Judgment of the Regional Administrative Tribunal of Veneto no. 1110, March 17, 2005, available at: http://www.federalismi.it/ApplOpenFilePDF.cfm?artid=17792&dpath=document&dfile=22032011171925.pdf&content=TAR+Sentenza+/2005,+in+tema+di+crocifisso+(Lautsi+TAR+Veneto)+-+documentazione+-+documentazione+-+.

64 See Ceccanti S., E se la Corte andasse in Baviera?, in Bin et al. (eds), *La laicità crocifissa?*, 10.

The TAR adopted the concepts of "laicità" and "neutralità" in its decision. While opponents of the crucifix's display claimed that the symbol could not be displayed because the majority of Italy was Catholic, the Court held that, actually, the crucifix was a symbol of Italy's deeply Christian and Catholic roots, and so must be displayed in reference to that.

Drawing from the new Concordat between the state and the Catholic Church, both of which had acknowledged the social and historical role played by Catholicism in Italy, the TAR rewrote 2,000 years of religious liberty and of "laicità," in the light of Christian doctrine, to conclude that Christian theology set the seeds for modern religious liberty in Italy.[65] According to the TAR's decision, the Waldensians, a Christian minority that survived persecutions through isolation in the Alps and later embraced Protestantism, especially played a role in shaping the idea of "laicità" and anticipated the ideas that were later enshrined in the Italian Constitution.[66]

In its opinion, the TAR explicitly investigated Christian attitudes towards religious freedom and education, and debated universal legal values in order to understand the compatibility of the Christian symbol of the crucifix with the public school environment. It affirmed that the ideals of tolerance and human dignity are trademark values of Christianity, which has always stressed the importance of love. Ideas of "tolerance, equality and liberty upon which the modern neutral ('laico') state is built" would therefore derive and be enforced by these foundational Christian values.

In the TAR's view, crucial historical rights such as the evolution of *habeas corpus*, the Enlightenment and the Universal Declaration of Human Rights are merely episodes of a story that has its origins in Christianity. Non-Christian behaviors such as the Inquisition, the Crusades and outbreaks of anti-Semitism are aberrations and errors that betrayed the basis tenets of Christianity.[67]

After providing a broad overview of the history of human rights and "laicità," the TAR concluded that in a nutshell, the crucifix, with its deep religious significance, represents a system of values that are key features of the Italian Constitution, such as liberty, equality, human dignity and religious tolerance—in other words, "laicità."[68]

In the TAR's reasoning, the Christian foundation behind Italian constitutional values justifies the public display of the crucifix. Removing the crucifix in the name of "laicità" would mean removing a Christian symbol in the name of a Christian value. Moreover, the religious symbol would also be positive for contemporary social challenges. The Court held that the public

65 Cavana, La questione del crocifisso in Italia, 7.

66 Section 9.2 of the judgment.

67 Section 11.6 of the judgment.

68 Section 11.1 of the judgment.

display of the crucifix would play an important role in aiding the integration of immigrants and facilitating a peaceful coexistence of different cultures in Italy. The Christian values that are embedded in the crucifix, the Court stated, would deter religious as well as extreme secular fundamentalism and would be inclusive of religions since the Christian value of charity does not advocate for discrimination between believers and unbelievers of any faith.

The judge in this case undoubtedly lacked any self-restraint in the religious field and, in giving his opinion, indulged in serious and debatable theological considerations. However, his opinion reaffirmed the strong relationship between law and religion seen in the early conception of "laicità" in the decisions of the Constitutional Court.

Soile Lautsi, having lost before the TAR, appealed before the Council of State to have the first judgment reversed and the crucifix removed. The Council affirmed the decision of the TAR and cited the TAR's arguments, but avoided delving into theology to the same degree that the TAR did.[69]

The Council of State affirmed that "laicità" is a broad, general principle that is best understood in the framework of each specific country that enforces the principle. It stated that there are several conceptions of "laicità" that are all deeply different and legitimate in their own context. Italian "laicità," for the Council, could best be understood only in the light of the constitutional articles on religious freedom, equality and fundamental rights.

With this set of constitutional articles providing a background, "laicità," the Council of State maintained consists in an affirmation of constitutional fundamental values. It is a symbol of the core values of the Italian law and, as such, it would extend to educational values as well. Non-discrimination, liberty of conscience, dignity, tolerance and a relationship—not separation—between church and state are all included in that symbol of "laicità" and the crucifix. Because the crucifix resonates with these Italian values, the Council ruled that the crucifix could be publicly displayed.

The Crucifix in the European Court of Human Rights

After losing before the domestic courts of Italy, Soile Lautsi applied to the ECtHR.[70] The ECtHR is an international jurisdiction that polices the enforcement of the European Convention on Human Rights, an international

69 Session VI, judgment of February 13, 2006, no. 556, available at: http://www.federalismi.it/ApplOpenFilePDF.cfm?artid=4056&dpath=document&dfile=17022006041629.pdf&content=Consiglio+di+Stato,+Sentenza+n.+556/2006,+In+materia+di+laicità+dello+Stato+e+di+esposizione+dei+simboli+religiosi+negli+ambienti+scolastici+-++-++-+.

70 *Lautsi v. Italy (*App. no. 30814/06).

treaty that has been signed by 47 states throughout Europe.[71] The ECtHR exercises its jurisdiction in favor of individuals and groups only after the domestic jurisdictions that are available to them have been exhausted.[72] Applicants can apply to the ECtHR claiming that one of their rights enlisted in the Convention has been violated or has not been protected by the relevant state; therefore, the respondent is always a state. The ECtHR normally judges in sections; after the decision, the losing part can appeal before the Grand Chamber of the ECtHR, which can decide to hear the case and release the final judgment or to dismiss the appeal without hearing.

If the ECtHR finds a violation of a right enshrined in the Convention, the state is committed to do whatever is in its power to fix the violation,[73] and can also be condemned to indemnify the victim of the violation.[74] This means that, in itself, the decision does not directly affect domestic law, but only imposes on the state an obligation under the Convention. However, the Italian Constitution obliges the state and its legislation to respect the Convention in the interpretation given to it by the ECtHR.[75] In practice, this would entail that if the display of the crucifix is found to be in violation of the Convention by the ECtHR, the state has the constitutional obligation to adhere to this interpretation of the Convention, and therefore domestic judges can also order the removal of the crucifix.

Soile Lautsi claimed that Art. 9 of the European Convention on Human Rights, which protects the freedom of religion, and its Additional Protocol no. 1, Art. 2, which protects a parent's right to educate their children according to their own beliefs, had been violated by the public display of the crucifix. It is necessary to analyze the European Court's response to these claims in order to further understand Italy's attitude towards public displays for religion within the broader European context.

---

71 Art. 19 of the European Convention: "To ensure the observance of the engagements undertaken by the High Contracting Parties in the Convention and the Protocols thereto, there shall be set up a European Court of Human Rights, hereinafter referred to as "the Court." It shall function on a permanent basis."

72 Art. 35, par. 1: "1.The Court may only deal with the matter after all domestic remedies have been exhausted, according to the generally recognised rules of international law, and within a period of six months from the date on which the final decision was taken."

73 Art. 46, par. 1: "1. The High Contracting Parties undertake to abide by the final judgment of the Court in any case to which they are parties."

74 Art. 41: "If the Court finds that there has been a violation of the Convention or the Protocols thereto, and if the internal law of the High Contracting Party concerned allows only partial reparation to be made, the Court shall, if necessary, afford just satisfaction to the injured party."

75 Judgment nos. 348 and 349 of 2007, Italian Constitutional Court, available at: http://www.cortecostituzionale.it/actionPronuncia.do.

The Second Section of the ECtHR held in favor of the claimant, stating that there is:

> an obligation on the State's part to refrain from imposing beliefs, even indirectly, in places where persons are dependent on it or places where they are particularly vulnerable. The schooling of children is a particularly sensitive area in which they compelling power of the State is imposed on minds which still lack (depending on the child's level of maturity) the critical capacity which would enable them to keep their distance from the message derived from a preference manifested by the State in religious matters.[76]

According to this judgment, the crucifix had a clear Christian connotation and the placement of it in public schools went "beyond the use of symbols in specific historical contexts."[77] The circumstances in which the crucifix was displayed conflicted with the state's duty to "uphold confessional neutrality in public education."[78] The ECtHR held that therefore this symbol was emotionally disturbing for pupils of other religions and for those of no religion, and infringed upon "the rights of parents to educate their children in conformity with their convictions and the right of schoolchildren to believe or not believe."[79] In short, the ECtHR concluded that the crucifix violated both Art. 9 and Protocol no. 1, Art. 2 of the Convention, and declared that the public display of the crucifix was incompatible with the state's duty of impartiality and neutrality.

The decision prompted a wide cultural and legal reaction. Italy appealed to the Grand Chamber against the Second Section's decision, and several other Member States of the Convention intervened in Italy's favor. The Grand Chamber reversed the judgment and found no violation of either Art. 9 or Protocol no. 1, Art. 2 in the public display of the crucifix.[80]

While ruling against the Second Section, the Grand Chamber did reaffirm two crucial aspects of the previous ECtHR's decision by stating that a state has a duty towards both neutrality and impartiality. It acknowledged that the crucifix, despite its traditional cultural value to Italians, is "above all a religious symbol."[81] However, it also stated that "a crucifix on a wall is an essentially passive symbol and this point is of importance in the Court's view, particularly regarding the principle of neutrality."[82] Therefore, the Grand Chamber held, the

76 Decision of November 3, 2009, par. 48.

77 Par. 52.

78 Par. 56.

79 Par. 57.

80 Decision of March 18, 2011.

81 Par. 66.

82 Par. 72.

presence of a crucifix in classrooms did not necessarily imply the indoctrination of students into Catholicism.

Of relevance to the Grand Chamber's reasoning was the open attitude towards all religions found in Italian law and the fact that the presence of a crucifix was but one of many religious symbols found in Italian classrooms. As the Grand Chamber stated:

> Italy opens up the school environment in parallel to other religions. [It is] not forbidden for pupils to wear Islamic headscarves or other symbols or apparel having a religious connotation; alternative arrangements [are] possible to help schooling fit in with non-majority religious practices; the beginning and end of Ramadan [are] often celebrated in schools; and optional religious education [can] be organized in schools for all recognized religious creeds.[83]

In other words, the ECtHR's final decision found that the Italian version of "neutrality" welcomed religious symbolism and activities beyond Catholicism, and therefore concluded that this religion did not monopolize the public school environment. It concluded that as a passive symbol does not always affect religious conscience, as Italy is open to religious pluralism and as the crucifix did not violate the religious rights of other students, then the public display of a crucifix was not inconsistent with the Italian state's duty of "neutrality."

Conclusively, the Grand Chamber acknowledged that the Italian legal system protected the religious rights of individuals and endorsed "neutrality." "Neutrality," it stated, was such a broad concept that it included the possibility for states to display religious symbols such as a crucifix in public places without infringing upon the religious rights of any individuals if these public places are also open to other religions.

Overall, drawing from the utilization that has been made of it by the ECtHR, Italy has developed several understandings of "neutrality" over time, both in favor and against a close relationship between church and state. It will be good to analyze the cultural underpinnings of such conflicting approaches to neutrality in more depth.

Religious Freedom, "Laicità" and Neutrality: The Conceptions behind the Words

The driving forces that have shaped the complex concept of "laicità," with all its evolutions since its inception in the Constitutional's Court's case law, need to be briefly explored. Different understandings of "laicità" can prompt different

83 Par. 74; internal quotations omitted.

results in terms of religious rights and church–state relations. It is important to now turn to the conceptual frameworks that have been decisive in developing this principle through several different stages.

The early Constitutional Court's case law (1989–91) drew from the constitutional text and attempted to summarize its relevant provisions through the innovative use of the word "laicità." These initial cases endorsed a strong collaboration between religion and the state in the educational field and legitimized the teaching of Catholicism in public schools. Later, the Constitutional Court's decisions (mostly from 1995) trended towards, and finally embraced, a more separatist understanding of "laicità," now drawing from such expressions as "neutrality," "impartiality," and/or "equidistance, and from a more classical understanding of "laicità," and detaching itself from a textualist reading of the Constitution. Recently, Italy's domestic courts have re-embraced the historical connotations of "laicità," especially in relation to the public display of crucifixes. This regression to a traditional understanding of "laicità" was embraced by the ECtHR's Grand Chamber when it found that the public display of a crucifix was not incompatible with European case law concerning a state's study of neutrality.

The tension between these two different attitudes is not merely historical, it is a tension that influences Italian law to this day. The Court of Cassation's holding that individuals working at a ballot can object to working there because the display of a crucifix violates an individual's religious rights has not been overruled. At the same time, holdings that students must attend their lessons in the presence of crucifix also remain good law. These two trends coexist and, since both of these courts have parallel powers, no decision of one court can overrule the other.

Increasingly, the religious climate in Italy demands that both the Italian legislature and the judiciary make a choice between the two options. The needs of Muslims must be met in a way that respects both their religious rights and the Italian Constitution.

The Italian state could either choose a path of greater separation between church and state or a path that fosters a closer church–state relationship. Controversial topics, from same-sex partnerships to bioethics, have highlighted the importance of religious debate and church–state relations. Framing these debates are the different perceptions of "laicità," which has recently become one of the core political as well as legal religious–state concepts.

Religious groups, and especially the Catholic Church, have openly debated these topics. This has opened the forum to a statewide discussion of the relationship between law and religion, the place of religion in public life, and how religion should affect public institutions. Essentially, the debate about "laicità" that initially characterized the relationship between church and state has come to also encompass the role of religion in the fields of law and politics.

Strictly Separatists and Friendly Neutralists

Opponents of an open debate of religion in public policies have relied on the meaning of "laicità" as shaped by the Constitutional Court in 1995.[84] From the standpoint of these opponents, religion is being progressively removed from public places in the name of equality and neutrality as one of the prerequisites of democratic and constitutional statehood.[85] Religious arguments should also be removed from the public arena. These opponents argue that in order to protect democracy and the Constitution with neutrality, the state must protect the public sphere—a concept that encompasses both law and politics—from religious influences.[86]

This interpretation of "laicità" and of neutrality not only advocates for a religious disengagement from politics, it also advocates specific conceptions of political life. Opponents of a church–state relationship argue that churches should remove themselves from public debate because religion and law have different authority and foundations, and law can only be understood as an outcome of just political procedures.[87] These opponents claim that religions should stay out of public life because they do not have the right to interfere with political life and because political life is unrelated to religious values.[88]

The advocates of strict separatism can be persuaded that, thanks to the multi-centennial process of secularization,[89] political and democratic life are disconnected from the research of ultimate meanings in life, and have a purely immanent frame.[90] Alternatively, they can still believe that democratic procedures are based on core human and moral values or that they are related with the human research of truth;[91] however, justice and good, they argue, cannot be attained through and within religious traditions, but only through non-religious, purely rational, speculations, which utilize the doubt as the metholodogical approach

84 Colaianni N., La fine del confessionismo e la laicità dello Stato. Il ruolo della Corte costituzionale e della dottrina, in *Political del diritto*, 2009, 45 ff.

85 Kis J. State Neutrality, in Rosenfeld M. and Sajó A. (eds), *The Oxford Handbook on Comparative Constitutional Law*, Oxford University Press, Oxford, 2013, 332.

86 Zagrebelsky G., Stato e Chiesa. Cittadini e cattolici, in *Diritto pubblico*, 2003, 3, 706.

87 Spadaro, Libertà di coscienza e laicità nello Stato costituzionale, 57 and 81.

88 D'Amico M., I diritti "contesi" fra laicità e fondamentalismi, available at: www.statoechiese.it.

89 Hervieu-Léger D., La religion des Européens: modernité, religion, secularisation, in Davie G. and Hervieu-Léger D., *Identités religieuses en Europe*, La Découverte, Paris, 1996, 12.

90 Colaianni N., *Diritto pubblico delle religioni. Eguaglianza e differenze nello Stato costituzionale*, il Mulino, Bologna, 2012.

91 Rusconi G.E., *Non abusare di Dio. Per un'etica laica*, Rizzoli, Milan, 2007, 8.

to scientific and moral enquiry.[92] Yet, they are all skeptical that religious tradition can play a role in identifying and nurturing public and democratic values. They all believe that contemporary "constitutional secularism" simultaneously commands separation of faith from reason and equal liberty for all.[93]

Both these strands believe that "laicità" should involve the separation not only of the church from the state, but also of law from religion, even though only some of them submit that law should be disconnected from truth claims altogether. Overall, they claim that religions cannot assist in understanding core human values.

These readings of "laicità" are far from being a mere consequence of religious freedom or belief;[94] such a conception of "laicità" stands above religious values, as a thick political and moral concept, as is the case in France, where "laïcité" was born as a thick republican value[95] and a political utopia.[96]

This hostile approach towards religion would create a wall between truth, religion and legal norms.

In contrast, more religious-friendly advocates accept that religion has a role in the public space. To them, moral values and beliefs about human society are considered a legitimate part of public discourse, and so there should be an open forum in which individuals and religions can exchange opinions on such matters.[97] These advocates for a closer church–state relationship believe that all opinions should be welcomed, from those that derive from severely rational scientific language to those that derive from religious sources or authority. But they differ significantly in terms of how the articulate the role of religion in the public sphere. Some of them accept religious language in the public debate, whereas others expect religious thinking to be rendered in secular terms.[98]

---

92 Baubérot J., *Laïcité falsifiée*, La Découverte, Paris, 2012, 135.

93 Mancini S. and Rosenfeld M., Introduction, in Mancini S. and Rosenfeld M. (eds), *Constitutional Secularism in an Age of Religious Revival*, Oxford University Press, Oxford, 2014, XV.

94 But see Bielefeldt H., Liberal Secularism and European Islam: A Challenge to Muslims and Non-Muslims, in Cole Durham, Jr. W., Kirkham D. and Lindholm T. (eds), *Islam and Political-Cultural Europe*, Ashgate, Farnham, 2012, 8–9.

95 Baubérot J. and Milot M., *Laïcités sans frontières*, Seuil, Paris, 2011, 12.

96 Remy J., Laicité et construction de l'Europe, in Vincent G. and Willaime J.P. (eds), *Religions et Transformations de l'Europe*, Presses universitaires de Strasbourg, 1993, 367.

97 Cardia C., *Le sfide della laicità. Etica, multiculturalismo, islam*, San Paolo, Milan, 2007, 115.

98 Neuhaus R.J., Human Dignity and Public Discourse, in Human Dignity and Bioethics, Essays Commissioned by President's Council on Bioethics, Washington D.C., March 2008, available at: https://bioethicsarchive.georgetown.edu/pcbe/reports/human_dignity/chapter9.html, 219 and 223.

The contrast between these two conceptions of political "laicità" is deep, and parallels the global contrast between those who advocate and those who oppose a public role for religion. On one side stand those who believe that religion is irrelevant or even damaging to democratic life and law, and that it interferes with public institutions by influencing believers and criticizing legislation.[99] On the other side stand those who are mainly believers, but also some non-believers, who argue that religious traditions retain some basic truths that should be publicly shared, and that basic human truths could be legally enforced through public debates and the democratic process. Both parties use the same word to describe their differing ideologies: "laicità." "Laicità" has therefore come to encompass both the relationship between church and state, and the (dis)connection between law and religion.

Neutrality and "Laicità" in the Face of Religious Diversity: The Multicultural Impasse and the Way out

These two alternative—separatist or friendly—approaches to law and religion as well as to the relationship between church and state have different implications on the treatment of religious groups in Italy. If a rigid separatism—which, as we have seen, is not requested even by the ECtHR—is endorsed in Italy, the Italian legal system would not be able to fully understand or meet the needs of religious groups, whether large or small. A greater gap between church and state can result in a greater misperception of religious needs and can lead to a state giving a standard "package" of rights to each religious group without taking into account what that group actually needs: this is what we have already seen in Chapter 2 as a result of undertheorized, politicized negotiations between religions and the state. But rigid separatism can lead to the same result, since it is unable to detect and appreciate religious values and priorities. Instead, the Italian legal system should recognize if and how religious values are really at stake in religious groups' claims.

Religions claim to embed values and truths about human life. By definition, they enrich social and democratic life through sharing their standpoints on values and truth. To deny this is to demean them.[100] To deny that democracy relates to exchanging opinions on justice and truth is to underestimate democracy as well as the text and intent of the Italian Constitution. The framers clearly opted for a constitutional text that places human relations at its core, starting with Art. 2,

99 Zagrebelsky G., *Contro l'etica della verità*, Laterza, Rome-Bari, 2008, 5.

100 Häberle P., *Diritto e verità*, Einaudi, Turin, 2000, 93; Scola A., Tavola rotonda. Laicità dello Stato, confessioni religiose e multiculturalismo, in *Quaderni di diritto e politica ecclesiastica*, 2006, 359.

which states: "The Republic recognises and guarantees the inviolable rights of the person, as an individual and in the social groups within which human personality is developed." Men and women are understood as embedded in social relations and being enriched by them.

This point was understood by the ECtHR's Grand Chamber decision in *Lautsi* when it framed the situation of public classrooms as follows:

> [T]he presence of crucifixes is not associated with compulsory teaching about Christianity ... Secondly, according to the indications provided by the Government, Italy opens up the school environment in parallel to other religions. The Government indicated in this connection that it was not forbidden for pupils to wear Islamic headscarves or other symbols or apparel having a religious connotation; alternative arrangements were possible to help schooling fit in with non-majority religious practices; the beginning and end of Ramadan were "often celebrated" in schools; and optional religious education could be organised in schools for "all recognised religious creeds" ... Moreover, there was nothing to suggest that the authorities were intolerant of pupils who believed in other religions, were non-believers or who held non-religious philosophical convictions.[101]

In the Grand Chamber's words, the crucifix is but an element of a lively community, which creates religious and philosophical diversity, instead of forcing it out of school.

If the interpreters of the Italian Constitution endorse strict separatism as depicted here, they do not make a good service to democracy or to religion, even though they affirm that they are protecting both.

Islam: Striking a Balance between Neutrality and Pluralism

The increase of Italian religious groups is particularly apparent in relation to the Muslim community. Islam in Italy consists of scattered groups whose requests diverge among themselves as well as compared to those of other religions.

Muslims' needs must be detected in order to understand them and reconcile internal Muslim disagreements into a cohesive agreement with the state in line with earlier understandings of "laicità" based on earlier decisions of the Constitutional Court.

The non-ideological understanding of the principle of "laicità" which was behind judgment no. 203 in 1989 offers a guideline for how to establish an open relationship between Islam and Italy. If "laicità" is considered a summary of

101 Par. 74.

the constitutional principles that can govern church–state relations, then it can be used as a guideline to capture the essential needs of a religion and make a church–state agreement feasible. The collaborative approach stemming from this understanding of "laicità" contemplates and justifies a closer look at the tenets of Islam in order to satisfy Muslims' religious needs.

It is actually impractical to understand religion and what religious freedom is without accepting some degree of the relationship between the legal field and the religious field. To give an example, we can recall judgment no. 44 in 1995 of the Constitutional Court. Despite its inclination towards a more hostile conception of "laicità," the judgment used religious concepts to substantiate its reasoning. When the Court stressed the difference between "adoration" and "veneration" in order to separate a prohibition to offend God from a prohibition of offenses against persons and symbols venerated by the Catholic faith, it captured an understanding of religious terms and used those terms for state purposes. Although the decision advocated a rigid separation between religion and state, it actually drew from religious doctrine to decide the case. It engaged in an open confrontation with the Catholic doctrine in order to detect its basic tenets and use these when interpreting the state law at issue. The Court openly affirmed a quite separatist reading of the Constitution, but concretely used the Catholic legal tradition, with its difference between adoration and veneration to solve the case. In this respect, the decision was much less "separatist" than it appeared to be.

As we will see in the following chapter, a similar understanding of Islamic law and Islamic doctrine is essential to addressing Muslims' religious needs and protecting religious freedom for Muslims.

Chapter 7
State "Laicità" vis-à-vis the Muslim Community's Demands

Introduction

After reflecting on the principle of "laicità" and on its implications when addressing Muslims' religious needs, we can turn to some requests that have been submitted by Muslim groups in Italy and see how the term "laicità" resonates with these groups.

This chapter will focus on some requests made by religious Muslims and will ponder how they can most realistically be addressed. In addition, we will consider if these requests truly derive from Islamic tradition or if these requests are more symbolic with little foundation in religious belief. Requests granted that do not have their roots in Islam do not truly fulfill the mission of religious pluralism.

To understand what requests have religious foundations and which do not, we will contrast Islamic tradition and Italian law. Religious law is central in this respect. It is only through consideration of Islamic law and tradition that we can explore the possibility of integrating Islam in Italy,[1] as well as avoid endowing some religious groups with legal grants or exceptions that have no religious justification.

Islamic requests are the starting point of this investigation, but they are only just the starting point. Religious requests only show that an entity wants something to be enforced, but these requests do not necessarily provide a justification for any enforcement. Arts. 8 and 19 of the Italian Constitution command that all religious groups be allowed to enjoy as much religious freedom as possible, as long as an individual's constitutional values are not endangered. Any deviations from the ordinary regime must have an explanation, even when such deviations do not conflict with fundamental constitutional provisions. When the fulfillment of a request entails an imposition of a burden on Italian society or institutions, an explanation must be provided for the acquiescence of such a request. Here, we maintain that these explanations are normally rooted in the very religiously legal systems that govern each religious group. Through

1 Botta R., La condizione dei gruppi religiosi di più recente insediamento in Italia, in *Il diritto ecclesiastico*, 2000, 364.

understanding these explanations, we can understand what requests are merely symbolic and could therefore be rejected. This rejection, though, would be based on objective grounds.[2]

This chapter will ponder which Islamic requests should take precedence and which should be rejected based on their more symbolic nature. Following that, we will explore the religious and normative character of such beliefs and requests. The Spanish experience with Islam, the ECtHR's case law and the US Supreme Court, with its deep introspection on balancing public interest with the requirements of religious freedom, all provide useful precedents on the granting of religious rights.

Through analysis of case studies that mainly pertain to the most visible and public aspects of Islamic belief, we will be able to exemplify how the Italian constitutional understandings of the relationship between state, religion and religious freedom address the true exigencies of religions and foster a realistic policy of religious freedom. Islamic needs can be understood through understanding religious values—and this is true for religions more broadly. The depth of religious practices and obligations can help us to assess how to accommodate religious needs.[3] Any objections, exceptions and special regimes can be granted according to the level of cogency of each request and not merely according to whether other religions have been granted similar exemptions. A universal granting of the same request can brush over different religious backgrounds.

Understanding a religion's needs means understanding the religious spirit, goal and rationale. No real religious freedom reform can be achieved without this understanding and no state can recognize the uniqueness of each religion if it fails to understand the reasoning behind a religious request.

The Church and State Agreement Methodology

A full recognition of Islamic needs can be complicated by several factors. Islam has unique features compared to other religions, it is not traditionally present

2 Lillo P., *Diritti fondamentali e libertà della persona*, Giappichelli, Turin, 2001, 144; Pizzorusso A., Libertà religiosa e confessioni di minoranza, in *Quaderni di diritto e politica ecclesiastica*, 1997, 55; Vitale A., *Corso di diritto ecclesiastico. Ordinamento giuridico e interessi religiosi*, Giuffrè, Milan, 1998, 105; Colaianni N., *Confessioni religiose e intese. Contributo all'interpretazione dell'art. 8 della Costituzione*, Cacucci, Bari, 1990, 122–29; Cardia C., Matrimonio, famiglia, vita privata. Spunti di analisi ricostruttiva, in *Quaderni di diritto e politica ecclesiastica*, 2002, 53.

3 Esposito C., Il nesso tra "fondamentalismo" e "relativismo," in Prades J. (ed.), *All'origine della diversità. Le sfide del multiculturalismo*, Guerini, Milan, 2008, 131.

in Italy, its relationship with the political sphere is normally strict, and its mainstream theology embraces religious and political connections; moreover, the acceptance of these connections is affected by widespread Islamophobia and by international relations that see Islam playing an ambiguous global political role—a sort of "moral panic,"[4] whose implications for religious freedom of Muslim individuals and groups can be significant. All these factors shape the religious cultural situation in Italy and play a role in the conclusion of a state–Islamic agreement or, alternatively, in shaping a general law that advocates and respects the needs of Muslims.

Italian agreements are largely discretional. While parts of the negotiation are disputed, the general assessment is that public institutions have no obligations other than negotiating with religions.[5] In those agreements, the state is not obliged to accommodate all religious requests.[6]

The political discretion of the agreement process is when a broad consideration of the constitutional directives on state, religion and religious freedom come into play. Through such directives, state institutions can draw distinctions between what is forbidden, what is mandatory and what is only discouraged or recommended, or even merely permitted. The state can prioritize some religious requests, especially those that are particularly important for a religious group.

The varieties of religious rules allow for different treatments. Such rules are not characterized by the very same prescriptive tone. Sometimes they only allow people to keep certain practices; some other customs are merely recommended. For example, Islamic law clearly says that pork meat is forbidden, that daily prayers are mandatory and that polygamy is, at most, permitted.

The distinctions among the normativity of religious laws are not made by the state; they are made by the very same religious law. Religious law normally determines the normativity of religious prescriptions. And it is their specific tone that distinguishes them from individuals' desires and decisions, and allows the state to understand them with particularity. Individual determinations are a product of a self-determined individual liberty; religious norms, as well as religious ethos, are determined by the divine being or by the entity that is the

4 Ryan P., *The Multicultural State and the Religiously Neutral State: A Reply to Paul Cliteur*, 2 *International Journal of Constitutional Law*, 2014, 12, 463.

5 Corvaja F., Rimedi giuridici contro il diniego di intesa con le confessioni religiose, in *Quaderni costituzionali*, 2002, 228.

6 Randazzo B., La legge "sulla base" di intese tra Governo, Parlamento e Corte costituzionale. Legge di approvazione?, in *Quaderni di diritto e politica ecclesiastica*, 2001, 216 and 223; Analogamente Colaianni N., A vent'anni dalla prima intesa. Un'analisi economica, in *Quaderni di Diritto e Politica Ecclesiastica*, 2004, 240.

object of belief.[7] If a state navigates the requests depending on the normative value of each of them, it does not intrude into the area of religious affairs or the conscience of religious individuals.

State institutions need to understand the distinctions in the cogency of religious rules. For example, for a religious believer, it is more important to avoid what is forbidden than to do what is encouraged or even permitted by the religion.[8] The state can provide for a religious conscious environment exactly through the term "laicità," as shaped by the Constitutional Court's decisions.

Agreements are conceived as a means to provide religious freedom and to make it possible for believers to participate both in their religion and political society at the highest achievable level. To provide this, the state must understand the individual's conflict between his religious and political life. This means that the state must guess when there is a direct conflict between religious law and political law.

Religious law permits the state to identify religious priorities and the most problematic of religious needs,[9] since the state can single out religious norms that command or prohibit certain acts from those that only encourage or discourage them.[10]

This state investigation is particularly important when a religion has no central unified hierarchy or clear list of priorities.[11] This is the case for Italian Islam. It is not possible execute a difficult agreement or legislation without understanding what is most important to Muslims.

Understanding what is allowed, forbidden and required according to the Muslim faith is possible. In fact, Islamic doctrine normally distinguishes between obligatory and prohibited acts, while other acts are only recommended, discouraged or simply religiously indifferent.

It must be a priority to understand which acts Islam forbids or mandates. The mere detection of these priorities is not enough, obviously. Once they are singled out, these acts will need to be balanced with constitutional constrains and public interests.[12] But this balancing test can only be achieved after understanding an act's importance to religious believers.

---

7 Sandel M.J., *Democracy's Discontent. America in Search of a Public Philosophy*, Harvard University Press, Cambridge, MA, 1996, 65–66 and 345.

8 Casuscelli G. and Domianello S., *Intese con le confessioni religiose diverse dalla cattolica, Digesto—Discipline pubblicistiche*, UTET, Turin, 1993, 529.

9 Ferrari S., *Lo spirito dei diritti religiosi*, il Mulino, Bologna, 2002, 34.

10 Facchi A., *I diritti nell'Europa multiculturale*, Laterza, Rome-Bari, 2001, 66–67.

11 Castro F., *Diritto musulmano, Digesto—Discipline civilistiche*, UTET, Turin, 1994, 290–91.

12 Witte Jr. J., The Future of Muslim Family Law in Western Democracies, in Ahdar R. and Aroney N. (eds), *Shari'a in the West*, Oxford University Press, Oxford, 2010, 286.

This balancing test provides a safeguard for both the state and Islam. The state can ponder religious needs objectively and Islam can receive a treatment based on its individual and unique needs as opposed to a boilerplate solution that replicates previous agreements.

The approach that I propose is compatible with the ECtHR's case law. It is also, to some extent, akin to American jurisprudence and case law, and Spanish law on this subject.

I will analyze each contribution, many of them case studies, and will then offer an in-depth analysis of some Islamic requests and how to best respond to them. I will consider how, as the first good template, the Islamic holy day of Friday should be respected and the state treatment of religious ministers.

The Conflict of Loyalties

The Conflicts between Constitutional and Religious Values

A primary conflict between constitutional and religious values takes place in the context of military service,[13] which is, according to the Italian Constitution, a sacred duty for every citizen.[14] Military service was compulsory for men until recently[15] and this compulsion forced the Constitutional Court to strike a balance between the political duty of military enlistment and religious and moral obligations. These decisions demonstrate how state and religious obligations can be reconciled.

It is not necessary to analyze every judgment as these decisions are varied and encompass a range of circumstances from complete objection to all military service, to only objecting to service in military prisons. It will suffice to broadly highlight the Court's attitude towards obligations of the conscience.

The Court has attempted to accommodate moral objections to service while holding that the defense of a nation is a duty that can admit no exception. Concerns of conscience are given the highest consideration, but such concerns are difficult to navigate when there is a fundamental duty at stake.[16] The Court has

---

13 Guazzarotti A., La Corte costituzionale "a colloquio con se stessa." Un'additiva "con vincolo di risultato" sull'obiezione di coscienza al servizio militare, in *Giurisprudenza costituzionale*, 1997, 395–419.

14 Art. 52: "The defence of the Fatherland is a sacred duty for every citizen.

Military service is obligatory within the limits and in the manner set out by law. Fulfilment thereof shall not prejudice a citizen's employment, nor the exercise of political rights."

15 Law no. 226, August 23, 2004.

16 Randazzo B., *Obiezione di coscienza, Dizionario di diritto pubblico*, Giuffrè, Milan, 2006.

held that when such conflict of conscience and duty exists, the legislature must be in charge of balancing and acting on these competing interests. In the Court's words, "it is up to the legislature to find the point of equilibrium between individual conscience and this need, on one hand, and the fundamental duties of political, economic and social solidarity (among which the military service stands)."[17] In other words, when fundamental duties are at stake, determinations of conscience are not forfeited, but must be balanced—and this task is for legislators.[18]

A discussion of this pivotal role of individual conscience is found in judgment no. 467 of 1991, where the issue at hand was an objection to military conscription by the applicant after his service has already begun.[19] This decision has been referenced as a milestone in the history of the Constitutional Court.[20] In fact, it has, almost literally, affirmed that in human conscience, constitutional rights find their origin.

At that time, the Court drew from Art. 2 of the Constitution, which protects an individual's fundamental rights to affirm that a person's own relationship with his self and his morals must be protected. Individual conscience, the Court stated, lies at the core and is the origin of human rights. It is an "engine" that gives birth to fundamental freedoms and is a space in which individuals can further associate with others.[21]

This decision was not only important for how it protected the right of human conscience, it also identified the extension of such protection. The Court stated that freedom of conscience extends to behaviors attached to non-negotiable values of personhood and dignity, and to acts directly related to an individual's liberty.

In a later judgment no. 422 of 1993, the Court sharpened its understanding of conscience. The Court stated that reasons pertaining to conscience "don't coincide with any moral imperative"—on the contrary, only "inner commands that derive form general conceptions of life" fit in the picture. In the eyes of the Court, the legislator can only allow "limited exceptions and exemptions

---

17 Judgment no. 43, 1997.

18 Law no. 772, December 15, 1972; it was later repealed.

19 Di Cosimo G., Coscienza individuale e momento di manifestazione dell'obiezione al servizio militare, in *Giurisprudenza costituzionale*, 1991, 3818–33.

20 Pastori G., L'obiezione di coscienza nell'ordinamento italiano, in Perrone B. (ed.), *Realtà e prospettive dell'obiezione di coscienza. I conflitti degli ordinamenti*, Giuffrè, Milan, 2002, 149–50.

21 "[L]a sfera intima della coscienza individuale deve esser considerata come il riflesso giuridico più profondo dell'idea universale della dignità della persona umana che circonda quei diritti, riflesso giuridico che, nelle sue determinazioni conformi a quell'idea essenziale, esige una tutela equivalente a quella accordata ai menzionati diritti, vale a dire una tutela proporzionata alla priorità assoluta e al carattere fondante ad essi riconosciuti nella scala dei valori espressa dalla Costituzione italiana."

to specific constitutional duties" in the name of freedom of conscience.[22] To make a long story short, the Court's discussion implicitly acknowledged that not all moral obligations are equal and that some obligations are more related than others with fundamental decisions that each individual takes. Only the latter enjoy the greatest constitutional protection.

Reasons of conscience are always built upon sincere, strongly held beliefs, but that does not mean that each reason should be treated the same: the level of cogency varies, for religious consciences, with the normative value of each religious rule.[23]

This returns us to our initial reflections on the level of discretion a government has in negotiating a state–religion agreement and the duties that the Italian Parliament has in crafting generally applicable law on religious freedom. Sincerely, strongly held and deep beliefs must be carefully protected and balanced with political concerns.[24]

The Relevant ECtHR Case Law

The European Convention on Human Rights institutions have paid growing attention to conscience claims, grounding them in Art. 9 of the Convention protecting freedom of religion[25] and enumerating what circumstances could limit religious freedom.

These institutions have consistently held that freedom of religion, as enshrined in Art. 9, not only covers the practice and adherence to a religion; expressions and objections of conscience must also be protected, especially if they derive from an individual's deep and sincere belief.

---

22 "[M]otivi di coscienza … non coincidono con qualsiasi imperativo morale, ma riguardano … i comandi del foro interno riconducibili a concezioni generali, ai quali, in ragione del pluralismo dei valori di coscienza susseguente alla garanzia costituzionale delle libertà fondamentali della persona, può esser attribuita dal legislatore una determinata e limitata capacità di deroga a specifici doveri costituzionali di solidarietà civile o politica."

23 Bertolino R., *L'obiezione di coscienza moderna. Per una fondazione costituzionale del diritto di obiezione*, Giappichelli, Turin, 1994, 90.

24 Ibid., 29.

25 Art. 9: "1. Everyone has the right to freedom of thought, conscience and religion; this right includes freedom to change his religion or belief and freedom, either alone or in community with others and in public or private, to manifest his religion or belief, in worship, teaching, practice and observance.

2. Freedom to manifest one's religion or beliefs shall be subject only to such limitations as are prescribed by law and are necessary in a democratic society in the interests of public safety, for the protection of public order, health or morals, or for the protection of the rights and freedoms of others."

The European Commission on Human Rights (which used to police the European Convention on Human Rights alongside the Court, and should not be confused with the EU's Commission) was used to address claims of human rights violations and was the first European Convention institution to clarify that freedom of conscience claims were protected only when there is a strict and evident relationship between the belief and the behavior.[26]

Later, the ECtHR went further in explaining the connection between belief and behaviors and when the latter is protected. This relationship cannot be merely tenuous; there must be a solid connection between the two. The Court has maintained that such religious freedom protection does not cover mere "opinions," or "ideas":[27] "it cannot be said that every act which is in some way inspired, motivated or influenced by a belief constitutes a manifestation of that belief."[28]

This protection has to do with personal "convictions," which are characterized by a specific and close relationship with the individual and are therefore worthy of protection under Art. 9 of the European Convention.[29] If Art. 9's protection extends beyond religious practices, it still requires "a sufficiently close and direct nexus between the act and the underlying belief," which "must be determined on the facts of each case." However, "there is no requirement on the applicant to establish that he or she acted in fulfillment of a duty mandated by religion."[30]

Connection, seriousness, depth and strength of a belief help to distinguish beliefs that must be protected funder Art. 9 from mere opinions or ideas. These beliefs do not necessarily need to reflect religious obligations per se, but they must have a deep religious or moral conviction backing them.[31]

The European Convention's institutions demonstrate a striking resemblance to the Italian Constitutional Court's attitude towards a claim of conscience. Both allow room for distinguishing religious rules on the basis of cogency, and ground the protection of conscience on the meaning and the depth of the belief of the claimants.[32]

---

26 *Arrowsmith v. United Kingdom* (App. no. 7050/75), October 12, 1978, par. 71.

27 *Campbell and Cosans v. United Kingdom* (App. nos. 7511/76, 7743/76), February 25, 1982, par. 36.

28 *Eweida and Others v. United Kingdom*, (App. nos. 48420/10; 59842/10; 51671/10; 36516/10), January 15, 2012, par. 82.

29 Marie J.B., La liberté de conscience dans les instruments internationaux des droits de l'homme: reconnaissance et interprétation, in *Revue de droit canonique* 52(1), 2002, 46.

30 *Eweida and others v. United Kingdom*, par. 82.

31 Berlingò S., Stato democratico sociale e obiezione di coscienza: profili di diritto comparato, in Perrone B. (ed.), *Realtà e prospettive dell'obiezione di coscienza. I conflitti degli ordinamenti*, Giuffrè, Milan, 2002, 398.

32 See also *Sessa v Italy*, (App. no, 28790/08), Second Section, April 3, 2012, par. 37: "It is not disputed between the parties that the applicant was able to perform his religious duties.

The Contribution of US Supreme Court Case Law on the Relationship between Civil Institutions and Religious Doctrines

It is important to briefly illustrate the standpoint of the legal culture of the US regarding the protection of conscience claims and to the inspection that can be undertaken to ensure that such claims are well founded. The American legal culture has repeatedly dealt with freedom of conscience claims deriving from its very strong protection of freedom of religion. It therefore provides an excellent comparison to assist in understanding the connection between religious rules and political obligations.

The protection of religion is a matter of endless debate in the US. The treatment of religious claims, in order to allow conscientious objections without leaving the door open to any claim, either well founded or rootless, has not been addressed in a consistent way or ended in a well-settled jurisprudence.[33] The US Supreme Court, however, has delved into such issues multiple times and has had to balance and understand religious tenets in order to ascertain the fervency and importance of a religious belief.

In the nineteenth century, the Court hesitated to delve into matters of faith, mostly because Christian beliefs were sacred in the religious and well as political climate.[34] In 1944, in *United States v. Ballard*,[35] the Court changed its position. It still affirmed that the judiciary must be removed from the theological realm, but only because of the intrinsic limits on the judicial power and not because of the infallible veracity of any religious doctrine.[36] The dissent in *Ballard* expanded that notion and maintained that it is not possible for the judiciary to even investigate whether a religious opinion is sincerely believed among its members.[37]

Furthermore, he could have expected that his request for an adjournment would be refused on the basis of the statutory provisions in force and could have arranged to be replaced at the hearing in question to ensure that he complied with his professional obligations."

33 Helfand M.A., Litigating Religion, in *Boston University Law Review* 2013, 93, 501.

34 Goldstein J.A., Is There a "Religious Question" Doctrine? Judicial Authority to Examine Religious Practice and Beliefs, in *Catholic University Law Review*, 2005, 54, 506.

35 322 U.S. 78, 86.

36 "Man may believe what they cannot prove. They may not be put to the proof of their religious doctrines or beliefs. Religious experiences which are as real as life to some may be incomprehensible to others" (ibid., 86).

37 Justice Jackson: "The most convincing proof that one believes his statements is to show that they have been true in his experience. Likewise, that one knowingly falsified is best proved by showing that what he said happened never did happen. How can the Government prove these persons knew something to be false which it cannot prove to be false? If we try religious sincerity severed from religious verity, we isolate the dispute from the very considerations which in common experience provide its most reliable answer" (ibid., 93).

The Court's new approach was affirmed through a series of judgments in the 1960s,[38] 1970s[39] and 1990s,[40] and foreclosed the concept of a relationship between political and religious institutions. However, this absolute abstention has not always been favorable to religion and has in fact inadvertently legitimized some religious frauds. Self-proclaimed religious therapists or healers, or *Kosher* caterers who did not provide the kind of food they had contracted to provide, found judicial protection for their frauds precisely because the judiciary could not step into the religious realm.[41]

However, here and there in the Supreme Court's case law, there are some attempts to connect the religious and political sphere and address freedom of conscience claims after a consideration of the basic tenets of a religion.[42]

An empirical and realistic approach, albeit one that has been widely criticized, is found in the Supreme Court case *Wisconsin v. Yoder* (1972).[43] In *Yoder*, an Amish family was protected in their right to withdraw their children from school and educate them in isolation from modern civilization and influence.

The Court protected this school exemption because the teachings of the school were contrary to central tenets of the Amish faith. This decision stressed the importance of the Amish concern in having their children attend state school and stressed that, far from being merely an individual preference, this concern was deeply rooted in the Amish lifestyle, as confirmed by its own history and third party experts.[44]

38 *Presbyterian Church v. Hull Church* 393 U.S. 440, 450 (1969): "the interpretation of particular church doctrines and the importance of those doctrines to the religion. Plainly, the First Amendment forbids civil courts from playing such a Role."

39 *Md. and Va. Churches v. Sharpsburgh Ch.* 396 U.S. 367, 369 (1970): "to permit civil courts to probe enough into the allocation of power within a church so as to decide where religious law places control over the use of church property would violate the First Amendment in much the same manner as civil determination of religious doctrine."

40 *Employment Division v. Smith* 494 U.S. 872, 887 (1990): "It is no more appropriate for judges to determine the 'centrality' of religious beliefs before applying a 'compelling interest' test in the free exercise field than it would be for them to determine the 'importance' of ideas before applying the 'compelling interest' test in the free speech field. What principle of law or logic can be brought to bear to contradict a believer's assertion that a particular act is 'central' to his personal faith?"

41 Goldstein, Is There a "Religious Question" Doctrine?, 499.

42 See Helfand, Litigating Religion, 493 ff.

43 406 U.S. 205.

44 "In sum, the unchallenged testimony of acknowledged experts in education and religious history, almost 300 years of consistent practice, and strong evidence of a sustained faith pervading and regulating respondents' entire mode of life support the claim that enforcement of the State's requirement of compulsory formal education after the eighth grade would gravely endanger if not destroy the free exercise of respondents' religious beliefs" (ibid., 220).

In 1979, *Jones v. Wolf*,[45] a case concerning ecclesiastic real estate, provided another opportunity for the Court to expand on how to best protect religious beliefs. When deciding this case, the Court found it was indispensable to consider the doctrines of the relevant religious as well as religious texts. It tried to balance the competing needs of the religious and secular realm in order to both provide a remedy and respect the gap between these two realms. The Court lauded the examination of religious texts, but warned that "a civil court must take special care to scrutinize the document in purely secular terms, and not to rely on religious precepts," in order to maintain a state's neutrality and protect religious autonomy.

Justice Powell's dissent criticized the contradiction in which he thought the Court was falling.[46] He warned that the Court was pushing the judiciary to interpret religious documents in "purely secular terms," an approach that he feared would bring more confusion than clarification to both the documents and the political–religious relationship.

The attitudes of the Court's opinions in *Wisconsin* and in *Jones* differ greatly: in the first case, the Court investigated the religious doctrines through reading its sacred history and through the contribution of experts during the trial hearings, while in *Jones*, it shied away from inspecting religions and wanted religious texts to be read secularly. But, in both cases, the Court resolved to tackle the religious doctrines. Regardless of whether it opted for religious or secular readings of them, in neither instance did it shy away from dealing with the religious doctrines.

If domestic courts cannot judge religious disputes, they should still be able to grasp religious doctrines.[47] This would help in addressing religious frauds[48] and protecting religious freedom.

The Court recently affirmed this idea in *Buckwell v. Hobby Lobby* (2014),[49] a decision that protected the owner of a for-profit organization from refusing to provide abortifacient contraceptives coverage to its employees. The Court's decision, drafted by Justice Alito, briefly discussed the importance of sincerity in beliefs. Alito stated that "it is not for us to say that their religious beliefs are mistaken or insubstantial"; however, the Court could still conclude that in this present case, "there is no dispute" that the "case at stake involves an honest conviction." Congress, the opinion observed, had already recognized that the "ability of the federal courts to weed out insincere claims" and thus single out situations in which an exemption might be well founded based on a sincere belief from those in which an exemption would not be appropriate.

45 443 U.S. 595.

46 Justices Powell, Stewart and White.

47 Goldstein, Is There a "Religious Question" Doctrine?, 501.

48 Ibid., 550–51.

49 134 S.Ct. 2751.

This deference from a domestic court to a religious legal system is not considered bizarre. Religious laws are, after all, laws as well. Domestic courts draw from the laws of other countries constantly, most commonly when deciding how to enforce or apply a foreign law.[50] In fact, when an Iranian or Israeli law is applied to another state, a consequence could be that an Islamic law or Jewish law is enforced in a foreign supposedly secular country, since Iranian law has partially assimilated Islamic law and Israeli law has partially assimilated Jewish law.[51]

The American experience, ignoring its broad fluctuations, confirms the idea that the reception of religious tenets is feasible, and even laudable, in order to give room to presuming religious issues and protect religious freedom.[52]

Contrasting Religious Requests with Religious Needs: Is it Feasible?

When addressing a religious request, there are only two options.[53] The first is to explore the religious claims in order to detect that claimant's sincerity. It is not clear, however, where a state can lawfully detect its sincerity.[54] The second option consists of relying only on a claimant's declaration concerning his sincerity. This option could grant exemptions and special treatments to people who do not actually have a need to be treated differently from the general applicable norms and could be given unjustified benefits.[55]

The circle can be squared through a placement of the *onus probandi* on the part of the state. The claimants should not need to prove that their belief is sincere.[56] It is easier, and more just, for the state to delve into the facts in order to examine whether a belief is rooted in religious beliefs.

---

50 Kim E.J.K., Islamic Law in American Courts: Good, Bad, and Unsustainable Uses, in *Notre Dame Journal of Law, Ethics & Public Policy*, 2014, 28, 287 ff.

51 Goldstein, Is There a "Religious Question" Doctrine?, 538.

52 Nussbaum M., *Liberty of Conscience. In Defense of America's Tradition of Religious Liberty*, Basic Books, New York, 2008, 170.

53 Di Cosimo G., *Coscienza e Costituzione. I limiti del diritto di fronte ai convincimenti interiori della persona*, Giuffrè, Milan, 2000, 32–33.

54 Ibàn I., Nuovi movimenti religiosi: problemi giuridici, in Ferrari S. (ed.), *Diritti dell'uomo e libertà dei gruppi religiosi. Problemi giuridici dei nuovi movimenti religiosi*, Cedam, Padua, 1989, 96.

55 Di Cosimo G., Privilegi per le confessioni religiose: chi certifica l'autenticità dei motivi di coscienza?, in *Giurisprudenza costituzionale*, 1992, 4228.

56 But, as for the European Court of Human Rights' jurisprudence, see *Kosteski v. The Former Yugoslav Republic of Macedonia* (App. no. 55170/00), April 13, 2006, par. 46: "However, insofar as the applicant claims that he is the only person of the Muslim faith who has been required to prove his adherence to that religion, the Court considers that any resulting difference of treatment may be regarded as based on objective and reasonable justification.

The state has the ability, and right, to ascertain if a relevant religious duty exists. If the claimants had acted differently from the action requested, then a neutral third party would be led to believe that the request was largely fabricated and the state would be justified to deny this request.[57]

Breaking though this veil of religion to inspect its nature and value was a problem that particularly troubled Italian institutions in terms of how to treat a group called *Dianetics*. With the Dianetics, the Constitutional Court had to decide what level of scrutiny was appropriate to be adopted in order to ascertain the religious nature of the group.[58] It began with the assumption that self-qualification is a good starting point in determining a group's religious beliefs, but then added that the state institution should be able to investigate in order to ascertain whether the group's characteristics confirm or deny its self-declaration.

From the *Dianetics* case, we can infer that a similar approach could be taken regarding all religious practices, and not just the religious nature, of an organization. State institutions should be able to check if religious data confirm or deny a religious request or claim. If Italian "laicità" is understood as a device that connects, and not only separates, church and state, then the government can inspect religious tenets to ascertain their consistency with the claims that a religious organization makes.[59]

The Spanish experience of state–religion relationships confirms how this approach of drawing from a religious-friendly understanding of state neutrality can be good and fruitful. In political decisions in this field, Spanish institutions took into account the doctrinal heritage of the religious agreements with which they negotiated.

The Lesson from Spain: An Important Parallel

Separation of Church and State in Spain

The Spanish constitutional infrastructure is similar in many ways to the Italian one.[60] Since Spain has reached an agreement with the Islamic community, it will

---

The applicant was making claim to a privilege or exemption to which he was not entitled unless he was a member of the faith concerned and in circumstances which arguably gave rise to doubts as his entitlement. As found above under Article 9, it was not unreasonable or disproportionate to require him to show some level of substantiation of his claim."

57 Di Cosimo, *Coscienza e Costituzione*, 220–21.

58 Judgment no. 467, 1992.

59 Di Cosimo, Privilegi per le confessioni religiose, 4243.

60 Garcimartín Montero M.C., La laicidad, en las Cortes Constituyentes de 1978, in *Ius Canonicum*, 1996, 539 ff.

be helpful to give a short overview of how Spain has shaped the relationship between church and state.

Religious freedom, state disestablishment and a collaborative approach between state and religion were all concepts used in Spain[61] and made it possible to conclude an agreement with Islam,[62] Judaism,[63] Orthodox and Protestant Christianity,[64] and special pacts with the Catholic Church.[65]

Furthermore, in Spain, the constitutional system of the relationship between church and state is commonly described as "laico" or "laicidad," the same wording used to depict a similar concept in the Italian legal system. Like Italy, the Spanish Constitutional Tribunal has used this wording even though such a concept was not found in the Spanish Constitution.[66]

In Spain, as in Italy, the concept of "neutralidad" or "neutrality" is used circumspectly.[67] "Neutrality" is described attentively in order to avoid conveying a hostile state approach towards religion and the complete removal of religions from the public sphere.[68]

In addition to the above-mentioned similarity, there are additional common features found in both legal regimes. For example, the Spanish Constitution (like the Italian Constitution) explicitly references the Catholic faith, but the Constitutional Court jurisprudence in both countries does not believe this to be an exception or deviation from equality and "laicità" (or "laicidad"). For both countries, religious freedom, non-establishment, and cooperation between church and state remain at the core of the systems.

Catholic teaching is imparted in Spanish public schools pursuant to an agreement between the state and the Holy See along similar lines to those that legitimized the teaching of Catholicism in Italian schools.[69] There is a striking parallel to the Italian

---

61 Giménez y Martínez De Carvajal J., Los acuerdos Iglesia-Estado de 1979, in Pérez De Laborda A. (ed.), *Existencia en libertad*, Madrid, 2004, 176.

62 Law no. 29, issued on November 10, 1992.

63 Law no. 25, issued on November 10, 1992.

64 Law no. 24, issued on November 10, 1992.

65 Agreement of January 3, 1979.

66 This word is used for the first time in judgment no. 46, 2001.

67 González Vila T., Laicidad del Estado y libertad religiosa, in Pérez De Laborda A. (ed.), *Existencia en libertad*, Facultad de Teología San Dàmaso, Madrid, 2004, 213–14.

68 Martínez-Torrón J., La contribución del la Ley Orgánica de Libertad Religiosa a la transición democrática en España, available at: www.olir.it, 8; Roca M.A., La neutralidad del Estado: fundamento doctrinal y actual delimitación en la jurisprudencia, in *Il diritto ecclesiastico,* 1997, 407; Llamazares Fernandez D., *Derecho a la libertad de conciencia I*, Civitas, Madrid, 1997, 37.

69 See the agreement on teaching and cultural issues made on January, 3, 1979 following after the general agreement between the Spanish State and the Holy See, signed on July 28, 1976.

Constitutional Court's judgment no. 203 of 1989: as early as 1981, the Spanish Constitutional Tribunal had rooted this subject in a pluralist, non-denominational Spanish regime which allows religion to play a role in the public sphere—even to the extent of allowing Catholicism to be taught in its public schools.[70]

In short, if the fundamentals of the Spanish constitutional attitude towards religion have been depicted or characterized as "laicidad," this wording must be further understood, as in the Italian legal system, as a synthetical description of the constitutional values of church and state collaboration, non-establishment of religion and religious freedom.

Given the striking similarities between the Italian and Spanish models, it is even more essential to consider how the Spanish law has assessed the Spanish Islamic community's requests. Referencing Spain's navigation through various opinions and tendencies can help Italy shape its policy towards Muslims in Italy.

Islamic Beliefs and Religious Needs

The statute law in Spain is preceded by a detailed description of its motives in a provision entitled "Exposición de motivos." The introductory description of the legislation embedding the agreement between the Spanish state and Islam is highly illustrative of what Spain understood its role to be and how it formatted an agreement that best reflected Islamic tenets.

The wording of the "Exposición" is similar to other religious state agreements. However, the "Exposición" stresses that it is intended to address Muslims' religious needs[71] and make their enjoyment of religious freedom "real and effective." It gives a detailed account on how state institutions behaved with Muslims and the consideration in which Islamic requests have been taken in order to respect Islamic precepts and doctrines as much as possible.[72] An open reception of Islamic requests was central to the Islamic–Spanish agreement.

---

70 Judgment no. 5, 1981, par. 9: "En un sistema jurídico político basado en el pluralismo, la libertad ideológica y religiosa de los individuos y la aconfesionalidad del Estado, todas las instituciones públicas y muy especialmente los centros docentes, han de ser, en efecto, ideológicamente neutrales. Esta neutralidad, que no impide la organización en los centros públicos de enseñanzas de seguimiento libre para hacer posible el derecho de los padres a elegir para su hijos la formación religiosa y moral que esté de acuerdo con su propias convicciones (art. 27.3 de la Constitución), es una característica necesaria de cada uno de los puestos docentes integrados."

71 "Dando respuesta a los deseos formulados por ambas Federaciones, expresión de la voluntad de los musulmanes españoles, y tras las oportunas negociaciones, se llegó a la conclusión del presente Acuerdo de Cooperación."

72 "En la negociación del presente Acuerdo, se ha procurado siempre tener el más escrupuloso respeto a la voluntad negociadora de los interlocutores religiosos, como la mejor expresión de los contenidos específicos del credo religioso islámico y de las

The "Exposición" focuses on the consistency between the Islamic group that has negotiated the agreement, the claims that it made and the doctrines of the Muslim faith. In so doing, this agreement magnifies the role of Islamic representation while also pointing out the connection between the Islamic doctrine and requests of Spanish Muslims.

The Spanish "laicidad" provides a rationale for this approach that links religious requests to religious doctrines. Spanish "laicidad," as a form of collaboration between church and state, focuses on the state's respect for religious freedom according to what a religion commands. The state–religion agreement is the means through which religious freedom may be protected.

Spanish "laicidad" can illuminate what can be expected from the Italian term "laicità." "Laicidad" can show how Italy can single out religious priorities and what requests correspond to a Muslim's religious need to exercise their freedom.

Representation of religion is necessary for religious communication with the state. However, if different groups of the same religion diverge in terms of their requests, a type of compass is needed in order to detect more prevailing and essential needs. The principle of "laicità," as well as its Spanish counterpart of "laicidad," confirms that this could be accomplished. Proposals that stem from the basic tenets of Islam can prevail and become a state priority.

Religious doctrines or commands cannot be changed or modified by the state, but they should be observed. The state modification of religious doctrine would conflict with religious rights as well as church autonomy, as established through the Italian Constitution and the European Convention on Human Rights. However, it is possible to distinguish between what is not important and what doctrines compose a fundamental component of religious heritage.

Given inner religious conflicts, if a Muslim group makes a request, this does not necessarily mean that there is a religious need behind it. On the contrary, the differences between the Italian groups' proposals make it necessary to distinguish between which requests parallel Islamic religious tenets and which do not.

The principle of "laicita" justifies this approach. The use of this concept can help in protecting religious freedom for Muslims without interfering with Islamic texts.

Friday as the Muslim Holy Day: The Requests for a State–Religion Agreement

We can start with considering Friday as the Muslim holy day and pondering whether in an agreement, it is possible to include an allowance for Muslims to abstain from work and school lessons during Friday in accordance with Islamic law doctrines.

---

peculiares exigencias de conciencia que de ellos se derivan, para hacer posible que sea real y efectivo el ejercicio del derecho de libertad religiosa de los creyentes musulmanes."

Here we will need to contrast Italian Islamic groups' requests with what Islamic doctrine instructs and the regular working-week schedule in Islamic countries in order to ascertain whether a request for a Friday holy day is backed by a religious obligation. In the presence of such a sincere religious obligation, a state refusal to allow Muslims to abstain from working on Fridays would create a conflict of conscience.

According to the Italian Constitution, rights may be limited only for a reason proportionate to the right. In particular, according to Italian case law, a right may be limited if it is "necessary and able to achieve the legitimate aim, because, amongst a set of appropriate measures, it is least restrictive of competing rights and establishes not disproportionate burdens in pursuing of such aims" (judgment no. 1, 2014).[73] Therefore, the limitation to the free exercise of religious freedom must be grounded in objective reasons, be minimally restrictive while balancing state interests and not disproportionately burdensome to believers.

The European Convention on Human Rights institutions have developed case law fleshing out how the conscience must be protected.

The European Commission addressed violations of Convention rights until 1998, when it was shut down. Such protection used to be subordinate to competing claims. A prime example of this took place in the field of labor law. In *Konttinen v. Finland*,[74] the Commission wrestled with the case of a worker claiming his right to leave his job during prayer hours and the competing interest of the employer, who fired the employee for abandoning his job. The Commission recognized the legitimacy of the employer's decision, claiming that the employee was "free to relinquish his post." The Commission regarded leaving a job not as a disproportionate burden for the employee, but as a safeguard of his religious freedom. Relinquishing the post was "the ultimate guarantee of [the] right to freedom of religion." In sum, the dismissal determined, in itself, no interference with the exercise of the freedom of religion of the applicant before the Commission, and the Commission found no violation of such a right.[75]

The European Convention on Human Rights' case law has since evolved. For example, while, as discussed in *Konttinen*, the Commission stated that if an employee disliked an employer's business practice because it restrained his religious freedom, the employee was free to resign, the Court held that this approach was too rigid. "The better approach," the Court stated in *Eweida and others v. UK*, "would be to weigh that possibility in the overall balance when considering whether or not the restriction was proportionate."[76] A resignation, the Court elaborated, should be a last option and should only be used if all

73 Par. 3.1.

74 (App. no. 24949/94), December 3, 1996.

75 Par. 1.

76 Par. 83.

other possibilities are exhausted. Therefore, the Court settled the ground for overruling its case law. But at the same time, it balanced its own affirmation with its quite traditionally deferential approach towards states' choices in balancing competing rights and interests. In fact, it continued to state that members of the Convention retain significant discretion in terms of how and the extent to which they accommodate religious employees.[77]

Current agreement drafts proposed by Islamic religious groups have differed in relation to whether they wish to instate Friday as a holy day. All proposals have requested that the day of Friday be given religious significance. However, groups differ on what this religious significance would mean. Some groups seek for the entire day of Friday to be protected entirely as a holy day, while other groups only seek permission for Muslims to attend the liturgy at the midday prayer.

The COREIS draft[78] proposes that Muslims who, through job constraints, are exceptionally impeded from enjoying Friday as a holy be allowed to participate in the midday prayer. Excepting extreme circumstances though, the COREIS agreement implicitly asks that Muslims be permitted to abstain from work on Friday.[79]

In contrast, the UCOII draft agreement has evolved over time. Originally, this agreement permitted public and private employees to attend Friday prayer only if this did not conflict with their duties.[80] A Muslim student's absence from Friday lessons was automatically legitimized in the agreement.[81] However, the school provision was later modified and now a student is permitted to leave school only for the time necessary to attend prayer.[82]

All draft agreements agree on one point: school examinations must be allowed to be taken on days other than Fridays.[83]

Whether the state pursues the project of a state–Islam agreement or legislates through general law, state institutions must navigate these agreement proposals and choose the best solution following Islamic doctrine while minimally inconveniencing working and educational activities.[84]

Precedents: Saturday as a Holy Day

According to Art. 36, par. 3 of the Italian Constitution: "Workers have the right to a weekly rest day and paid annual holidays. They cannot waive this

77 Par. 84.
78 Art. 5, last par.
79 Art. 3.
80 Art. 3.
81 Art. 3
82 Art. 3.
83 Art. 10 AMI; Art. 15 COREIS; Art. 3 UCOII.
84 Botta, La condizione dei gruppi religiosi di più recente insediamento in Italia, 399.

right." The Civil Code has normally designated the weekly rest day as Sunday with some exceptions.[85] This choice of Sunday as the rest day is clearly tied with the Italian Christian tradition that prevails in Italy. This is legitimized by the European Social Charter (1996), which was adopted by the state parties to the Council of Europe. This Charter stated that in order "to ensure a weekly rest period which shall, as far as possible, coincide with the day recognized by tradition or custom in the country or region concerned as a day of rest" (Art. 2, par. 5).

The core constitutional value that underpins the obligation of a weekly rest day is the protection of employees' health as understood in both psychological and physical terms.[86] In addition, this value promotes the right of a worker to enjoy free time, socialize and spend time with their family.[87]

Public institutions have repeatedly tried to accommodate other minority religious groups such as the Jews and the Adventists whose religious holy day does not fall on a Sunday. Agreements with both these religions protect their right to abstain from work and schooling on Saturdays.

Jewish tradition has its holy day on Saturdays under the belief that, according to Genesis, God, after creating the world, rested on the seventh day of the week. Since under the Jewish tradition days commence at sundown, the Jewish holy day begins on Friday at sunset and ends on Saturday at sunset.

The Jewish–Italian agreement in Italy has permitted the use of Saturday as a Jewish holy day and Jewish employees, both private and public, are permitted to abstain from work on that day. Pursuant to that agreement, abstention from school is also permitted on Saturdays.

The state–Adventists agreement has provided similar accommodations. Adventists, like Jews, regard Saturday as their holy day.[88] Like the Jewish day, the Adventist holy day begins on Friday at sundown and ends on Saturday at sunset. During that time, Adventists abstain from ordinary occupations and devote themselves to religious education, visiting the sick and other charitable activities. The Adventist agreement with the state has allowed public and private employees to enjoy their Shabbat by abstaining from working and Adventists students are allowed to not attend lessons for the entire day.

---

85 Art. 2109, par. 1: "Il prestatore di lavoro ha diritto ad un giorno di riposo ogni settimana di regola in coincidenza con la domenica." See also law no. 470, February 22, 1934, Art. 3.

86 Art. 31, first paragraph, of the Constitution: "The Republic shall safeguard health as a fundamental right of the individual and as a collective interest and shall guarantee free medical care to the indigent."

87 Lillo P., Rilevanza civile delle festività religiose in Spagna e in Italia, in *Il diritto ecclesiastico*, 1995, 415; Colaianni, *Confessioni religiose e intese*, 154.

88 Genesis 2:2–3.

The use of Saturday as a holy day for the Jews[89] and the Adventists,[90] as provided by the state–religious agreements, has lead to Saturday being even more protected as a holy day than the day of Sunday is for Catholics and other Christian denominations. Sunday is a regular day of rest and so exceptions to this day of rest requiring an employee to work are easily made. In contrast, Saturday enjoys greater protections, such as those enforced through religion–state agreements. Requiring work on these days entails a violation of these agreements and, consequently, of the Constitution.

This additional protection of Saturday as a holy day is justified by the fact that the use of the Sabbath is deeply embedded in religious doctrine. This commandment of keeping the Shabbat day holy is more pronounced in current Jewish and Adventist practice than it is in Catholic practice.[91] There is no additional religious privilege that is introduced through the religion–state agreements, but only a means through which Jews can avoid conflict between their religious ordinances and secular obligations. Jews and Adventists are given only what they require to enjoy religious freedom in the context of labor law.

The use of a religious agreement to protect a holy day provides a powerful precedent in terms of how best to approach Muslims' requests for Friday as a holy day. Because the Italian state has already granted a Saturday holy day for Jews and Adventists, many argue that similar treatment should be granted to Muslims.[92] However, the Muslim request for a Friday holy day should be reconsidered for two reasons.

First, the Muslim use of Friday as a rest day would have a statewide impact on society and the economy. Friday is considered a day of work in Italy. Both private and public business and school institutions are typically open Monday through Friday. Saturday is considered, for the most part, a vacation day in which most organizations, and all schools, are closed. There is minimal impact in allowing Jews and Adventists to abstain from school and work on those days. In contrast, allowing Muslims to abstain from work on Friday would have a much greater impact on both educational and working institutions.

Second, Muslims in Italy comprise a substantially larger proportion of the working population than do Jews or Adventists. Jews and Adventists comprise a small percentage or demographic minorities, while Muslim residents in Italy comprise of more than one million individuals. Both the holy day and the percentage of religious adherents make the use of a Saturday holy day and a Friday holy day very different from each other.

---

89 Art. 3 of the Agreement.

90 Art. 17 of the Agreement.

91 Rimoldi T., La Chiesa avventista del 7° giorno, available at: www.olir.it, 57.

92 Botta R., L'intesa con gli israeliti, in *Quaderni diritto e politica ecclesiastica*, 1987, 101; Vitale, *Corso di diritto ecclesiastico*, 71.

In order to balance this decision, the religious rest obligation in the Islamic tradition must be weighed before the secular concerns of losing a substantial part of its working class on a traditional work day. If there is no religious obligation, then there is no individual conflict between religious and secular authority, and so there is no constitutionally grounded reason why a holy day provision should be provided for in a religion–state agreement. Below, we will consider Islamic legal doctrine as well as common practices in Islamic countries regarding the use of Friday as a holy day.

Friday in the Muslim Faith According to Islamic Law

According to the Islamic faith, daily prayers are one of the five "pillars of Islam" along with the profession of faith, a pilgrimage to Mecca, the ritual donation and fasting during Ramadan. Muslims must perform their ritual prayers five times a day, each time at a particular time of the day.

The Friday midday prayer must be recited with other believers in a Muslim mosque.[93] In fact, the word for Friday in Arabic (*yaum al-juma'a*) is the same word to describe an assembly of believers gathered together to pray.

The day of communal prayer in Islamic tradition is not the day of rest. In fact, there is no connection between the two. On the contrary, Muslims initially began to gather on Fridays precisely because it was a working day. For example, the Bedouin tribes would gather in Medina to sell their wares. Friday was traditionally a market day and was used to sell goods to the Jews before the Shabbat commenced and they were religiously forbidden from commerce. Friday was chosen as a day of communal prayer because Muslims were already in the city and thus were saved from making an additional journey to it.[94]

The day of Islamic prayer was knowingly placed on a day of work.[95] Islamic doctrine does not believe that a day of rest for God was necessary. God, Muslims believe, does not need to rest; in fact, it would be blasphemous to believe that God could have such a human sensation as tiredness.[96]

Islamic doctrine does not command rest on Fridays; instead, it merely commands that Muslims gather and pray in the mosque on Fridays.

Exceptions are even permitted from prayer in mosques under the Islamic principle of "darura," which allows transgressions of religious commands for

93 Cilardo A., *Il diritto islamico e il sistema giuridico italiano*, Esi, Naples, 2002, 229.

94 Ibid., 229.

95 Ibid.

96 Aluffi Beck-Peccoz R., *Tempo, lavoro e culto nei paesi musulmani*, Fondazione Agnelli, Turin, 2000, 4–5 and 45.

the sake of the greater good.[97] Islamic doctrine provides mosque attendance exemptions for those who are too far away from a mosque. In addition, the communal prayer commandment is satisfied if three or more Muslims are gathered privately.[98]

The Holy Day in Traditionally Muslim States

In addition to examining Islamic doctrine, domestic traditions of the countries from which Muslim believers emigrated must be considered in order to understand how Friday should be interpreted as a holy day. In this, we find that the majority of Italian Muslims are originally from countries that do not traditionally keep Friday as a holy day.

Senegal and Tunisia traditionally have Sunday as their holy day; Algeria has Friday; Morocco varies its day of rest according to the day on which the market is held in each city—Friday, Saturday or Sunday. In these states, employers and schedules are generally flexible and so believers are able to pray at the mosque during their lunch break on Fridays.[99]

Islamic countries have begun to choose a day of rest due to international pressure and in order to comply with international labor standards and law. In reality though, it is still not typical for Muslim countries to have all their citizens take a break from work for a whole day every week.

Once countries decided to grant a day of rest, these countries took into account factors such as the need to proclaim their own Islamic identified (which had led countries to choose Friday), the protection of religious minorities (some of which require a specific rest day) and, finally, the need to align themselves with the weekly schedule of the international economy and more influential countries.[100]

Finally, it should be considered that Islamic law is, in fact, flexible and mostly adapts itself to the legal context of Islamic believers. Therefore, it is the prevailing tradition, and not necessarily the Islamic law, that will dictate the legal obligations of Muslims to their home state. It is difficult and unnecessary to transfer the norms of one country to those of another, since an Italian Muslim no longer owes any duty to his country of origin—he has no obligation to follow that country's laws.

---

97 Castro F., L'islam in Italia: profili giuridici, in *Quaderni di diritto e politica ecclesiastica*, 1996, 1279.

98 Navarro Valls R. and Martínez Torrón J., *Le obiezioni di coscienza Profili di diritto comparato*, Giappichelli, Turin, 1995, 151.

99 Aluffi Beck-Peccoz R., *Tempo, lavoro e culto nei paesi musulmani*, Turin, 2000, 46–47.

100 Ibid.

Conclusion: Holiness on Fridays

According to Islamic doctrine, the Friday holy day is not supposed to be treated in the same way as the Jews or the Adventists treat their holy day. Friday is special for Muslims only in the sense that believers are supposed to gather and pray in the mosque.[101] Legislation from majority Muslim countries has confirmed that the contemporary understanding of an Islamic holy day has not significantly altered from the traditional understanding. Many of these countries have simply established Friday as a rest day. This concession, though, is made mostly to highlight a connection between its Muslim citizens and does not come from Islamic tradition.

It would be difficult to Italy to grant Muslims a rest day on Friday both because of Friday's status as a work day and the fact that Muslim tradition does not necessarily require a full day of rest for Muslims. However, Italy should allow students and workers to abstain from work and lessons during the midday prayer as long as this does not prejudice the operation of private and public organizations. The midday prayer is the only religious practice required of Muslims; therefore, it must be protected either through a state–religion agreement or generally applicable legislation on religious freedom.

Spanish law has largely embraced this option of protecting the midday prayer while not granting an entire day of rest. The state–Islam agreement allows students and workers to leave for the Friday prayer between 1.30 and 4.30 pm, which roughly corresponds to the normal Spanish lunch break.[102] Noticeably,

---

101 Domianello S., *Giurisprudenza costituzionale e fattore religioso (1987–1998)*, Giuffrè, Milan, 1999.

102 See Art. 12 of the Agreement: "Los miembros de las Comunidades Islámicas pertenecientes a la 'Comisión Islámica de España' que lo deseen, podrán solicitar la interrupción de su trabajo los viernes de cada semana, día de rezo colectivo obligatorio y solemne de los musulmanes, desde las trece treinta hasta las dieciséis treinta horas, así como la conclusión de la jornada laboral una hora antes de la puesta del sol, durante el mes de ayuno (Ramadán). En ambos casos, será necesario el previo acuerdo entre las partes. Las horas dejadas de trabajar deberán ser recuperadas sin compensación alguna.

Los alumnos musulmanes que cursen estudios en centros de enseñanza públicos o privados concertados, estarán dispensados de la asistencia a clase y de la celebración de exámenes, en el día del viernes durante las horas a que se refiere el número 1 de este artículo y en las festividades y conmemoraciones religiosas anteriormente expresadas, a petición propia o de quienes ejerzan la patria potestad o tutela.

Los exámenes, oposiciones o pruebas selectivas convocadas para el ingreso en las Administraciones Públicas, que hayan de celebrarse en los días a que se refiere el número anterior, serán señalados, para los musulmanes que lo soliciten, en una fecha alternativa, cuando no haya causa motivada que lo impida." In so doing, the Agreement distinguishes between Muslim employees and students: workers must negotiate with their employers for permission to leave their duties to join the communal prayer,

the Spanish has offered different protections to Jews and Evangelicals. The agreements with the Jewish and the Evangelical communities allow religious participants an entire day of rest in accordance with the religious demands from both groups.[103] But it must be noted that this allowance is given only to those Evangelicals for whom the religious obligation to abstain from work does exist: namely, only to Adventists, who keep a full day of rest. Other Evangelicals do not enjoy such a right.

This action permitting Jews and Adventists an entire day of rest while only granting Muslims a midday prayer is not pejorative or arbitrary; instead, it is a logical consequence of providing protection in accordance with the religious needs of each group.

Ministers of Islamic Worship

Defining the Muslim Minister's Role

The definition and the powers of the ministers of a religious group are problematic both in the Italian and the European legal systems. The ECtHR has

---

whereas students are automatically exonerated from attending lessons during Friday prayer hours and festivities.

103 Art. 12, par. 1, of the Agreement with the Evangelicals: "El descanso laboral semanal, para los fieles de la Unión de Iglesias Adventistas del Séptimo Día y de otras Iglesias evangélicas pertenecientes a la Federación de Entidades Religiosas Evangélicas de España, cuyo día de precepto sea el sábado, podrá comprender, siempre que medie acuerdo entre las partes, la tarde del viernes y el día completo del sábado, en sustitución del que establece el artículo 37.1 del Estatuto de los Trabajadores como regla general."

Art. 12, par. 1, of the Agreement with the Jewish groups: "El descanso laboral semanal, para los fieles de las Comunidades israelitas pertenecientes a la F.C.I., podrá comprender, siempre que medie acuerdo entre las partes, la tarde del viernes y el día completo del sábado, en sustitución del que establece el artículo 37.1 del Estatuto de los Trabajadores como regla general."

Art. 12, par. 2, of the Agreement with the Evangelicals: "Los alumnos de las Iglesias mencionadas en el número 1 de este artículo, que cursen estudios en centros de enseñanza públicos y privados concertados, estarán dispensados de la asistencia a clase y de la celebración de exámenes desde la puesta del sol del viernes hasta la puesta del sol del sábado, a petición propia o de quienes ejerzan la patria potestad o tutela."

Art. 12, par. 2, of the Agreement with the Jewish groups: "Los alumnos judíos que cursen estudios en centros de enseñanza públicos y privados concertados, estarán dispensados de la asistencia a clase y de la celebración de exámenes, en el día de sábado y en las festividades religiosas expresadas en el número anterior, a petición propia o de quienes ejerzan la patria potestad o tutela."

repeatedly struggled with the status of those invested with religious or liturgical functions.[104] The US Supreme Court dealt with this exact issue in 2012.[105]

The role of the minister differs based on the religion. All religions have some higher authority who distinguishes normal believers from believers and who can allow a certain amount of religious guidance. These religious guides are normally protected by the Italian state through either normal legislation or a state–religion agreement, and these ministers are granted a special status both in the religious and the secular world.

Islam is characterized by a couple of distinguishing features which make the religious protection granted to its religious leaders a little different.

First, Islamic doctrine, as opposed to those of other religions, does not clearly define what and who is a religious minister. While some members of the Islamic community have traditionally been respected interpreters of Islam, these members were not really leaders.[106] In the Italian context, there are two ways to become a respected Muslim leader: there are charismatic leaders who rise to prominence through their charisma and leadership; and there are politically backed leaders who rise to prominence largely by a foreign country providing and funding for a religious building and community. This practice of Muslim countries choosing Italian religious leaders has the effect of often embedding political thought in what would normally be a more religious function.

Second, Islam tends to be schismatic in Italy.[107] The growth of prayer centers has prompted disputes and conflicts within local Muslim communities. Some charismatic leaders oppose other leaders who are protected by Muslim states. The growth of the Muslim community has led to a diverse group of religious ministers.

All these aspects of the Islamic ministry pose problems in Italy and the Italian legal system is struggling to both define and protect a religious minister.

The category of religious ministers was initially coined by Italian law and legal doctrine to protect Catholic figures[108] and analogous figures found in non-Catholic religions. According to canon law, a religious minister is someone who is a cleric, has been ordained by a deacon and has the role of teaching, sanctifying and leading a religious group.

104 See the following cases: *Obst v. Germany* (App. no. 425/03); *Schüth v. Germany* (App. no. 1620/03); *Siebenhaar v. Germany* (App. no. 18136/02); *Fernandez Martinez v. Spain* (App. no. 56030/07).

105 *Hosanna-Tabor Evangelical Lutheran Church and School v. Equal Employment Opportunity Commission* 132 S. Ct. 694 (2012).

106 Fregosi F., Islam, una religione senza clero? Una riflessione comparata, in *Daimon*, 2003, 107.

107 Fumagalli Carulli O., Dai "culti ammessi" alla libertà religiosa: un cammino incompiuto, in *Iustitia*, 2004, 186.

108 Ferrari S., *Ministri del culto, Digesto—Discipline Pubblicistiche*, UTET, Turin, 1994, 533.

The extension of this definition to other non-Catholic religious is problematic because other religions differ on how they understand and define their religious leaders. There is no single criterion when defining religious leaders that can be applied to all religions.[109]

For example, Christian denominations such as the Baptists have a greater variety of religious leaders, which hardly fit under the same umbrella of "ministers."[110] Lutheran doctrine does not contemplate the sacrament of priesthood.[111] The Adventists–state agreement has incorporated a special protection for Adventist missionaries,[112] or "colporters,"[113] whose status is now different from that of any other religious minister.

Agreements not only diverge in terms of the figures they qualify as ministers, but also in terms of how this qualification is given. For example, Baptist churches tell the state who must be considered as Baptist ministers for the purposes of celebrating marriages and of spiritual counseling;[114] Lutherans,[115] Buddhists[116] and the Jewish communities,[117] following their agreements with the state, provide their own ministers with a special certification.

The definition of a religious guide or personnel has become so expanded and is now so flexible that agreements usually defer to however the religious group has chosen to define their guide. The Italian state normally blesses as ministers those figures who each religion wants to be protected by law, on the basis of the 1929–30 legislation on "Allowed religions."[118]

The types of ministers and how they receive their qualifications for the purpose of state agreements have mushroomed, paralleling the increasing religious pluralism. Since religions differ in their concept of ministers as well as in terms of how they want to qualify them, the state justly defers to religions and how they choose to define their religious leaders.

However, this means that religious groups might be tempted to use the qualification of minister to grant protection to someone who does not actually play a religious role. The protection granted by religious certification can easily

109 Ibid.

110 Colombo S., I rapporti tra lo Stato e l'Unione Cristiana Evangelica Battista d'Italia: l'Intesa del 1995, available at: http://www.olir.it.

111 Saracino R., L'intesa con la Chiesa evangelica luterana in Italia, available at: http://www.olir.it, 4.

112 Art. 4, par. 2 of the Agreement.

113 Art. 5 of the Agreement. Colportors are those who spread the Evangelical message and support themselves through selling religious goods.

114 Art. 3 of the Agreement.

115 Art. 8 of the Agreement.

116 Art. 7 of the Agreement.

117 Art. 3 of the Agreement.

118 Art. 3.

abused since the state has no role in ascertaining whether an individual should actually be qualified as a minister.[119]

The religious qualification must be investigated by the state, and state institutions should ensure that the individual in question is actually a minister to the religious group. The state should also ensure that a professed minister's activities parallel those of an actual minister. A declaration that an individual is a minister should be fact-checked by the state. Domestic judges have begun to take this approach.[120]

The importance of this check must be understood in light of the special protection that Italian law grants religious ministers. We will consider this special protection briefly below.

Muslim Ministers, State–Islam Agreements and the Law on Religious Freedom

Italian law has provided religious ministers with strong legal protections. Many agreements were drafted when male military service was still compulsory and so those agreements that have followed even once military service was made voluntary still have a clause in it in reference to service. Many religious agreement excused religious ministers from military service and other agreements allowed ministers to abstain from fighting in exchange for offering spiritual counseling while in the army.[121]

All agreements allow religious ministers to give spiritual counseling in the army, in hospitals and in prison.[122] All agreements except that with the Buddhists also allow ministers to celebrate religious marriages with civil effects.[123]

---

119 La Croce L., I ministri di culto nel vigente sistema normativo. Una prima ricognizione, in *Quaderni di diritto e politica ecclesiastica*, 2003, 368.

120 Bettetini A., Alla ricerca del "ministro di culto." Presente e futuro di una qualifica nella società multireligiosa, in *Quaderni di diritto e politica ecclesiastica*, 2000, 256.

121 For example: Art. 5 of the Agreement with the Waldensians; and Arts. 6, 7, 8, and 9 of the Agreement with the Adventists.

122 Arts. 3 and 4 of the Agreement with the Jehovah's Witnesses; Arts. 5 and 8 of the Agreement with the Waldensians; Arts. 4 and 6 of the Agreement with the God's Assemblies; Arts. 7, 8, 9 and 11 of the Agreement with the Jewish Communities; Arts. 5, 6 and 7 of the Agreement with the Baptists; Arts. 5, 6 and 7 with the Agreement with the Lutherans; Arts. 4, 5 and 6 with the Agreement with the Orthodox community; Arts. 8, 9 and 10 of the Agreement with the Mormons; Arts. 4, 5, 6 and 7 of the Agreement with the Apostolics; Art. 4 of the Agreement with the Buddhists; Arts. 4 and 5 of the Agreement with the Hindus.

123 For example: Art. 6 of the Agreement with the Jehovah Witnesses; Art. 11 of the Agreement with the Waldensians; Art. 12 of the Agreement with the God's Assemblies; Art. 18 of the Agreement with the Adventists; Art. 10 of the Agreement

A special protection is also granted to those who are spiritually assisted by religious ministers. General legislation allows ministers to protect the confidences made by those to whom they provided spiritual ministers and prosecutes ministers who violated this religious duty.[124] However, the ministers who can remain silent are those whose religious doctrine or structure does not collide with the Italian legal system.

Similar protections are included in almost all agreements. Information discovered under ministerial obligations cannot be revealed according to pacts with the Holy See,[125] the Jews,[126] the Lutherans,[127] the Buddhists,[128] the Jehovah's Witnesses,[129] the Apostolics,[130] the Mormons,[131] the Orthodox community[132] and the Hindus.[133] Agreements with other religious regimes do not include such clauses and so these religious ministers fall under the umbrella of general legislative religious protection.

Because of their social and religious role, religious ministers may not participate in politics. They cannot run for regional, provincial or local elections,[134] and they cannot be selected as members of a jury.[135] Such limitations prevent them from using their religious popularity to collect votes and ensures that their religious duties to not conflict with their political ones.

Islamic organizations have requested a special protection to be granted to their ministers in agreement drafts.[136] Only the UCOII draft specifically lists these figures as Alim, Ami and Imam,[137] but all agreements seek the same protection for their religious guides as those provided for other religions. According to these agreement drafts, Islamic leaders should be allowed to give spiritual

with the Baptists; Art. 13 of the Agreement with the Lutherans; Arts. 9 and 14 of the Agreement with the Mormons; Art. 13 of the Agreement with the Apostolics; Art. 9 of the Agreement with the Hindus.

124 Arts. 200, n. 1, lett. *a*), and 256 of the Code of Penal Procedure; Art. 622 of the Penal Code; Arts. 210 and 249 of the Code of Civil Procedure.

125 Art. 4, par. 4, of the Agreement of Modification of the Concordat (1929).

126 Art. 3, par. 1.

127 Art. 4, par. 3.

128 Art. 8, par. 2.

129 Art. 2, par. 2.

130 Art. 3, par. 2.

131 Art. 4, par. 4.

132 Art. 3, par. 2.

133 Art. 3, par. 2.

134 Law no. 154, April 23, 1981, Art. 2.

135 Law no. 287, April 10, 1951, Art. 12, lett. *c*).

136 Agreement proposals from AMI, Art. 2; UCOII, Art. 2; COREIS, Art. 13.

137 Art. 2 of the Agreement proposal.

counseling to the armed forces, hospitalized people and jailed inmates.[138] In addition, in order to protect this ministry, the drafts have exempted them from communicating to state institutions based on information they have collected in the course of religious counseling.[139] Finally, COREIS[140] and UCOII[141] both ask that their religious leaders be permitted to celebrate Islamic marriages with civil effects.[142] So far, no Islamic religious figure has been blessed with the official recognition by the state under the "Allowed religions" legislation.

We will consider some duties and rights that such Islamic figures are supposed to enjoy in the agreement drafts and will explore their justifications and feasibility in light of the Islamic doctrine as well as of Italian constitutional precepts.

The Training of Imams

One of the greater contemporary needs for European Islam is the creation of its own leaders.[143] This includes the training of Imams and of other leading authorities.

Islamic figures who perform religious rites or activities with civil effects, or represent the community in public, need to be adequately trained and later identified by the Muslim community as being representative of their religion.

Educating Imams lies at the intersection of state interests and religious interests. Islam and the state must be both reassured that Islamic personalities such as Imams are well trained, responsive to their community, reliable to the state and faithful to Islamic doctrine.[144]

The issue of religious training is where the lack of concordance among Islamic groups is particularly evident and counterproductive. Given the principle of "laicità," the state cannot step in and impose a uniform training for Muslims interested in performing religious rites. The teaching of doctrine must be completely run by the religious groups.[145] Piecemeal solutions that have taken place at the local level outside Italy do not work here, since it is through the religion–state negotiation of an agreement that the religious training and leaders can receive formal recognition.

---

138 COREIS: Arts. 17, 18 and 19; AMI and UCOII: Arts. 7, 8 and 9.

139 COREIS: Art. 13 COREIS; AMI and UCOII, Art. 2.

140 Art. 22.

141 Art. 12.

142 The AMI Agreement proposal foresees only the freedom to celebrate and dissolve Islamic marriages without civil effects: Art. 12.

143 Ferrari S., The Training of Imams, in Cole Durham, Jr. W., Kirkham D.M. and Lindholm T. (eds), *Islam and Political-Cultural Europe*, Ashgate, Farnham, 2012, 107.

144 Carnì M., Islam e ministri di culto, in Cardia C. and Dalla Torre G. (eds), *Comunità islamiche in Italia. Identità e forme giuridiche*, Giappichelli, Turin, 2015, 233.

145 Ferrari, The Training of Imams, 109.

The state needs to stay away from defining religious teaching programs. Contrary to other European countries such as Germany, Austria and the Netherlands, the Italian state has traditionally deferred in relation to religious culture to private institutions: state universities do not teach religious doctrines of any kind, including Catholic doctrines.[146] Italian state educational institutions shy away from teaching theological disciplines and therefore offer no venues for Islamic groups to consolidate and start crafting shared Islamic programs under state courses umbrellas.

But disagreement on Imams' training among Islamic groups does not derive solely from their different religious attitudes; the national origins of Imam candidates also make a difference. Here the immigration bias steps in again and affects state policies on Islam.[147] State institutions have consistently insisted that Imams must become familiar with the Italian cultural and legal environment so that they can align their preaching to the society in which they live. But this is a concern for groups that are mainly composed by immigrants.[148] In the long run, it is quite likely that this preoccupation will fade away, and it is certainly already inappropriate for groups that are mainly composed of Italians who converted to Islam. They surely do not need to familiarize themselves with Italy and the national culture, since they were born in it.

Until Islamic groups gather and agree on how to select and train Imams, the official recognition of Imams and of their religious acts seems precluded.

Confessional Secrecy and Islamic Law

As stated above, religious secrecy is already protected by law. This is done on a general basis for all religious groups whose doctrines or structure do not conflict with Italian legal system, and specifically through state–religion agreements. Such protection allows any religious minister to perform his acts of spiritual counseling freely, with full protection against the disclosure of information exchanged during counseling.

Following agreements already in force, all Islamic groups' draft agreements aim to protect information that ministers have collected in religious counseling through a state–religion agreement. However, this protection granted in a religious agreement would have some disagreeable consequences.

First, the general applicable law is flexible. Any state–religion agreement can be modified only with the agreement of both parties, while, in contrast, a generally applicable law can be modified by the state provided that a strong

146 Ibid., 108.

147 Carnì, Islam e ministri di culto, 241.

148 Ferrari, The Training of Imams, 108.

protection of ministerial secrecy is granted, since it is rooted in Art. 19 of the Constitution on religious freedom.[149]

Second, the information exchanged in counseling is protected unless it is contrary to Italian law. This provision, paralleling Art. 8 of the Constitution, which states that "religious confessions other than Catholicism have the right to organize themselves with their own statutes, to the extent that these are not in conflict with the Italian legal system," must be understood as referring only to Italian core legal values, whereas religious doctrines can certainly depart from and even collide with specific Italian law provisions.[150] Religions whose values conflict with constitutional values have the full freedom of expression and organization, and are limited only when their activities could jeopardize the survival of the Italian legal and democratic order. Therefore, under general applicable law, all Islamic groups already retain full freedom. The exception to this is terrorist organizations whose activities are not covered by the ministerial secrecy clause. But if the state–Islamic community agreement included a protection for religious secrecy, religious ministers could remain silent in trials on terrorism under the agreement. Therefore, Islamic doctrine does not need an additional degree of protection concerning ministerial secrecy.

This conclusion, however, is in line with the original scope and purpose of ministerial secrecy protection. Such protection springs out of the special protection that has been granted to the Catholic sacrament of confession.[151] This protection was later extended to other religions, even those that did not have a confessional sacrament.[152]

Often this protection is unnecessary.[153] The feared "horrible dilemma" of conscience, where a priest or minister could be torn between revealing a secret or preventing justice, has no place outside of confession or those times when a person is in need of guidance from a religious minister.[154]

Including a ministerial secrecy clause would not be necessary for Muslims to enjoy religious freedom. Not all religious groups have confession, and Islam certainly does not. Moreover, adequate protection is already accorded through general applicable law. Under the current regime, only gross violations of constitutional core values, such as terrorist activities, enjoy no protection through ministerial secrecy.

---

149 Paladin L., *Le fonti del diritto italiano*, il Mulino, Bologna, 1996, 197–98.

150 Botta R., *Confessioni religiose, Enciclopedia giuridica*, vol. VIII, Treccani, Rome, 1994, 5.

151 Palomino R., Una aproximacion al secreto religioso, in Reyna V. and Ballesta M.A.F. (eds), *Acuerdos del Estado español con confesiones religiosas minoritarias*, Marcial Pons, Madrid, 1996, 734–35.

152 Ibid., 739 and 742.

153 Milani D., *Segreto, libertà religiosa e autonomia confessionale*, Eupress, Lugano, 2008, 100–105.

154 Nussbaum, *Liberty of Conscience*, 127.

Islamic Marriage and Islamic Ministers

In the Italian legal context, marriage is a public institution that is regulated according to the Civil Code and on which spouses can negotiate only the patrimonial side. The Italian Constitution affirms that "The Republic recognises the rights of the family as a natural society founded on marriage" (Art. 29) and the Constitutional Court has also recently labeled the preservation of marriage as a "State interest" (judgment no. 170, 2014). Far from being merely a private agreement, marriage is considered to be a vital institution and its celebration has powerful implications on the spouses as well as on the overall national community.

COREIS and UCOII drafts empower Islamic ministers to celebrate Islamic marriages with legal effects. In so doing, the drafts align themselves with other religion–state agreements that have been signed in Italy, with the exception of that with the Buddhists. The largest majority of agreements has provided religious ministries with the right to celebrate marriages that, through their transcription, receive legal effects before the states, so that if some formal requisites are respected, the spouses do not need to perform another wedding to receive full recognition as husband and wife from the state.

The expanding praxis of empowering religious ministers to celebrate religious marriages and provide for their transcription in the public registries stems from the multicenturial praxis of endowing Catholic marriages with state effects. According to Catholic doctrine, religious marriage is also to be considered as such for secular purposes—hence the attachment of secular effects to Catholic religious marriage.

This request of recognizing the effects of Islamic marriages is of some interest because although there is no conflict of conscience, it shows how astray a legal regime can go if it does not take into account religious needs and doctrines. In fact, notwithstanding the COREIS and UCOII requests, according to Islamic law, a religious minister is not in a position to perform a marriage.

In Islamic law, marriage is a mere contract made between two private parties. It does not need to be written and public authority has no role in it.[155] Originally, the parties had unequal powers to conclude a marriage contract, with the man having the greater role. Over time, the balance has shifted to a more equalitarian contract.[156] However, public authorities as well as religious ministers remain

155 Benkheira M.H., Matrimonio, in Amir-Moezzi A.A. (ed.), *Dizionario del Corano,* Mondadori, Milan, 2007, 499. See also Schacht J., *Nikah*, *Encyclopaedia of Islam*, Brill, Leiden, 2003.

156 Aluffi Beck-Peccoz R. and Ferrari S. (eds), *Il matrimonio. Diritto ebraico, canonico e islamico: un commento alle fonti*, Giappichelli, Turin, 2006, 205.

outside of the marriage contract.[157] Today, the most common practice is that the parties involve an Imam in their celebration in order to demonstrate the religious and social implication of the contract.[158]

Conclusively, Islamic marriage, as a private contract, does not require the intervention of either religious or state institutions. Paradoxically, some *fatawa* (legal opinions) given in Europe attach Islamic legal effects to civil marriage between Muslims as long as the Islamic law formalities have been respected.[159] In other words, the modern practice consists of recognizing religious effects and implications to marriages that are celebrated under the state law and before state officials. This is the opposite solution that previous agreements have disciplined and that the COREIS agreement foresees. Islamic doctrine and practice both run against the state recognition of Islamic marriage celebrated by religious ministers: none of these aspects is in line with Islamic doctrine and therefore is not a need that deserves the protection of religious freedom.

This obviously does not mean that Islamic guides do not have the right to celebrate purely private marriages, with no religious effects. This remains in the religious sphere and deserves full constitutional protection under religious freedom rights. But this right does not include having such marriages (which are not consistent with Islamic doctrine) fully recognized by the state.

Islamic Teaching in Public Schools

The overwhelming majority of Muslims attend public schools in Italy. A total of 70 percent of the Italian Islamic school population would like to have Islamic teaching imparted at school.[160] The agreement proposals made by Islamic groups, however, diverge significantly on this point, and it is hardly foreseeable which trend will prevail, although Islamic lessons are already disciplined by the Spanish Islam–state agreement.[161] Nevertheless, it is worth mentioning the issue here, in the context of the Islamic ministers' topic, since their choice would be crucial in this respect.

The legislation that the state and the Catholic Church have negotiated with the Concordat's revision in 1984 disciplines the teaching of Catholic

157 El Alami D.S. and Hinchcliffe D., *Islamic Marriage and Divorce Laws of the Arab World*, Kluwer, London, 1996; Doi A.R.I., *Shari'ah: The Islamic Law*, Taha, London 1984, 138–40.

158 Ferrari S., Matrimonio e alterità. La rilevanza interordinamentale del matrimonio nei sistemi giuridici religiosi, in *Daimon*, 2005, 199.

159 Ibid.

160 Acquaviva A., Scuola pubblica e privata e islam, in Cardia and Dalla Torre (eds), *Comunità islamiche in Italia*, 453.

161 Art. 10, par. 1 of the Agreement.

religion in public schools,[162] and grounds it in the inherent value of "religious education" and in the historical connection between Catholicism and Italian culture. The teaching is imparted for one hour per week and is based on an active collaboration between the state and the religion: the topics covered are mutually agreed; the teachers that are appointed by the school to impart the subject must have attended Catholic programs[163] and need to receive the local bishop's approval.[164] This teaching, which is paid for by the state, is not compulsory, but merely elective. The agreements with non-Catholic religions do not include such provisions. Instead, they contemplate the possibility that religious groups are invited to lecture at school on religion and on their specific traditions. However, this is done outside the scope of the ordinary school curriculum.

Therefore, there is a huge difference between the provisions that are included in the agreement with the Catholic Church and those that discipline the state's relationships with other religions. The Catholic Church is the only religion that is involved in the school curriculum; Catholic institutions do not teach directly, but they do oversee the subjects and prepare the teachers. To some extent, the teaching is consequently inherently confessional. This does not mean that the lessons are confessional, though: Catholic and non-Catholic students alike are allowed to attend such lessons, and both of them can opt out under the same conditions.

Among the Islamic groups that have proposed an agreement with the state, only AMI has proposed that Islam is taught in public schools;[165] COREIS, instead, has followed the usual lines of non-Catholic religions and has proposed that Islamic figures, if requested, can lecture at schools about Islam.[166] The AMI proposal follows the line of the state–Catholic Church agreement rather coherently, as it says that AMI will compile a list of teachers and share it with schools. There is, however, at least one essential difference: AMI proposes that only Muslim students have the right to attend lessons on Islam. This specification is also included in the Spanish state agreement with Islam. But this accentuates the confessionalization of the teaching: lesson are not just *on* Islam or taught *by* figures selected by the religions, but they address specifically *Muslim students*. It singles out students depending on their faith.

162 Art. 9, par. 2 of the new Concordat.

163 The Constitutional Court (judgment no. 390, 1999) endorsed this provision.

164 Madonna M., L'insegnamento della religione cattolica nelle scuole pubbliche tra amministrazione ecclesiastica e pubblici poteri. Brevi note sullo status dei docenti, available at: http://www.statoechiese.it.

165 Art. 19.

166 Art. 20.

A second difference between imparting Catholicism and Islam as school subjects lies in their justifications. Both surely incarnate the value of religion for humanity; however, only Catholicism is deeply tied to Italian cultural roots. Teaching Islam at school would need to be rooted elsewhere.

Obviously, teaching Islam at school can be seen as an exercise of religious freedom: the community of Muslim believers and Muslim students could exploit school time and places to impart Islamic doctrine. This does not seem to be in conflict with the Italian understanding of "laicità," which—as the ECtHR's Grand Chamber in *Lautsi* noted—understands schools as places where students and teachers comprise a diverse community through bringing in their own personal and collective identities.

It must be pointed out, however, that the specification that only Muslim students have the right to attend lessons on Islam conflicts with "laicità." In fact, this provision does not utilize the school as a place where students display and exchange their opinions on life and faith, but instead isolates Muslims from the rest of the school population.

More broadly, having Islam imparted in schools still seems problematic because of the programs and the teachers involved. Programs must be agreed upon by the state and the Islamic community. This is a particularly difficult task, given the disparate ideological approaches that characterize Islamic groups in Italy. The same teaching of Islam at schools seems rather unlikely given the composition of the Islamic community itself. Unless there is a substantial agreement between Muslim groups that Islamic doctrine be taught as quintessentially pluralistic and composite, the possibilities that such a school subject sees the light of day are extremely poor. In order to solve this problem, Islam should probably take a inner pluralistic approach and impart lessons on different readings of Islam. If one strand of Islam monopolizes the political representation before the state and is able to impose its own interpretation of Muslim belief, it is fairly likely that students who belong or are familiar with other strands of Islam will desert the subject, and that the teaching itself will disrupt the fragile cohesion of the Muslim community.

The Boundaries of Religious Freedom for Muslims: The Case for Mosques

A broader and more challenging issue pertains to the extension of religious freedom that should be granted to Muslim practices and, more specifically, to mosques as places of worship.

Religious practices vary according to each religion. This is evident from the various state–religion agreements. With the exception of the first religion–state agreement, which was signed with the Waldensians, the state has constantly included in the agreement a list of activities that must be legally considered "religious or cultic activities."[167] In contrast to the standardized approach that tends to assimilate religious differences into a uniform model, this "list" has varied significantly from religion to religion. Evidentially, religions pay special attention to attempting to enumerate their practices according to their own doctrines.

Generally speaking, agreements draw a distinction between religious and cultural activities. This stems from religious freedom and the "laicità" principle: religious affairs fall outside of state affairs and therefore are not subject to state approbation. Moreover, organizations in charge of religious activities are entitled to protection under Art. 20 of the Constitution:[168] this protection applies to all religious activities and organizations, regardless of whether the organization involved has signed an agreement with the state. Religious activities include spiritual counseling, religious education, ministerial training, social and charitable work, education and culture, and excludes commercial and for-profit activities.[169]

The content of this first category will vary according to the religion. For example, Reformed Christian communities have referenced the role of the Gospel in their agreements, while the Mormons have included genealogical research within their list of activities; meditation is mentioned in the Buddhist–state agreement. The list of religious activities in the state–Jewish agreement includes "Jewish education," "study of Judaism," and social service.

As is apparent, religious activities and practices vary significantly. Abandoning some religious practices entails curtailing a part of a religious experience. However, it is still reasonable and even necessary to distinguish between religious and non-religious activities,[170] as religious activities justifiably enjoy greater constititutional and legal protection.

However, distinguishing between religious and non-religious activities is rather problematic in the Islamic context, as the issue of mosques demonstrates.

Traditionally, the construction of religious buildings is favored in Italian law as long as it complies with existing state and local regulations that discipline the

167 The only exception is the Agreement with the Waldensians, the first agreement ever signed.

168 Art. 20 of the Constitution: "No special legislative limitation or tax burden may be imposed on the establishment, legal capacity or activities of any association or institution on the ground of its ecclesiastical nature or its religious or worship purposes."

169 See Art. 15 of the Agreement with God's Assemblies; Art. 21 of the Agreement with the Adventists; Art. 26 of the Agreement with Jewish communities; Art. 11 of the Agreement with the Baptists; Art. 22 of the Agreement with the Lutherans; Art. 15 of the Agreement with the Apostolics; Art. 21 of the Agreement with the Mormons; Art. 11 of the Agreement with the Jehovah's Witnesses; Art. 14 of the Agreement with the Orthodox community; Art. 9 of the Agreement with the Buddhists; Art. 10 of the Agreement with the Hindus.

170 Licastro A., *I ministri di culto nell'ordinamento giuridico italiano*, Giuffrè, Milan, 2005, 161–63.

development of urban areas, and even more robust protection and benefits are accorded to buildings that are specifically conceived for worship and prayer.[171] As early as 1958 (judgment no. 59), the Constitutional Court stated that the creation of a religious building is an inherent aspect of religious freedom. This approach has subsequently been adhered to in the following years. Italian law has accorded tax and property advantages, such as non-confiscatory guarantees, to buildings that have been officially recognized as religious,[172] and the Constitutional Court has enforced a strict equality principle in this field: religious groups of any kind—regardless of whether they have reached an agreement with the state or not—stand on an equal footing and therefore cannot be discriminated against. As a result, funds or fiscal benefits must also be accorded to religions without an agreement.[173] Different treatments and benefits among religious groups are legitimate if they reflect the demographic proportionality among resident religious communities: groups of different sizes can be justifiably granted benefits of different extents.[174]

The most delicate aspect, however, lies in the definition of what a "religious" building is. Only if it is "religious"—and more so if it is a place of worship—does it enjoy specific protection. Defining what a religious building is requires investigation of the nature of the building and of how the practices that are held inside are related to the religious creed.[175]

Religious protection is especially significant with regard to Islam. The deep connection between religion and politics makes it more difficult to understand what is a political activity and what is a religious activity.

The issue of mosques and their role for Muslims is particularly exemplary of this aspect. The proliferation of mosques has prompted a debate on their

---

171 Bettetini A., Gli enti e i beni ecclesiastici, in Schlesinger P. and Busnelli F.D. (eds), *Il Codice Civile Commentato*, Giuffrè, Milan, 2005; Botta R., "Diritto alla moschea" tra "intesa islamica" e legislazione regionale sull'edilizia di culto, in Ferrari S. (ed.), *Musulmani in Italia La condizione giuridica delle comunità islamiche*, il Mulino, Bologna, 2000; Tozzi V., Le moschee ed i ministri di culto, available at http://www.statoechiese.it/index.php?option=com_content&task=view&id=103; D'Andrea L., Eguale libertà ed interesse alle intese delle confessioni religiose: brevi note a margine della sent. cost. n. 346/02, in *Quaderni di diritto e politica ecclesiastica*, 2005, 668–85; Mantineo A., La legislazione sull'edilizia di culto alla prova della giurisprudenza (nella Regione Calabria e altrove), in *Quaderni di diritto e politica ecclesiastica*, 2005, 675–705.

172 Bettetini A., La condizione giuridica dei luoghi di culto tra autoreferenzialità e principio di effettività, in *Quaderni di diritto e politica ecclesiastica* 1, 2010, 9–12.

173 Ibid., 12.

174 Fiorita N., La moschea, il consiglio comunale e il diritto di libertà religiosa, in *Quaderni di diritto e politica ecclesiastica*, 2, 2010, 461.

175 Bettetini, La condizione giuridica dei luoghi di culto tra autoreferenzialità e principio di effettività, 14.

religious nature as well as their possible utilization by Muslim terrorists, singling out the debate about their construction and presence within Italian territories from the rest of religious buildings.[176] Admittedly, state and—more frequently—local governments have paid special attention to the status of mosques because they fear that Islamic terrorists could make easy hideouts of them, and for broader concerns about Islam's compatibility with constitutional values.

Here and there, strong political and social opposition to the construction of Mosques has appeared at the regional and local level. This is because the location and the structure of religious buildings fall within the shared state–regional competence of "land-use planning":[177] regions and local bodies play a crucial role when it comes to religious buildings. Regional and local regulations or legislation attempted to deny the construction of a mosque for different reasons: [178] because of concerns expressed by the local community; or requests that Islamic organizations include women on their leading boards; or requests that Italian be the liturgical language of the prayer.[179] Such regulations or requests were nullified by Italian courts citing the constitutional protection of religious freedom and autonomy of religious organization.

As local opposition and fears have impeded the construction of places where Muslims can practice their faith, such delays have increased the number of prayer rooms and buildings put in place under the table. Since such prayer activities are run outside the law, they have both attracted extremism and expanded the fear that terrorist activities flourish there.[180]

The most recent attack on the right of Muslims to have buildings for their commonal prayers comes from the Lombardy region. The regional law no. 2, issued on February, 3, 2015,[181] is now under the scrutiny of the Constitutional Court for some provisions that limit the freedom to establish religious buildings, which indirectly targets the Islamic faith.

In fact, this new piece of legislation allows for local referenda on the construction of prayer buildings: this makes the enjoyment of the right of religious minorities—such as Muslims—subject to the will of local majorities.[182]

176 Allievi S., *La guerra delle moschee. L'Europa e la sfida del pluralismo religioso*, Marsilio, Venice, 2010, 13–16.

177 Art. 117, par. 3, Italian Constitution.

178 Bettetini, La condizione giuridica dei luoghi di culto tra autoreferenzialità e principio di effettività, 14.

179 Colaianni N., Come la xenofobia si traduce in legge: in tema di edifici di culto, available at: www.olir.it.

180 Bombardieri M., *Moschee d'Italia. Il diritto al luogo di culto il dibattito sociale e politico*, EMI, Bologna, 2011, 105.

181 Modifiche alla legge regionale 11 marzo 2005, n. 112—Principi per la pianificazione delle attrezzature per servizi religiosi.

182 Art. 1, par. 4.

Moreover, a video surveillance system must be set up at the expense of the religious group and connected with police forces as a prerequisite for the approval of the construction project: here the fear that terrorism infiltrates Islamic religious activities is evident. The Constitutional Court is likely to strike down the new Lombardy legislation since it violates religious freedom for minorities, overburdening them with disproportionate security measures and with a generalized suspicion of terrorism.

However, some fortunate experiences have also taken place at the local level. Negotiations and agreements have emerged, even if only in a piecemeal fashion, and have led to a fairly peaceful process of the construction of mosques. In some cases, Islamic groups have been able to access public funds to build their places of worship. For instance, the Florentine local body of Colle Val d'Elsa, in 2003, partially funded the construction of the local mosque alongside private donations from Muslim residents and from foreign donors. Interestingly, the local public institutions negotiated the creation of a scientific committee equally composed of state and Islamic religion representatives. Half of the committee's members are selected by the Islamic association that started the initiative, while the other half is selected by the local body. After all, the public institution of Colle Val d'Elsa co-runs a mosque,[183] which seems to be incompatible with the principle of "laicità" protects religious rites from the intrusions of public institutions.

The policies and the debate over mosques are on the whole extremely fluid and ambiguous because the nature of such buildings is not adequately understood by public institutions. The lack of agreement on the purpose and structure of the mosque facilitates political and legal delays and ambiguities at the local, regional and state levels. Unless mosques are understood as being fully religious buildings, their presence is felt as less necessary and urgent for the local Muslim community, and they are mainly subject to political accommodations.

The Committee for Italian Islam delivered an opinion in 2011 in which it expressed its wishes that Islamic mosques be open to everyone willing to engage in their activities—whether the individual be Sunni or Shiite, man or woman.[184] The opinion also stated that services should be open to all nationalities and should be given in Italian, with Arabic only utilized for a ritual prayer. This opinion, while helpful in demonstrating some characteristics of a mosque, failed to truly define a mosque.

---

183 Bettetini, La condizione giuridica dei luoghi di culto tra autoreferenzialità e principio di effettività. For more details, see Zannotti L., La costruzione di una moschea: l'esempio di Colle Val d'Elsa, available at: http://www.statoechiese.it.

184 Ministro dell'Interno, Comitato per l'islam italiano, Luoghi di culto islamici. Parere del Comitato per l'Islam Italiano, Rome, March 3, 2011, available at www.olir.it, 10.

Muslim tradition has largely preserved the role of the mosque over time.[185] Since the seventh century, mosques have been places where Muslims gather for activities ranging from judicial trials to politics. Mosques have provided a prime example for how, for Muslims, religion, law and politics are closely intertwined.

Islam religion, society and law are all combined in the communal prayer and sermon (*khutba*).[186] The *khutba*, which is spoken by the *Khatib*,[187] distinguishes itself from the prayer traditionally led by the *Imam*,[188] although the *Khatib* and the *Imam* are often the same person. The sermon normally focuses on socio-political issues. As of 2011, there was knowledge of no more than three mosques in Italy and more than 700 Islamic *mussallat*, which is a sort of chapel devoted only to Muslim prayer.[189]

A mosque is often a place of political activity; this, however, does not affect the fact that a mosque is legally qualified as a place of religious activity and worship. On the contrary, it makes sense that political activities would be conducted in a mosque since religion, law and politics are so connected and embedded in Islamic doctrine.[190]

The constitutional principle of "laicità," understood as a means through which religious needs are made known by the state and eventually regulated through applicable law and agreement, allows political activities to be included as a part of the Muslim faith and doctrine. "Laicità" leads Italian law and institutions to expand their standardized conception of "religious activities" in order to fully appreciate the nature of Islamic doctrine.

In the same way as how cultural activities were considered a part of religious activity in the Jewish agreement, so must political activity be included in a mosque's religious activity.

Therefore, there is little doubt that mosques fall squarely within the scope of religious and even worship buildings for Muslims, and that they consequently need full protection. Their presence or their benefits—on an equal footing with the places of worship of other religions—on the territory cannot be negotiated; only their locations can legitimately be planned, bearing in mind the necessities of the local Muslim community and other public interests that must be taken into account in the context of land-use planning.

---

185 Maréchal B., Mosquées, organisations et leadership, in Dassetto F., Maréchal B. and Nielsen J. (eds), *Convergences musulmanes*, L'Harmattan-Bruylet, Louvain, 2001.

186 See Wensink A.J., *Khutba*, *Encyclopaedia of Islam*, Brill, Leiden, 2003.

187 Pedersen J., *Khatib*, *Encyclopaedia of Islam*, Brill, Leiden, 2003.

188 Monnot G., *Imam*, *Encyclopaedia of Islam*, Brill, Leiden, 2003.

189 Wensink, *Encyclopaedia of Islam.*

190 Colaianni N., *Diritto pubblico delle religioni. Eguaglianza e differenze nello Stato costituzionale*, il Mulino, Bologna, 2012, 195.

The same can be said with regard to the language utilized during the religious service. Although the Committee for Italian Islam proposed that the Italian language be used during ceremonies, "laicità" creates a space of free exercise of religion in which political, social or other kinds of constraints cannot enter: since religious worship is entirely left to religions, the way in which this is held is absolutely free, as long as it does not interfere with specific constitutional values. The choice of Arabic as the ritual language remains within the boundaries of religious freedom and therefore cannot be controlled by the state.

On the contrary, the requirement that mosques that have received official recognition and benefits accept people of all nationalities and of both sexes is constitutionally legitimate. This requirement reflects the public character of the service that is performed inside: such religious buildings enjoy special protection and are included in land-use planning precisely because they respond to the religious needs of the Muslim population that resides in the relevant area. It would be contradictory for Muslim groups to receive specific protection for their mosques, but prevent some Muslims residing there from taking advantage of them. Imposing a given language would affect religious ceremonies while imposing that officially recognized places of worship welcome everybody does not affect religious rites and therefore can apply to religious places.

Finally, the possibility of excluding Sunnis or Shiites from mosques depends on the nature of the Muslim groups operating in a given area and on their representativeness of the resident Muslim population. If a group represents both Sunna and Shia, it must take into account both traditions when it negotiates for mosques in the context of land-use planning, and therefore must either accept both strands of the Muslim tradition in the mosques it runs or, alternatively, devote a religious place to each of them.

Conclusion
Finding Religious Freedom in Today's "Hybridization"[1]

Religious Pluralism and New Constitutional Models of Church–State Relationships

The integration of Islam in Italy reflects many common problems in Europe. Countries are uniformly facing increasingly pluralistic societies in which modern faith coexists with more traditional faith.

Such highly hybridized societies see increasing contaminations of models and identities, which take the shape of judicial accommodations and political and legal negotiations. These accommodations are not merely small variations of the state models of state–religion relationships; sometimes they affect such relationships profoundly, urging states to take measures either to modify, reinforce or supplant pre-existing relationships.

State reactions to an increasingly pluralistic culture differ widely. Countries such as France have chosen to reinforce their traditional church–state separation and are pushing religious influence out of the public sphere, as demonstrated by their laws regarding religious symbolism in school and in public places. In Spain, equalitarianism has taken the shape of a standard boilerplate state–religion agreement with very minor, although sometimes significant, variations. The Spanish agreement with Islam was signed too quickly and was more concerned with a symbolic restoration of Islam in Spain after 500 years of separation than the goal of allowing Muslims to enjoy true religious freedom.

In Switzerland, a referendum amended the Federal Constitution in order to prohibit the establishment of minarets. At the moment, the Federal Constitution, although proclaiming religious freedom and deferring political relationships with religions to Cantons, prohibits only the realization of minarets: this is the only textual Federal limitation to religious freedom in the country.[2]

---

1 Gomarasca P., *Meticciato: convivenza o confusione?*, Marcianum Press, Venice, 2009.

2 Art. 72: "(1) The regulation of the relationship between church and state is a cantonal matter.

(2) Within the limits of their competencies, the Federation and the Cantons may take measures to maintain public peace between members of the various religious communities.

(3) The building of minarets is prohibited."

British society developed has a much more welcoming approach towards Muslims. The then Anglican Archbishop of Canterbury, Rowan Williams, advocated an acceptance of Muslims and their religious law in the state.[3] Also the US has tried to integrate Islam symbolically into its institutional life after the multiple terrorist attacks in September 11, 2001 by including leaders in public ceremonies alongside Jewish and Christian ministers.[4]

However, it must be added that terrorist threats, extremism and misperceptions of Islam have undermined the true integration of Islam in both the UK and the US. Great Britain is threatened by Islam's strong societal independence in British society. The US has experienced a degree of Islamophobia[5] which has prompted widespread initiatives at the state level that have been aimed at preventing, more or less explicitly, the enforcement of any Islamic law provisions in state courts.[6] Great Britain is threatened by Islam's strong societal independence in British society.[7]

Notwithstanding its national multicultural pedigree, Canada's province of Ontario erased from its law the possibility of having family disputes resolved through non-state tribunals because of the fear that this would pave the way for Islamic courts with detrimental effect for gender equality in the family context. This dramatic change in the legal realm of Ontario stemmed from the perception that the conservative portion of the local Muslim community was re-negotiating "the place and role of religion and sub-state authorities in regulating a significant aspect of their members' affairs—in this particular instance, the terms of entry into and exit from a marriage relationship—in lieu of the exercise of this authority by the seculars state itself."[8]

---

3 Available at: http://rowanwilliams.archbishopofcanterbury.org/articles.php/1137/archbishops-lecture-civil-and-religious-law-in-england-a-religious-perspective.

4 Pin A., Islam at the Threshold, in Ferrari S. and Cristofori R. (eds), *Law and Religion in the 21st Century*, Ashgate, Burlington, 2010, 359ff.

5 Uddin A.T. and Pantzer D., A First Amendment Analysis of Anti-Sharia Initiatives, in *First Amendment Law Review*, 2011–12, 10, 36 ff.

6 See the *American Laws for American Courts*, a bill proposal that was advanced by the Public Policy Alliance to promote anti-Shari'a state and federal legislation. The proposal is available at: http://publicpolicyalliance.org/legislation/american-laws-for-american-courts. A list of states that are trying to implement such pieces of legislation can be found at: http://www.islamophobiatoday.com/2014/03/01/new-anti-sharia-legislation-introduced-in-several-states.

7 Milbank J., Shari'a and the True Basis of Group Rights, in Ahdar R. and Aroney N. (eds), *Shari'a in the West*, Oxford University Press, Oxford, 2010, 147.

8 Shachar A., Demystifying Culture, in *International Journal of Constitutional Law*, 2012, 10(2), 448.

The aforementioned examples demonstrate the impact of the Muslim presence in Europe and in the Western world, and how the fears of terrorism, religious extremism and societal isolations prompt varied responses and legal, even constitutional, changes.

Such changes do not affect only Muslims or other religious minorities; they affect the whole of society. State–religion relationships are increasingly driven by the need to secure *equal rights*. The role of equality levels down all religions equally: measures that are intended to provide a special framework to some religious groups have side-effects for the general society. It is not by chance that the prohibition of religious symbols in public schools affected Muslims and Jews alike, since Jewish students were prohibited from wearing the kippah.

The Italian Approach to Separatism and Minority Religions

This emphasis on equalitarianism has impacted the Italian legal system's interpretation of its Constitution. State–religion relationships have been dominated by this standardized approach that has ignored essential language and principles in Art. 8. of the Constitution: state–religion agreements have not been tailored to meet each religion's specific needs, but instead have imposed a standardized regime onto what should have been unique and different religious agreements.

Failing to acknowledge religious principles is detrimental to both the state and religion. A religion's potential contribution is moulded to what has already been conceded in previous religious pacts. This mold does not reflect a religion's true spirit and structure, and prevents the religions from truly contributing to society.

Furthermore, a too standardized state–religion agreement betrays the constitutional principles that govern state–religion relations. The Italian constitutional system, with its pivotal principle of "laicità," already possesses the resources needed to address each religion's needs and balance them against constitutional values in an attempt to accommodate these needs. This was already starting to occur in the mid-1980s through legal decisions such as those allowing Catholicism to be taught in public schools, with no detriment to other religious or non-religious beliefs.

It has been only from the mid-1990s onwards, through overwhelming preoccupations with equality, that "laicità" has begun to assume more separatist features. The Constitutional Court's endorsement of this new interpretation of such principle has neutralized the public role of religion and has prompted a greater and stricter separation between law and religions.

This separatism approach has no foundation in the Italian Constitution, nor is it supported in the Constituent Assembly's legislation. On the contrary, the

Italian Constitution's text as well as the intent of the drafters show a desire to cultivate a coexisting relationship between the religious and legal fields.

A too strict separatism shares the shortcomings of strict equalitarianism, as well as those of multiculturalism. All of these approaches fall short of establishing true religious freedom. Equalitarianism pushes for a public arena deprived of any religious symbols, identities and feelings, and makes it impossible to distinguish between and address different religious needs; multiculturalism welcomes virtually all religious identities, but fails to capture or understand them.

The Implications of "Laicità" on Religious Freedom for Muslims and Italians

Respecting and Protecting Islamic Specificity

In order to understand and use Italian constitutional devices, we must go back to the Constitutional Court's original understanding of "laicità." Only through this understanding of "laicità" can the state and religions collaborate in a way that will allow the state to gain a greater understanding of religious doctrine while allowing Islam to assist in shaping a policy of integration and interaction with state institutions.

State institutions, according to the constitutional text and the Constitutional Court's interpretation, have the necessary powers to investigate each religion's priorities without interfering in religious life. For example, the use of a proper understanding of "laicità" could enable state institutions to undertake further examination of the request from Islamic groups for Friday to be a holy day and to see if this is consistent with Islamic tradition and practice, since Islamic groups in Italy diverge on this point. This research would allow state institutions to ascertain whether allowing Muslims to abstain from the workplace on Friday would truly protect their religious freedom—it would serve Muslims' religious freedom better.

This research or observation of religious doctrines does not violate the religious intimacy or rights on believers. On the contrary, it enables the state to adequately evaluate religious needs in order to tailor a specific and unique agreement for each religion that protects the tenets of that religion.

The Relationship between Freedom of Conscience and Freedom of Religion

This renewed understanding of "laicità" can also shed light on the quintessence of religious freedom and on its relationship with the freedom of conscience. In fact, the case law of the Italian Constitutional Court and the ECtHR has largely elaborated on the freedom of conscience, but, in so doing, has inadvertently downplayed the specifics of religious freedom.

The Constitutional Court has developed the idea of freedom of conscience drawing from Art. 19 of the Constitution, which literally speaks only of religious freedom. The Court has articulated freedom of conscience as the common thread that unites atheists, agnostics and religious believers, going beyond the conception of freedom of religion as covering only the right to profess a creed.[9] Conscience has become the foundational aspect of all rights, not just of freedom of religion.[10] The ECtHR has similarly crafted the idea that freedom of conscience includes ideals and values that are cherished as fundamental for a human being, and drew a distinction between them and mere opinions. Opinions do not have the same importance for the subject and therefore deserve less substantial protection.

This interpretation of freedom of conscience as a constitutional and human right has qualified the uniqueness of religious freedom. Religious freedom has been equated with freedom of conscience, without any significant distinction. It has been portrayed as a sphere of autonomy for individuals in which they can cultivate their relationship with the divine sphere.

Religious freedom is more specific and narrow than freedom of conscience. It covers only transcended beliefs, not just opinions or beliefs that are firmly believed as true.

In addition, freedom of religion is a right that belongs to a group or community, whereas freedom of conscience is normally articulated as applying only to a single individual.[11] In the field of religious freedom, a man or woman participates in a community bonded by a group adhesion to an outside doctrinal or moral proposal.[12] Through "laicità," state institutions can take into account these external and collective dimensions of religious freedom. "Laicità," as initially understood by the Italian Constitutional Court, can appreciate the difference between freedom of conscience and freedom of religion.

9 Judgment no. 117, 1979: "l'opinione prevalente fa ormai rientrare la tutela della c.d. libertà di coscienza dei non credenti in quella della più ampia libertà in materia religiosa assicurata dall'art. 19."

10 Cardia C., *Libertà di credenza, Enciclopedia giuridica*, Treccani, Rome, 1990, 6; Spadaro A., *Libertà di coscienza e laicità nello Stato costituzionale. Sulle radici "religiose" dello Stato "laico,"* Giappichelli, Turin, 2008, 234.

11 See Rivers J., *The Law of Organized Religions: Between Establishment and Secularism*, Oxford University Press, Oxford, 2010, 35: "Religious liberty as freedom of conscience has a limit in its individualistic tendency."

12 Novak D., *The Jewish Social Contract. An Essay in Political Theology*, Princeton University Press, Princeton, 2005, 68; and Novak D., *In Defense of Religious Liberty*, Isi, Welmington, 2009.

It is only through a reconsideration of religious freedom in light of its transcendent, collective and intergenerational dimensions that the religious needs of Muslims and other religious groups can be fully evaluated. The appearance of Muslims—with their sense of community that transcends time and place, and connects them to a divine being—in the European public sphere provides a good opportunity to reconsider religious liberty and appreciate its uniqueness and specificity.

Index

Note: numbers in brackets preceded by n are footnote numbers.

For Product Safety Concerns and Information please contact our EU representative GPSR@taylorandfrancis.com
Taylor & Francis Verlag GmbH, Kaufingerstraße 24, 80331 München, Germany

www.ingramcontent.com/pod-product-compliance
Ingram Content Group UK Ltd.
Pitfield, Milton Keynes, MK11 3LW, UK
UKHW011013180926
475701UK00004B/726
* 9 7 8 0 3 6 7 5 9 7 4 4 3 *